STIEGLITZ STEICHEN STRAND

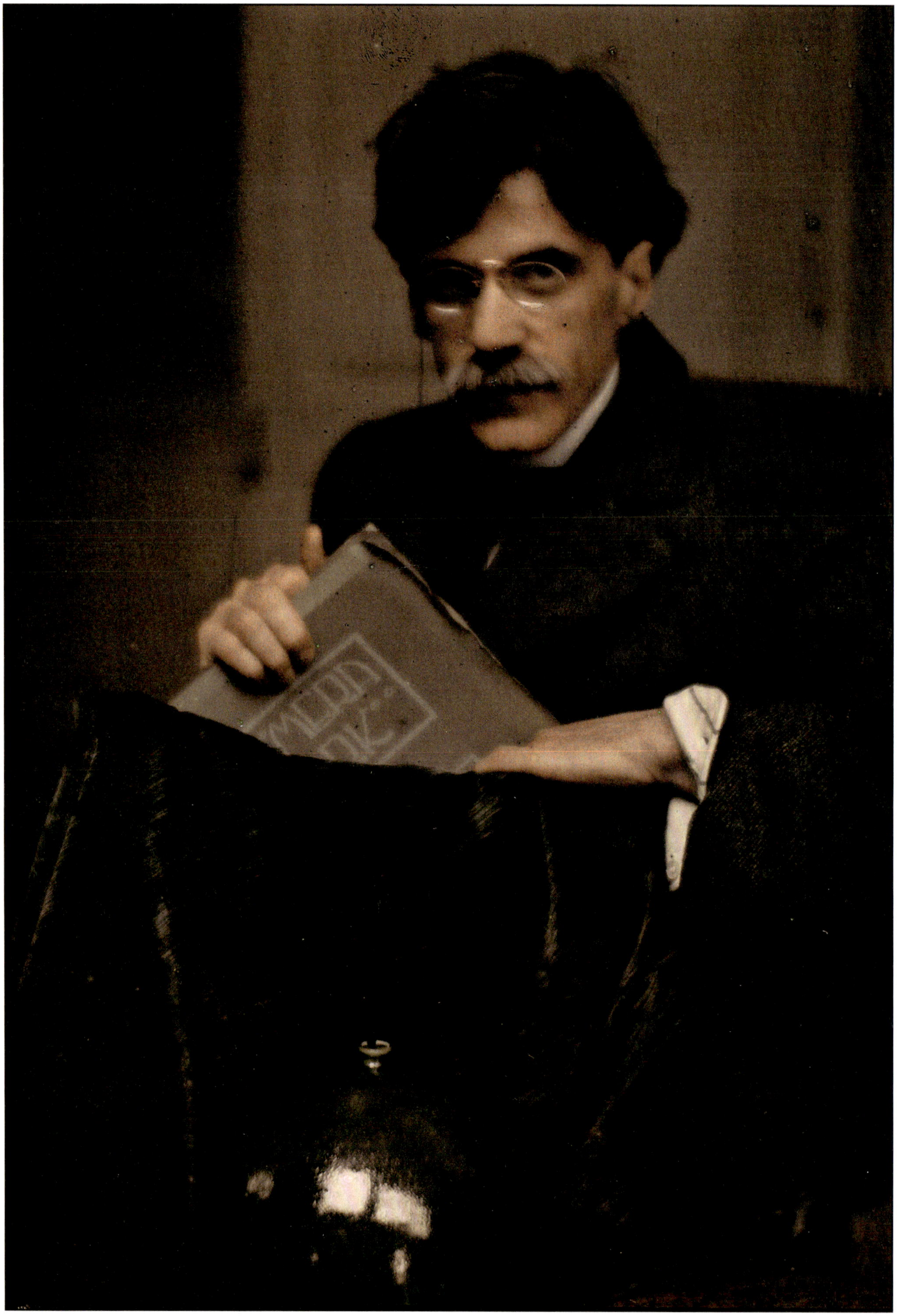

STIEGLITZ STEICHEN STRAND

MASTERWORKS FROM THE METROPOLITAN MUSEUM OF ART

Malcolm Daniel

The Metropolitan Museum of Art
Yale University Press

This volume is published in conjunction with the exhibition "Stieglitz, Steichen, Strand," held at The Metropolitan Museum of Art, New York, from November 10, 2010, to April 10, 2011.

The exhibition is made possible in part by Joseph M. Cohen.

Published by The Metropolitan Museum of Art, New York
Gwen Roginsky, General Manager of Publications
Peter Antony, Chief Production Manager
Dale Tucker, Senior Editor
Chris Zichello, Production Manager
Bonnie Laessig, Assistant Production Manager
Jane S. Tai, Image Research and Permissions

Book design by Abbott Miller and Kristen Spilman, Pentagram
Typeset in Sackers Gothic and Dada Grotesque
Printed on 130 gsm Gardapat Kiara
Color separations by Professional Graphics, Inc., Rockford, Illinois
Printed and bound by Conti Tipocolor, s.p.a., Florence, Italy

Front cover illustration: Alfred Stieglitz, *From the Back Window, 291*, 1915 (plate 49)
Back cover illustration: Paul Strand, *Geometric Backyards, New York*, 1917 (plate 100)
Frontispiece: Edward Steichen, *Alfred Stieglitz*, 1907. Autochrome, 9 x 6 3/16 in. (22.9 x 15.7 cm). The Metropolitan Museum of Art, New York, Alfred Stieglitz Collection, 1955 (55.635.10)

New photography by Eileen Travell, The Photography Studio, The Metropolitan Museum of Art

Library of Congress Cataloging-in-Publication Data
Metropolitan Museum of Art (New York, N.Y.)
Stieglitz, Steichen, Strand: masterworks from the Metropolitan Museum of Art/Malcolm Daniel
p. cm.
"This volume is published in conjunction with the exhibition "Stieglitz, Steichen, Strand," held at The Metropolitan Museum of Art, New York, from November 10, 2010, to April 10, 2011."
Includes bibliographical references.
ISBN 978-1-58839-405-7 (Metropolitan Museum of Art: hc)—ISBN 978-0-300-16901-0 (Yale University Press: hc) 1. Photography, Artistic—Exhibitions. 2. Photography—United States—Exhibitions. 3. Stieglitz, Alfred, 1864–1946—Exhibitions. 4. Steichen, Edward, 1879–1973—Exhibitions. 5. Strand, Paul, 1890–1976—Exhibitions. 6. Metropolitan Museum of Art (New York, N.Y.)—Exhibitions. I. Daniel, Malcolm R. II Title.
TR653.M48 2010
779.74'7471—dc22
2010034048

CONTENTS

DIRECTOR'S FOREWORD

Today there can be little question that photography has found a home both at The Metropolitan Museum of Art and in the hearts of our public. Few museumgoers are surprised to find galleries at the Met devoted to photography of the past and present. For many, this most modern of art media is especially accessible: a fly in amber revealing and reanimating something of the past; a lens through which to understand our fellow human beings; or a mirror in which to examine our own lives. Moreover, the language of photography, shaped by the perceptive eye and skilled hands of the artist, can be understood without a handbook of iconography, expertise in foreign languages, or archaeological training, and we now rarely hear that refrain so often repeated in the past: "But is it art?"

This was not true a century ago, when Alfred Stieglitz crusaded for the acceptance of photography alongside the traditional fine arts. I wish we could claim that the Metropolitan was among the prescient few who purchased photography—or avant-garde drawings, prints, or paintings, for that matter—from Stieglitz's galleries in the 1900s and 1910s, but we were not. Fortunately for us and for our public, Stieglitz was persistent. With a gift of his own photographs in 1928 and subsequent gifts of works by the photographers he most admired, Stieglitz laid the foundation for what is now one of the world's great collections of photography, spanning the medium's history from its invention to the present day. To the many collectors, donors, and supporters who have followed Stieglitz's lead and helped build the Museum's photography collection, we owe an equally great debt.

On the pages that follow, Malcolm Daniel, Curator in Charge of the Metropolitan's Department of Photographs, lays out the fascinating story of three early twentieth-century masters of the medium. The first is Stieglitz himself, who is renowned not only for his advocacy of photography and modern art but also for his own remarkable works, including his series of New York City views, photographs of clouds above Lake George, and, most of all, his many portraits of the painter Georgia O'Keeffe, whom he married in 1924. The second is Edward Steichen, whose large, colorful, and elaborately crafted portraits, nudes, and landscapes Stieglitz held up as the finest photography of the early 1900s, and whose collaboration was key to Stieglitz's influential series of avant-garde exhibitions. The third is Paul Strand, the young photographer who brought Stieglitz back to the promotion of photography in the mid-1910s and whose nearly abstract works blazed the trail of an emerging modernism. Their interwoven stories, and the remarkable pictures reproduced in this volume, map one of the most pivotal periods in the history of photography. The Metropolitan is fortunate to have deep, rich holdings of works by each of them. I hope you will enjoy these masterpieces on our walls in the exhibition "Stieglitz, Steichen, Strand" and that this book will help preserve that pleasure in the years to come. For the exhibition, we extend a very special thanks to Joseph M. Cohen for his generous and longtime support of the Department of Photographs.

Thomas P. Campbell
Director
The Metropolitan Museum of Art, New York

INTRODUCTION

On December 30, 1928, Alfred Stieglitz wrote to Ananda Coomaraswamy, curator at the Museum of Fine Arts, Boston, to herald momentous news: "The Metropolitan Museum has opened its sacred halls to Photography. . . . My photographs have performed the miracle!"[1] Stieglitz's gift of twenty-two recent photographs, just then accepted by the Metropolitan's board of trustees, were indeed the Museum's first acquisitions of photography as art, a goal long sought by Stieglitz and by the Met's founding curator of prints, William M. Ivins, Jr. Although Stieglitz had donated twenty-seven photographs to the Museum of Fine Arts four years earlier, it had been his dream to place photography alongside the other fine arts at the Metropolitan, the nation's most prominent museum, as early as 1902. That year, the Metropolitan's first director, General Luigi Palma di Cesnola, asked Stieglitz to organize the American photography section of the Esposizione Internazionale d'Arte Decorativa Moderna in Turin. Years later, Stieglitz remembered their conversation: "I told the General what my fight for photography had been, still was, and that I would let him have the collection needed for Turin if he, Cesnola, guaranteed that when it came back it would be accepted by the Metropolitan Museum of Art in toto and hung there. Cesnola gasped. He said, 'Why Mr. Stieglitz, you won't insist that a photograph can possibly be a work of art?'"[2] Cesnola initially refused, but when Stieglitz called his bluff by declining to organize the show, Cesnola gave in and accepted his terms. In the end, however, as Stieglitz recounted, Cesnola died before the material returned from Turin, and he felt it would be unfair to hold Cesnola's successor to their unwritten gentleman's agreement.[3] His dream would have to wait another quarter century.

If Stieglitz's 1928 gift pried open the Museum's doors, his second gift, in 1933, threw them wide open, fully realizing Stieglitz's dream and placing the Metropolitan at the forefront of museums collecting artistic photography. In that year, he gave more than four hundred photographs made by various artists during the fertile period between the turn of the century and the close of World War I. Most of them were the very prints he had exhibited in his galleries, sent to exhibitions around the world, and reproduced in his groundbreaking publications, *Camera Notes* and *Camera Work.* "Many have actual pedigrees—royal blood," is how he put it.[4] The collection comprised more than fifty photographs by Edward Steichen, including large exhibition prints from the early 1900s such as *The Flatiron* (in three variant printings), *The Big Cloud, Lake George*, *The Pond—Moonrise*, several versions of Rodin's *Balzac*, and numerous portraits; a half-dozen enlarged platinum prints, each one-of-a-kind, by Paul Strand, including *Blind*; more than fifty works by Clarence White, among them twenty studies of the nude from his 1907 collaboration with Stieglitz; and major groups of work by J. Craig Annan, Anne Brigman, Alvin Langdon Coburn, F. Holland Day, Frank Eugene, Gertrude Käsebier, Joseph Keiley, Heinrich Kühn, George Seeley, and Charles Sheeler. Along with some two hundred works donated by bequest following Stieglitz's death and about seventy-five examples of his work later placed at the Metropolitan by his widow, Georgia O'Keeffe, the Alfred Stieglitz Collection has long been both the foundation and core of the Museum's photography collection.

Additional works by Stieglitz, Steichen, and Strand from the Ford Motor Company Collection, formed by John C. Waddell and acquired by the Museum in 1987, and the Gilman Collection, acquired in 2005, have further enriched the Museum's holdings of photographs by these three early twentieth-century masters.

Stieglitz's portraits of O'Keeffe, Steichen's *Flatiron*, and Paul Strand's early platinum prints remain among the Metropolitan's most prized photographs and have been the subject of numerous publications and exhibitions over the years: Weston Naef's comprehensive catalogue and exhibition *The Collection of Alfred Stieglitz: Fifty Pioneers of Modern Photography* (1978); *Georgia O'Keeffe: A Portrait by Alfred Stieglitz* (1978), selected and prefaced by O'Keeffe herself (expanded with an afterword by Maria Morris Hambourg in 1997); Joel Smith's insightful and engaging *Edward Steichen: The Early Years* (1999); and Maria Hambourg's *Paul Strand circa 1916*, a 1998 exhibition and catalogue that examined photographs from the Met's collection along with many others from the artist's most creative moment.[5] The present volume, deeply indebted to each of these, brings the photographs of Stieglitz, Steichen, and Strand in the Metropolitan's collection back into print. The accompanying exhibition allows the public to savor a gallery of masterpieces by each artist in much the same way that elsewhere in the Museum visitors are able to contemplate an entire room devoted to the paintings of Rembrandt, Degas, or Manet.

Although these three giants of early twentieth-century photography each flourished at a different moment and with an oeuvre distinctly his own, their stories are interwoven. At the center is Stieglitz, a photographer of supreme accomplishment as well as America's greatest champion of photography and modern art at the turn of the twentieth century. Through the seminal journals he edited and his succession of galleries, Stieglitz introduced the American public to the new century's most advanced examples of photography, Parisian avant-garde art, and American painting. In turn, he helped shape the course of modern American art, both the public appetite for it and the critical response to it.

Steichen and Strand are, in a sense, bookends marking the beginning and end of Stieglitz's influential role as artistic impresario during the period of the Photo-Secession, the name he gave to the loose-knit group of photographers he exhibited, published, and promoted between 1902 and 1917. Their photographs illustrate perfectly the radical shift in Stieglitz's developing sense of photographic aesthetics. Steichen was heralded as the finest exemplar of artistic photography at the start of the Photo-Secession and was celebrated in early issues of *Camera Work*. He was also Stieglitz's link to modern European art and his collaborator on exhibitions at the Little Galleries of the Photo-Secession. Strand, in contrast, was a decade younger and represented a new generation: photographers who were influenced not by the fin de siècle Symbolist painting that inflected Steichen's early work but instead by the very type of European avant-garde art that Steichen had helped Stieglitz present to the American public. Strand's photographs of 1916–17, which filled the pages of the final double issue of *Camera Work*, led the way to a straightforward, modern photography unencumbered by the allegorical themes, celebrity subjects, and painterly techniques of turn-of-the-century artistic photography.

THE BIG THREE

"I was born in Hoboken. I am an American. Photography is my passion. The search for Truth is my obsession."[6] So began an autobiographical statement by Alfred Stieglitz (1864–1946) in the catalogue for a show of his photographs at the Anderson Galleries in 1921. Although born across the Hudson River, this son of well-off German-Jewish immigrants spent most of his childhood in Manhattan. He studied in Germany beginning in 1881, first in Karlsruhe and then Berlin, and remained there throughout the 1880s, absorbing European culture and immersing himself in the methods and aesthetics of amateur artistic photography. He chose subjects common among amateurs—portraits, "types," genre scenes, and historic or picturesque aspects of European cities—but his early photographs stood out, as they would throughout his life, as technically accomplished and meticulously printed. Back in New York in the 1890s, Stieglitz became a steady contributor and frequent award winner at photographic exhibitions across America and abroad as well as a forceful writer on both the chemistry and aesthetics of photography for magazines such as *American Amateur Photographer*. After taking charge of a photoengraving firm that his father had invested in (with the vain hope that Alfred might turn a profit in some aspect of photography, the only field he seemed to love), in 1893 Stieglitz entered a financially convenient but spiritually and intellectually vacant—and ultimately miserable—marriage to Emmeline Obermeyer, sister of his friend and business partner.

At the turn of the century, in nearly every city and town across America and Europe, amateur photographers were banding together to form photographic societies. These were typically one part social club, one part communal darkroom, and one part vehicle for promoting members' work through exhibitions and modest publications. New York, naturally, had two: the Society of Amateur Photographers, and the New York Camera Club. After helping to merge them in 1896 into a single large and wealthy Camera Club of New York—the most important such organization in America—Stieglitz proposed the following year that the club's newsletter be replaced with a substantial and beautifully illustrated quarterly magazine, to be titled *Camera Notes*. Stieglitz stipulated that he, as chairman of the Publications Committee and editor of the magazine, was to have "the unhampered and absolute control of all matters, direct or remote, relating to the conduct of the proposed publication."[7] As promised, *Camera Notes*, published beginning in July 1897, brought new members as well as notoriety to the Camera Club of New York, but most of all it provided Stieglitz a platform with international reach, and by 1900, at the age of thirty-six, he was already recognized as the leading tastemaker in American photography.

It was natural, then, that a twenty-one-year-old aspiring painter and photographer from Milwaukee—on his way to Paris to study painting and to see the Rodin Pavilion just outside the 1900 Exposition Universelle—would make a stop at the Camera Club of New York. Edward Steichen (1879–1973) was by that time an accomplished photographer in the soft-focus, self-consciously artistic style that distinguished serious amateurs from casual snapshooters and commercial studios alike, and he came to Stieglitz with the endorsement of one of the country's leading artistic photographers, Clarence White. Impressed by the young Midwesterner, Stieglitz bought three of his photographs—a self-portrait and two moody, atmospheric woodland scenes printed in platinum (plates 54, 55)—for the impressive sum of five dollars each. Elated, Steichen (who told Stieglitz that he'd never before sold a photograph for more than fifty cents[8]) left additional photographs from his portfolio for Stieglitz to publish or send to exhibitions, as he saw fit, and then boarded the ship for Europe.

Once in France, Steichen quickly abandoned his painting studies at the Académie Julian, but he took heed of both the French academic tradition and the latest trends in painting and sculpture, including the work of Whistler and Rodin. More important, he began to focus his energies on photography. He learned the technical intricacies of the gum bichromate process,[9] popular among the members of the Photo-Club de Paris; befriended Stieglitz's erstwhile friend and current rival, F. Holland Day; and happily participated in Day's exhibition, "The New School of American Photography," in London and Paris.[10] He also developed a reputation as a portraitist of noted artists, writers, and members of society. By the time Steichen returned from Paris, in August 1902, he was perfectly positioned to launch his own career and to serve as Stieglitz's chief acolyte. Arriving back in New York, where it was clear that he could make his fortune more easily than in Milwaukee, Steichen rented a studio on the top floor of a brownstone at 291 Fifth Avenue, between Thirtieth and Thirty-first streets, conveniently around the corner from the well-equipped darkrooms, library, and meeting rooms of the Camera Club of New York, on Twenty-ninth Street. He had a small, street-level showcase made and "hung out [his] shingle as a professional portrait photographer."[11]

Stieglitz, too, was ready to turn a corner in 1902. Longtime members of the Camera Club, increasingly rankled by his autocratic editorship of *Camera Notes*, grew disillusioned to find themselves excluded from the pages of their own organization's journal and, consequently, from the exhibitions selected by Stieglitz and his followers. Stieglitz, in turn, chafed at the club's resistance to the artists and aesthetic direction he championed. His opportunity to make a definitive break came in early 1902 with the invitation to organize a photographic exhibition at the National Arts Club. The 162 works by 31 photographers that Stieglitz selected—including large concentrations of photographs by Stieglitz himself, Day, William Dyer, Frank Eugene, Käsebier, Joseph Keiley, Steichen, and White—represented the clearest expression yet of his aesthetic vision. When it opened on March 5, 1902, the exhibition, billed as "American Pictorial Photography Arranged by The 'Photo-Secession,'" was Stieglitz's declaration that he and a group of like-minded artists (most without even knowing it!) had seceded from the photographic establishment and formed their own association. Never mind that nothing more than the name and a generalized desire yet existed, or that "secession" did not entail giving up membership in the Camera Club, with its excellent darkroom facilities. "In fact," recalled Steichen later, "no one but Stieglitz seemed to know just what 'Photo-Secession' meant."[12] At the opening Käsebier asked Stieglitz, "What's this Photo-Secession? Am I a photo-secessionist?" "Do you feel you are?" he responded. "I do," she said, to which Stieglitz replied, "Well, that's all there is to it."[13] In truth, that's not all there was to it; the Photo-Secession was entirely Stieglitz's invention, and the decisions as to who was or wasn't a "fellow," "associate," or "member" of the group would be

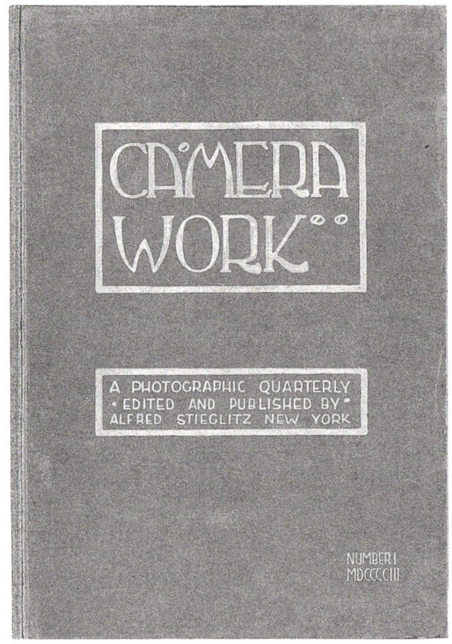

Figure 1. *Camera Work*, no. 1 (January 1903). Cover design by Edward Steichen. The Metropolitan Museum of Art, New York, Alfred Stieglitz Collection, by exchange, 1953 (53.701.1)

based on whether he alone felt the artist was worthy. The group he envisioned was modeled on the Brotherhood of the Linked Ring, a coterie of British photographers (and also Stieglitz) who had broken from the Royal Photographic Society, while the name recalled other artistic or aesthetic movements such as the Munich and Vienna Secessions. Only in December did Stieglitz announce a nominal governing structure, which consisted of a director (himself) and a council of twelve, but even then everyone in the group's orbit understood that, in reality, the Photo-Secession was Stieglitz. Unconstrained by the administrative strictures and political loyalties of the Camera Club, Stieglitz was free to chart a new course.

Over the next decade and a half, Stieglitz exercised his considerable influence by two means: publication and exhibition. First was *Camera Work*, a new journal, even more lavish than *Camera Notes*, in which he published poetry, exhibition reviews, and writings about aesthetics alongside illustrations, primarily hand-pulled photogravures printed on Japanese tissue and tipped into the magazine. The cover, with a hand-drawn Art Nouveau typeface, was designed by Steichen (fig. 1). Whenever possible the printing plates were made from original negatives, and Stieglitz considered the resulting illustrations to be not *reproductions* of photographs but rather *original* photographs printed in gravure. No journal before or since has matched *Camera Work*'s sumptuous production; indeed, photogravure illustrations from its pages are themselves highly prized today.

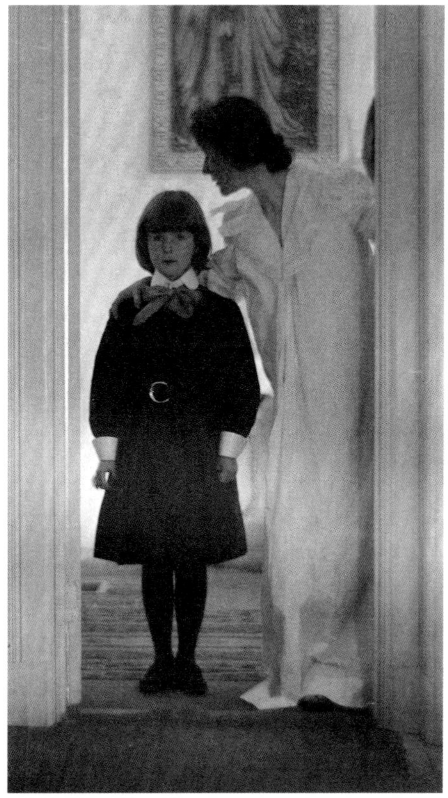

Figure 2. Gertrude Käsebier, *Blessed Art Thou Among Women*, 1899. Platinum print, 9 1/16 x 5 3/16 in. (23 × 13.2 cm). The Metropolitan Museum of Art, New York, Alfred Stieglitz Collection, 1933 (33.43.132)

The first number of *Camera Work*, issued in December 1902 but dated January 1903, featured the work of Gertrude Käsebier (fig. 2)—the grande dame of artistic photography in America—much to the chagrin of Steichen, who thought he deserved the honor of the premiere issue. The second issue was devoted exclusively to him, however, and contained eleven full-page images (seven of them gravures) as well as articles on Steichen by Charles Caffin and Sadakichi Hartmann (under the pseudonym Sidney Allan), an appreciation by Maurice Maeterlinck, and a short defense of photographic manipulation, "Ye Fakers," by Steichen himself. Over the fifteen-year, fifty-issue run of *Camera Work*, no other artist would be featured as prominently as Steichen, who had sixty-five photographs and three paintings reproduced in fifteen issues, including a "Special Steichen Supplement" in April 1906 and an all-Steichen double issue in 1913.[14] Among the works reproduced in the second issue were *The Pool—Evening* (one of Steichen's early woodland scenes; plate 56) and examples of the two principal genres that Steichen had pursued in Paris: painterly nudes in vaguely allegorical, decidedly artistic poses (*Dolor*, *Dawn Flowers*, *Nude with Cat*) and portraits of famous artists (Rodin, Albert Bartholomé, Paul-Albert Besnard, Franz von Lenbach). His portrait of Rodin (fig. 3), which he eventually combined with a second negative to make *Rodin—The Thinker* (plate 78), was particularly admired; Hartmann praised it as a man's whole life "condensed into a simple silhouette, but a silhouette of somber splendor, powerful and personal, against a vast background, where black and white seem to struggle for supremacy."[15] Only after a year of visiting the revered sculptor's studio each Saturday had Steichen dared to photograph him. Steichen's respectful persistence, and above all the power of the resulting picture, inspired mutual admiration and a genuine friendship that lasted until Rodin's death.

Equally important for broadcasting Stieglitz's view of artistic photography was the Photo-Secession's exhibition program, which at first consisted of groups of worthy works assembled by Stieglitz and "loaned by the Photo-Secession" to exhibitions around the country and abroad. Then, in the summer of 1905, a dedicated venue was inaugurated after Steichen moved his studio to larger rooms across the hall (actually in 293 Fifth Avenue) and arranged for Stieglitz to assume the lease on his former space and two recently vacated adjacent rooms for $50 a month. These modest quarters, christened the Little Galleries of the Photo-Secession but often referred to simply as "291," after its Fifth Avenue address, were envisioned as a place where New Yorkers could see the work of Photo-Secession artists and the best photography being produced overseas. Redesigned by Steichen, the gallery space was described in the April 1906 issue of *Camera Work*: "One of the larger rooms is kept in dull olive tones, the burlap wallcovering being a warm olive gray; the woodwork and moldings similar in general color, but considerably darker. The hangings are of olive-sepia sateen, and the ceiling and canopy are of a very deep creamy gray. The small room is designed especially to show prints on very light mounts or in white frames. The walls of this room are covered with a bleached natural burlap; the woodwork and molding are pure white; the hangings a dull *écru*. The third room is decorated in gray-blue, dull salmon, and olive gray."[16] Among the hundred photographs in the first show, which opened on November 25, 1905 (fig. 4), were eleven by Steichen, including *The Flatiron*, *In Memoriam*, *Portraits—Evening*, and *Rodin—The Thinker* (plates 61, 67, 73, and 78). The following year, Stieglitz selected works for exhibitions (which Steichen designed and hung) featuring the photographs of Pictorialists from France, Britain, Austria, and Germany; Käsebier and White; and Steichen himself, the first of four solo shows that Stieglitz would grant him.[17]

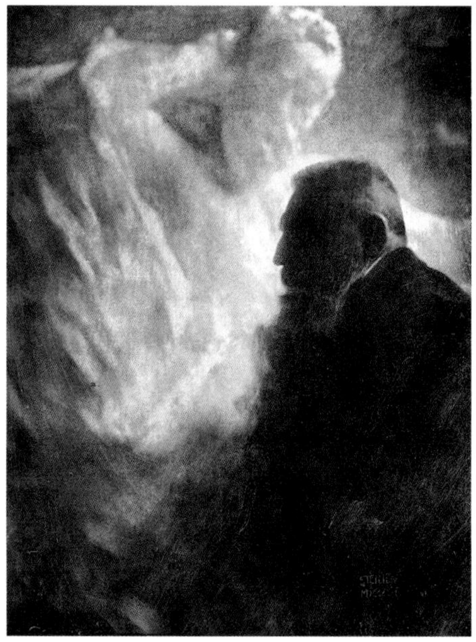

Figure 3. Edward Steichen, *Rodin*, 1901. Direct carbon print, 10$\frac{9}{16}$ x 8 in. (26.9 × 20.3 cm). The Metropolitan Museum of Art, New York, Alfred Stieglitz Collection, 1933 (33.43.4)

That first Steichen exhibition, on view from March 7 to April 5, 1906, included many photographs now deemed to be among his early masterpieces: *Rodin—The Thinker*; *Richard Strauss*; *Portraits—Evening* (titled *Mr. and Mrs. Steichen*); *Alfred Stieglitz and His Daughter Katherine*; *In Memoriam*; *The Little Round Mirror*; *La Cigale*; *The Brass Bowl*; *The Big Cloud, Lake George*; *The Pool—Evening*; and *The Pond—Moonrise*. Here were the themes that Steichen had already developed in Milwaukee and Paris: the celebrity portrait, the twilit woodland scene (though far more graphically powerful in *The Pond—Moonrise*; plate 60), and the painterly nudes that Hartmann called "the best and noblest aspirations of [Steichen's] artistic nature," seeing in them both mysticism and beauty.[18]

But there was something new as well: *The Flatiron*. In 1904, with the lessons of his first Paris sojourn still fresh in his mind, Steichen had turned his camera to his newly adopted city and to the astonishingly tall, 22-story skyscraper designed by Chicago architect Daniel H. Burnham for a triangular lot at the intersection of Fifth Avenue, Broadway, and Twenty-third Street. Stieglitz, whose earlier photograph of the building (fig. 5) Steichen surely knew, described the building's enormous height and unusual shape as "moving toward me like the bow of a monster ocean steamer, a picture of the new America which was in the making."[19] In *The Flatiron*, Steichen's chromatic range consciously echoed Whistler's Nocturne paintings, and the branch jutting in from the picture edge recalls similar devices found in Japanese ukiyo-e prints, which were very much in vogue in turn-of-the-century Paris. Although indebted to these influences, Steichen's iconic photograph is decidedly modern and American in its subject, with the soaring structure rising so high above the activity of the street that it cannot be contained within the frame.

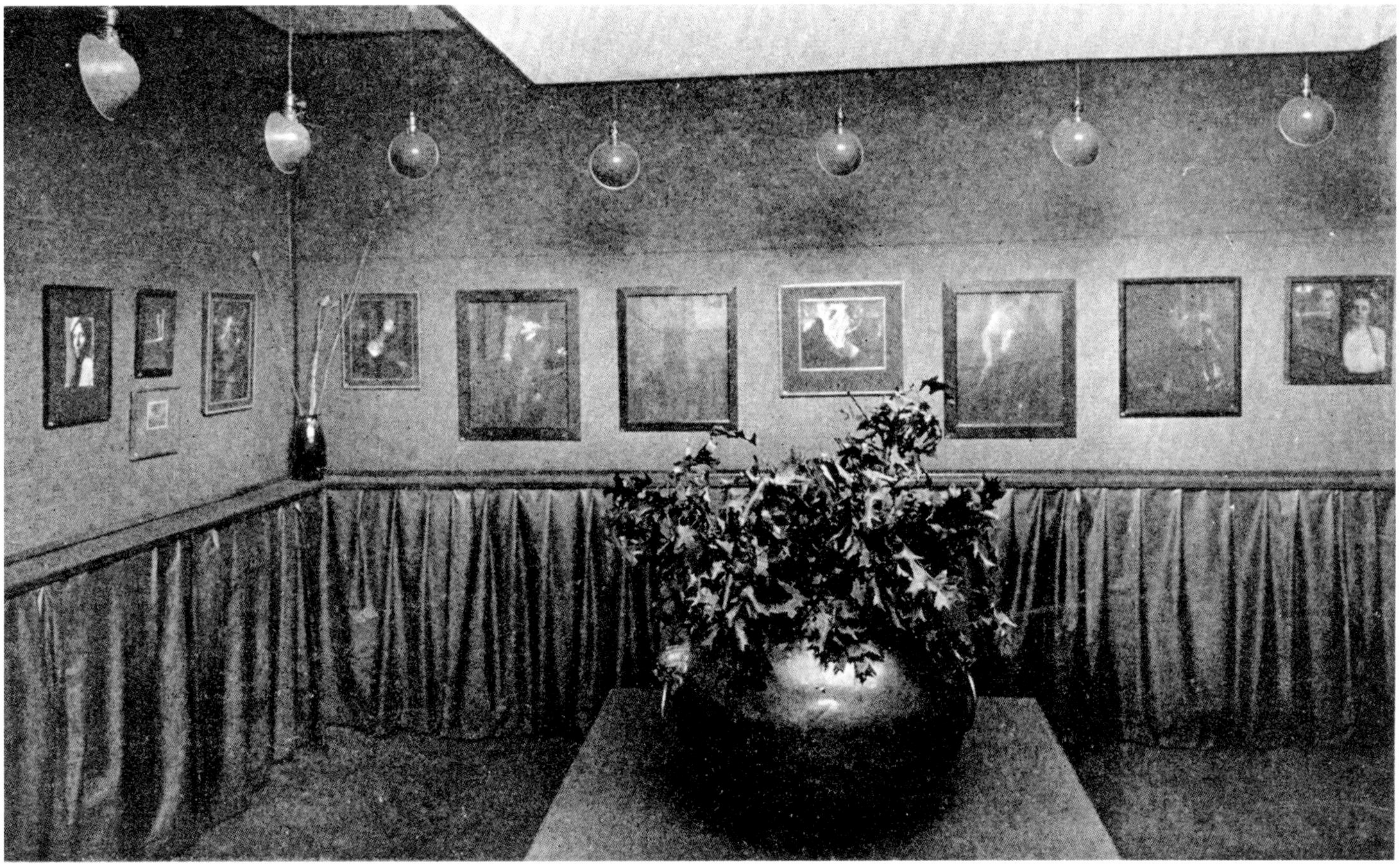

Figure 4. *The Little Galleries of the Photo-Secession . . . Decoration Designed by E. J. Steichen, Opening Exhibition, November 24, 1905–January 5, 1906*, in *Camera Work*, no. 14 (April 1906), p. 42. The Metropolitan Museum of Art, New York, Alfred Stieglitz Collection, by exchange, 1953 (53.701.14)

Although the three versions of *The Flatiron* (plates 61–63) were printed from the same negative, Steichen achieved varied coloristic effects, suggesting successive moments of twilight, by brushing layers of pigmented gum bichromate over platinum prints. Prints of *The Flatiron* were exhibited not only at the Little Galleries—in the inaugural show of 1905 and Steichen's first show, in 1906—but also at the Cincinnati Art Museum in the February 1906 "Exhibition of Photographic Art," the 1909 "International Photographische Ausstellung" in Dresden, and the landmark "International Exhibition of Pictorial Photography," held at the Albright Art Gallery (now the Albright-Knox Art Gallery) in Buffalo in 1910, the capstone of Stieglitz's efforts to promote Pictorialist photography as a fine art. It is likely that the blue-green print (plate 62) was made in 1909 especially for the Dresden show and was subsequently sent to Buffalo. All three prints—the *only* three prints of the image—were acquired by Stieglitz and ultimately given to the Metropolitan. Crown jewels of the Museum's collection, they remain prime examples of the conscious effort of Photo-Secession photographers to assert the artistic potential of their medium and to rival painting in scale, color, and individuality.[20]

Steichen's work as a professional portrait photographer flourished, not least in the wake of his famous portrait session with J. P. Morgan in 1903, which was initiated at the request of German painter Fedor Encke, who sought the assistance of a photographer to minimize the sitting time required of his busy subject. After photographing Morgan in the pose requested by the painter, Steichen was permitted to make a second negative for himself, one that shows an intense and assertive Morgan provoked by the photographer's posing instructions to reveal more personality than he intended. "Total time, three minutes," Steichen wrote. When later shown proofs of the two images, Morgan ordered a dozen copies of the first and ripped up the second, the image that would eventually become the iconic portrait of the banker. Despite (or because of) Morgan's initial hostile response, Steichen labored long to make a perfect print for presentation to Stieglitz, one that Morgan himself came to covet (plate 77).[21]

Notwithstanding his prominence in the pages of *Camera Work* and on the walls of the Little Galleries and his success as a portrait photographer, in the autumn of 1906 Steichen determined "to get away from the lucrative but stultifying professional portrait business" and return to France with his family in hopes of resuscitating his idled painting career.[22] It was a move with numerous consequences. For one, it positioned him to embrace the Autochrome, the process for making glass-plate color transparencies introduced by the Lumière brothers in 1907. Steichen—who had experimented with various methods, such as gum bichromate, to introduce color into his photographs—was enthralled by the technique, which he promptly introduced to Stieglitz, who was traveling through Europe that summer. In a long and technical article accompanying three color reproductions of his Autochromes in *Camera Work,* Steichen praised the luminosity of the medium, saying, "One must go to stained glass for such color resonance, as the palette and canvas are a dull and lifeless medium in comparison."[23] Steichen also made what he called his "first attempt at serious documentary reportage"[24] in the summer of 1907, using a borrowed hand camera to photograph the beau monde at Longchamp, the famous horse-racing venue in Paris's Bois de Boulogne. The results were startlingly fresh, unstructured pictures (plates 84, 85) far removed from the highly posed portraits that had long been his livelihood.

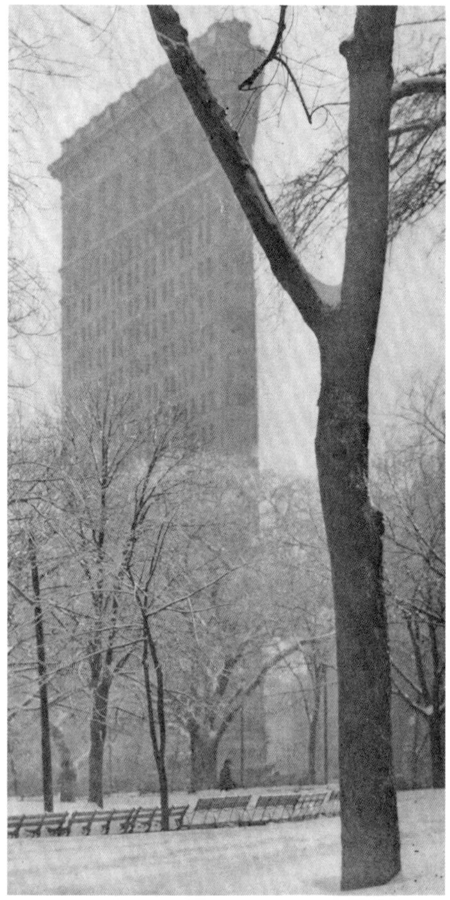

Figure 5. Alfred Stieglitz, *The "Flat-iron,"* 1903, printed 1910 or earlier. Photogravure, 12 15/16 x 6 9/16 in. (32.8 × 16.7 cm). The Metropolitan Museum of Art, New York, Alfred Stieglitz Collection, 1949 (49.55.16)

Steichen's return to Paris helped rekindle his friendship with Rodin and led to an invitation the following autumn to photograph the artist's monumental sculpture of Balzac, whose brooding hulk of a figure, the fruition of years of planning and countless studies, had remained covered in Rodin's studio since the 1900 exposition. Now, a decade after its rejection by the writer's group that had commissioned it, Rodin was trying anew to have the sculpture cast and erected in Paris in memory of the writer. (In fact, it would remain uncast during Rodin's lifetime.) In October 1908 Rodin moved the plaster to the terrace of his studio in Meudon, southwest of Paris, and invited Steichen to photograph it by moonlight. Steichen did just that, relying on exposures ranging from fifteen minutes to an hour. The resulting prints convey all of the commanding presence Rodin had envisioned for the piece: "You will make the world understand my Balzac with your pictures," he told Steichen when given a set of prints a few days later.[25] Steichen sent a second set of prints to Stieglitz for display at 291, and Stieglitz purchased them immediately for himself (plates 79–81).[26]

Of even greater consequence than these advances in his own career was Steichen's role as scout for 291, especially in expanding the gallery's brief to include avant-garde art other than photography, something he and Stieglitz had envisioned before Steichen left New York (and even at the first conception of the gallery). In many cases, the art that Steichen chose for exhibition at 291 constituted American debuts: drawings and watercolors by Rodin in 1908; works on paper by Matisse in 1908 and Picasso in 1911; and sculptures by Matisse in 1912. During a Stieglitz family visit to Paris in 1910, Stieglitz and Steichen attended an exhibition of Cézanne watercolors and "laughed like country yokels as [they] thought of what a red rag this would be in New York."[27] Steichen promptly arranged for the show to be sent to 291 the following winter, the artist's first solo show in America. Along with these artistic premieres, Steichen sent prints by Toulouse-Lautrec, Cézanne, Manet, and Renoir for exhibition in 1909 and 1910; sculpture by Brancusi in 1914; and a host of works by the American painter John Marin beginning in 1910. To this already estimable roster Stieglitz would add the painters Marsden Hartley, Arthur Dove, and Max Weber, the Mexican caricaturist Marius de Zayas, and others. Beginning in 1908, the pages of *Camera Work* and the shows of the Little Galleries of the Photo-Secession focused less and less on camera work and the Photo-Secession and increasingly became, prior to the Armory Show of 1913, the primary American venue for modern art.[28]

Steichen had played a critical role in broadening Stieglitz's interests, but the two began to grow apart in their aesthetic ideas about photography. In his introduction to the 1913 double issue of *Camera Work* (nos. 42/43), which was devoted to Steichen—the man he once held up as the most accomplished artist of the Photo-Secession—Stieglitz framed the issue's content more as repayment of a debt to an important collaborator than a celebration of work worthy in its own right. To glimpse this philosophical rift (which in turn led to a personal estrangement), one need only compare the now familiar style of Steichen's images in that issue with the provocative contents of the Armory Show, an exhibition bursting with the revolutionary ideas and artists that had been championed at 291 in the preceding years and which were already causing Stieglitz to rethink what a modern photograph could be.[29] What remained of their association ended with the outbreak of World War I and Steichen's return in 1914 from France, which over the years had become "another mother country" to him. Stieglitz, in contrast, was conflicted about the war and felt a continued fondness for the German people and culture. Those feelings, according to Steichen, were the catalyst that pushed him "then and there . . . to get into the war on the American side." As head of the photographic section of the Army Air Service Signal Corps, Steichen applied his skills to aerial photography of enemy lines, gun emplacements, and the like (plate 86). "I wanted to be a photographic reporter, as Mathew Brady had been in the Civil War," he later wrote.[30] With the Armistice, he returned to his former home in Voulangis to find his early negatives and prints deteriorated beyond salvation, leaving the photographs that Stieglitz had collected (and would eventually donate to the Metropolitan) as the best surviving representation of his early career.

The war had laid down a dividing line. The audience for Steichen's early photographs—readers of *Camera Work,* visitors to 291, and members of amateur camera clubs—were important within artistic circles, but their number was small compared to the audience he would address following the war. Indeed, Steichen's large and painterly early prints, perhaps because of their rarity, are now far less known by the general public than his portraits of Greta Garbo, Marlene Dietrich, Gloria Swanson, and other celebrities that appeared in Condé Nast's *Vogue* and *Vanity Fair* in the 1920s and 1930s, or his fashion and advertising photographs that shared those same pages (fig. 6).[31] Moreover, while the circulation of *Camera Work* never topped a thousand (and was often much less) and its intended audience was an intellectual elite, the Condé Nast publications catered to a much larger and broader readership, one hungry for just the sort of glamorous

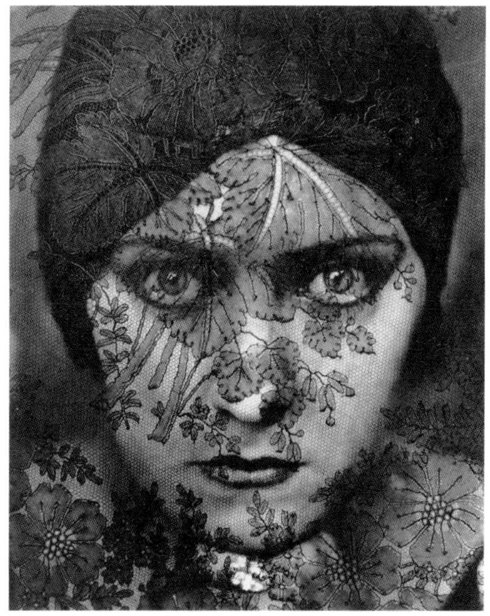

Figure 6. Edward Steichen, *Gloria Swanson,* 1924, printed 1960s. Gelatin silver print, 9 7/16 x 7 1/2 in. (24 × 19.1 cm). The Metropolitan Museum of Art, New York, Gift of Grace M. Mayer, 1989 (1989.1056)

celebrity portraiture at which Steichen excelled. Steichen's embrace of editorial and commercial photography in his own work—to Stieglitz's mind nothing less than apostasy—drove a still greater wedge between the former mentor and protégé. Similarly, Steichen's role as scout and collaborator for cutting-edge exhibitions at 291 contrasts dramatically with the content and popular impact of the single most memorable event of his tenure as curator of photographs at the Museum of Modern Art (1947–62), the 1955 exhibition "The Family of Man," a sentimental spectacle that, in various incarnations, was seen by nine million people around the world and whose frequently reprinted catalogue has sold more than four million copies.

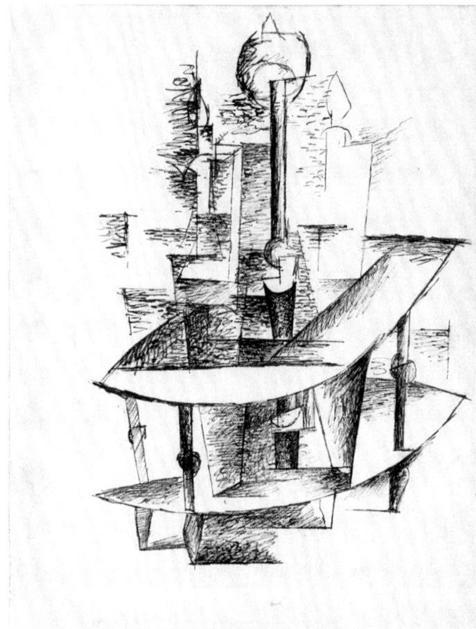

Figure 7. Pablo Picasso, *Still Life with Cruet Set*, 1911. Ink on white wove paper, 12⅜ x 9½ in. (31.4 × 24.1 cm). The Metropolitan Museum of Art, New York, Alfred Stieglitz Collection, 1949 (49.70.31)

In 1907, the pivotal year of Steichen's return to Paris, Paul Strand (1890–1976) was a seventeen-year-old student at New York's Ethical Culture School. His visit that year to a group show of Photo-Secession pictures at the Little Galleries with the school's camera club and its adviser, the pioneering social reformer and photographer Lewis Hine, was the inspiration for a career that would eventually take the medium in a bold new direction. From the moment of his high school graduation, in 1909, Strand devoted himself to photography. He steeped himself in the books and journals at the Camera Club of New York, learning from older members and working in its darkrooms. By the time he asked Stieglitz to critique his work in late 1914 or early 1915, Strand had amassed an impressive portfolio of platinum prints in the Pictorialist tradition of Gertrude Käsebier and Clarence White.

Stieglitz, however, was beginning to rethink the nature and potential of photography in light of the modernist art he had been showing—and studying—at 291. As he moved away from the soft-focus aesthetic he had once championed, Stieglitz abandoned in his own work the somewhat picturesque subjects of his early European photographs and the soft, sooty atmosphere of *The Terminal* and *The Hand of Man* (plates 5, 6). He sharpened his focus and began confronting his subjects squarely. Not surprisingly, he advised Strand to do the same, cautioning that the wide-open aperture Strand was using created a simplification of the image that looked good for a moment but was detrimental to the final expression. Strand took the advice to heart, and on a cross-country trip in 1915 he stopped down his lens and made blockier, more geometric compositions. Years later he recalled the profound change prompted by Stieglitz's admonition: "In 1915 I really became a photographer. I had been photographing seriously for 8 years and suddenly there came that strange leap into greater knowledge and sureness."[32] When he returned to New York he took his portfolio of recent photographs to Stieglitz, and this time the master's reaction was effusive. As Strand recalled, "He was very surprised, and he said 'I'd like to show these. And I'll put them in *Camera Work*.' It was like having the world handed to you on a platter."[33]

Having found a new home, one where Braque and Picasso, Cézanne and Brancusi were in the air, Strand set out to learn what he could from the modern art he had seen at 291 and the Armory Show, in particular how it might be applied to photography: "Not with the idea of imitating or competing with the painting," he said, "but trying to find out what might be its value to someone who wanted to photograph the real world."[34] In the summer of 1916, Strand tested out his new ideas in a groundbreaking series of nearly abstract photographs made at a cottage in Twin Lakes, Connecticut. It's not hard to feel the spirit of Cézanne working on

Strand in photographs such as *Pear and Bowls* (plate 96), with its interrelationship of elemental forms, or of Picasso (fig. 7) in the skewed and flattened spaces of the tabletop in *Jug and Fruit* (plate 97). In *Bowls* (plate 98), Strand pulls in so close as to nearly sever any connection between the real world and the objects themselves, which are reduced to a pattern of elliptical volumes. In the most radical of his images, *Porch Shadows* and its variants (plate 99), Strand used all of the means at his disposal to create an abstraction without resorting to darkroom manipulation. He first placed his subject in a disorienting situation by turning a round table on its side, so that it caught the pattern of sunlight and shadow through the porch balustrade. Then he moved in close with the camera, so that the objects are only partially recognizable. Finally, Strand rotated the print itself 90 degrees, further disorienting the viewer and emphasizing two-dimensional patterning over actual spatial relationships.

As innovative and satisfying as these abstractions were—and as celebrated as they remain today—Strand's "experiments," as he called them, lacked the human content that for him had made photography a worthwhile endeavor in the first place. When he returned to New York in the autumn, Strand set out to make a series of "portraits of people such as you see in the New York parks and places, sitting around, without their being conscious of being photographed."[35] In his earlier New York street scenes (plates 93–95), Strand framed his scene from a somewhat distant, elevated perspective and waited for passersby to be ensnared in his camera's trap. Now he adopted a new strategy to achieve the "candid" quality he sought: he rigged his camera with a prominent but false lens coming off the side, while hiding the real lens, on an extended bellows, under his arm. To casual observers Strand thus seemed to be photographing in one direction when in fact his real subject, which he could see in his viewfinder, was off to his side at a 90-degree angle. The most graphically and emotionally powerful of the resulting images shows a blind peddler (for whom, ironically, no right-angle lens would have been necessary). With *Blind* (plate 103), Strand integrated the boldly simplified forms of modernism with the humanist spirit and social concern that had been a part of his formation at the Ethical Culture School under Hine's tutelage, and which would become an ever greater element of his photographic work following World War I.

Six of Strand's photographs, including the now iconic *Wall Street* (plate 94), appeared in issue 48 of *Camera Work*, and in March 1916 still more were exhibited in a one-person show at 291. A double issue of *Camera Work* in 1917 devoted exclusively to Strand included eleven photogravures that were printed directly on the heavy journal page rather than on tipped-in Japanese tissue. The result was less precious, more direct, more modern—more "brutal," in Stieglitz's words. After years of relative disinterest in photography, of little picture making of his own and pallid enthusiasm for the work of others, Stieglitz wrote effusively about Strand's photographs: "The eleven photogravures in this number represent the real Strand. The man who has actually done something from within. The photographer who has added something to what has gone before. The work is brutally direct. Devoid of all flim-flam; devoid of trickery and of any 'ism;' . . . These photographs are the direct expression of today."[36]

The world was a different place after the upheaval of World War I, and Strand, like Steichen, emerged from the conflict a changed man. Gone was the heady spirit of 291, closed in 1917; the idealism of Strand's liberal schooling lay bruised by events of the war, and his personal pacifism fit awkwardly with his induction into the army in the summer of 1918. Although Strand saw no combat and was discharged the following year, his torrent of creativity in 1915–17 had been interrupted. A continuing interest in portraying people in motion can be seen in his day-in-the-life-of-a-city film *Manhatta* (1921), made in collaboration with the painter and photographer Charles Sheeler,[37] and his embrace of modernity and rigorous sense of a picture's formal structure are also evident in works such as *Akeley Motion Picture Camera*, from 1922 (plate 108). Nonetheless, the humanist roots instilled in Strand by family and schooling alike progressively led him, for the balance of his career, to focus his camera on more traditional subjects—portraiture, architecture, landscape, and nature study—that no doubt seemed even more relevant to him after witnessing the shipwreck of World War I.

Perhaps recalling the exquisite production values and wide impact of *Camera Work*, Strand increasingly turned his attention to making printed portfolios and books rather than fine platinum or gelatin silver prints. In 1940 he published a portfolio of twenty photogravures of images he had made in Mexico between 1932 and 1934, a period of postrevolutionary social reform and cultural efflorescence (plates 114–119). As with a half-dozen of his later book projects that focused on other parts of the world, *Photographs of Mexico* brought together images of traditional architecture, people, and religious subjects to form a collective portrait of place.[38] Whereas his groundbreaking photographs from 1915–17 were more closely related to Cézanne and Picasso than to any photography that had come before, Strand's later work fit squarely in the traditions of photographic practice and humanist concern that were, in fact, more deeply rooted in his soul than the avant-garde aesthetic ideas he had adopted as a young man exhilarated by the embrace of Stieglitz and his circle.

Just as 1902 had been a turning point for Stieglitz—from his break with the Camera Club of New York to the establishment of the Photo-Secession, the founding of *Camera Work*, and the beginnings of his collaboration with Steichen—so, too, was the period about 1917. The double issue of *Camera Work* devoted to Strand was the end of the publication's run, perhaps fittingly. Not only did it mark the journal's return to photography after years of focusing on avant-garde art in other media, it was as visually potent a repudiation of the soft-focus, painterly aesthetics of Pictorialism as the first issues, filled with photographs by Käsebier and Steichen, had been an endorsement. Since at least 1910 Stieglitz had all but abandoned his passionate promotion of Pictorial photography, devoting issues of *Camera Work* or exhibitions at 291 to Cézanne, Rodin, Picasso, Brancusi, and Matisse, and to the American painters Marsden Hartley, Arthur Dove, Charles Demuth, and Abraham Walkowitz. When Strand's exhibition opened in March 1916, there hadn't been a photography show at 291 (other than of Stieglitz's own work) since 1911.

In a sense, Stieglitz's battle for the acceptance of photography as a fine art had been won, even if it would take until 1928 for him to see it admitted into the "sacred halls" of the Metropolitan Museum. Stieglitz, meanwhile, was learning from the exhibitions of modern drawings, prints, paintings, and sculptures that he was presenting for the public's benefit. Finding himself less and less interested in the painterly print processes he had earlier championed (but never fully embraced in his own work), Stieglitz increasingly came to believe that the key to photographic

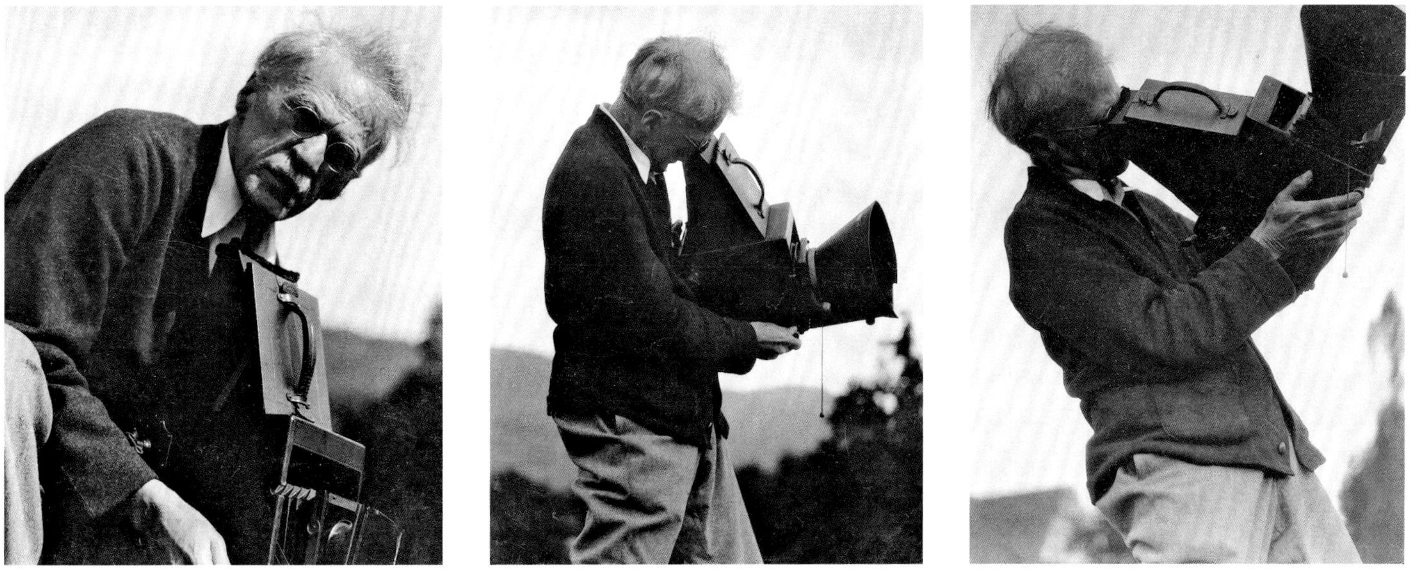

Figures 8–10. Paul Strand, *Alfred Stieglitz, Lake George, New York*, 1929. Gelatin silver prints, 4¾ x 3¾ in. (12 x 9.5 cm) each. Collection of Gary Davis

advancement was to emphasize the qualities unique to the medium rather than techniques that visibly allied it to painting and drawing.

Stieglitz's own photography had languished somewhat during the early years of the Photo-Secession, but beginning about 1910—perhaps energized by the work of modern painters—he made new images of a muscular and bustling New York, including *Old and New New York*, *The City of Ambition* (plates 8, 9), and *The Ferry Boat*. At the same time, he resurrected earlier negatives of New York—*Winter, Fifth Avenue* and *The Terminal* (both 1893), *The Street—Winter* (1897), *The Hand of Man* (1902), and *The "Flat-iron"* (1903)—for an issue of *Camera Work* in 1911 and for an exhibition and special edition of enlarged gravures in 1913. Also included was *The Steerage* (plate 7), which he had taken while en route to Europe in the summer of 1907 but not yet published or exhibited. If this signature image had gone unrecognized until that point, Stieglitz eventually found in it a perfect expression of Cubist ideals in photography. "You may call this a crowd of immigrants," he said. "To me it is a study in mathematical lines, in balance, in a pattern of light and shade."[39] And in 1915 he began a series of portraits of people connected with 291, primarily artists such as John Marin, Marsden Hartley, and Charles Demuth, but also Hodge Kirnon, the building's elevator operator (plates 12–14). Inspired by the lessons of the modern painters he had been displaying, Stieglitz's work of the mid-1910s had a directness and formal structure that his earlier work had not consciously possessed.

Ultimately more momentous for Stieglitz's personal life and his return to photography, however, was a group of drawings delivered to him in January 1916 and which he displayed at 291 the following May. The drawings were the work of a twenty-eight-year-old artist named Georgia O'Keeffe. O'Keeffe subscribed to *Camera Work*; she also had visited 291 in 1908, when she was at the Art Students League, to see the exhibition of Rodin drawings, and she returned in 1914 to see the Braque-Picasso show while a student at Columbia University's Teachers College, but on neither occasion did she speak to Stieglitz.[40] On another visit to 291, in early 1916, they conversed about art, but it was the exhibition of her drawings in May that sparked what became a voluminous correspondence and lifelong romance. In O'Keeffe, Stieglitz felt that he had found not only a painter who was both truly modern and purely American, but also his spiritual and intellectual soul mate. Indeed, it was O'Keeffe's presence and passion that propelled Stieglitz into the most productive years of his career.[41]

In April and May 1917 Stieglitz mounted a second show of O'Keeffe's drawings and watercolors, and the artist traveled by train from Texas for a spontaneous three-day visit to see her work on the walls of 291. During O'Keeffe's stay in New York, Stieglitz—already in love before her arrival—photographed her for the first time. Their brief summer romance and months of passionate correspondence led O'Keeffe to move to New York in June 1918, and although they would not marry until Stieglitz's divorce from Emmy was finalized, in 1924, they moved in together almost immediately. Shortly after the second O'Keeffe exhibition, Stieglitz closed 291. Free of the responsibilities of both the gallery and *Camera Work*, and clearly consumed by his desire for O'Keeffe, Stieglitz photographed her more than a hundred times in 1918 and 1919 in an unparalleled burst of activity.

Between 1917 and 1937, when Stieglitz set aside his camera for health reasons, he made some 331 photographs of O'Keeffe: of her face, torso, hands, or feet alone; clothed and nude; intimate and heroic; introspective and assertive (plates 23–39). His twenty-year-long portrayal of her, arguably his most complex and important body of work, was the most complete expression of his idea of the composite portrait: one that would record a single person throughout life, in many moods and many forms. More than mere documentation, the collective portrait records Stieglitz's psychological turns and charts the heartbeat of the couple's famous relationship, from their initial, rapturous collaboration in 1918 and 1919 through the alternating estrangement and attraction of the 1920s and 1930s, which saw O'Keeffe spending more and more time in the Southwest and Stieglitz lavishing affection and attention on others. Although the images of O'Keeffe gently caressing a horse's skull or the shiny spare wheel of her new Ford V-8 (plates 38, 39) were made at the Stieglitz family compound at Lake George, they evoke her life and art in New Mexico in the 1930s, when she was developing her own strong, independent persona, far from Stieglitz. Such photographs reflect a newfound self-sufficiency and mobility quite in contrast to the extraordinary intimacy that characterized the earliest works in the series. Despite the ups and downs of their relationship, the portrait sessions continued during O'Keeffe's summer visits to New York and Lake George, and their dance of mutual devotion and desire remained an underlying constant for most of Stieglitz's life.

The same notion of seriality—of changed meaning from the same subject—informed Stieglitz's two other important bodies of late work: the Equivalents (plates 40–46), and his late New York City views (plates 50–53). Beginning in 1922, when he was once again fully engaged in making photographs, and then from 1923 to 1934 with the added freedom of a handheld camera that used 4 × 5-inch negatives rather than his customary 8 × 10-inch tripod-bound camera, Stieglitz pointed his lens toward the clouds above Lake George (figs. 8–10). He eventually made more than two hundred photographs in the series, which he initially called Songs of the Sky. In some, such as *Music No. 1* (plate 40), he allowed the horizon to hug the bottom edge of the frame, but in most of the Equivalents all grounding elements have been banished. In these purposely disorienting and nearly abstract images, Stieglitz sought to arouse in the viewer the emotional equivalent of his own state of mind at the time he made the photograph, and to show that the content of a photograph was different from its subject. As visibly as the collective portrait of O'Keeffe charts Stieglitz's own life as much as hers, the Equivalents trace Stieglitz's emotional response to nature through periods of ecstasy and darkness, romantic engagement, and feelings of mortality.

In the spring of 1930, while still engaged in the ongoing portrait of O'Keeffe and with the Equivalents, Stieglitz returned to a subject that earlier had been central to his art: New York City. No longer a twenty-nine-year-old proving himself by braving a blizzard, as he had in taking *Winter, Fifth Avenue* and *The Terminal*, or aiming to convey the bustling metropolis, as he had done in 1910 with images such as *The City of Ambition* and *The Ferry Boat,* Stieglitz instead captured the city from the aerie of his thirtieth-floor rooms in the Shelton Hotel (on Lexington Avenue between Forty-eighth and Forty-ninth streets), where he lived with O'Keeffe from 1925 to 1937, or from the seventeenth-floor windows of An American Place, his final gallery, which opened at Madison Avenue and Fifty-third Street in 1929. From these lofty perches, the city became a slow symphony of abstract planes, ever changing as sunlit walls and tides of deep shadow shifted during the day or as the construction of new towers progressed. Here, finally, was Stieglitz's photographic corollary to high modernist painting, an expression of humanity's relationship to the modern city that was markedly different from the vertiginous street-level views of towers favored most frequently by painters and photographers alike.

In late 1928, as Stieglitz finalized his donation to the Metropolitan, he selected works that represented what was most alive to him at that moment—the sort of photographs he would want as his legacy. These images included seven portraits of O'Keeffe; nine Equivalents; photographs of the barn, trees, and landscape at Lake George; and portraits of Charles Demuth, Waldo Frank, and Dorothy True. How gratifying it must have been to learn that eight of these photographs were displayed in the Met's "Room for Recent Acquisitions" in early 1929, and to find that more visitors that year came to the Print Study Room to see his photographs than prints by Dürer, Rembrandt, Whistler, or Blake.[42] His subsequent gift, in 1933, of Photo-Secession masterpieces was very different: an unburdening of material that he knew to be historically important but that no longer held real interest for him and, moreover, cost him storage fees. He offered the collection to the Museum "without restrictions of any kind provided it would be called for within twenty-four hours," a condition that was promptly met.[43] By then, what must the author of the O'Keeffe portraits have thought of Steichen's Symbolist nudes or Käsebier's endearing portrayal of motherhood? Steichen's moody woodland scenes must have seemed positively old-fashioned compared to the Equivalents, and even *The Flatiron* would likely have struck him as more quaint than modern alongside his own city views. "Please don't fail to remember," he wrote to William Ivins, "that you are at liberty to throw out any print you feel not worthy of your institution. I will have no feelings about it."[44] Fortunately, the collection was both preserved and augmented, and now, with the perspective of history, we can recognize the varied works of Stieglitz, Steichen, and Strand as groundbreaking, influential, beautiful, and moving each in their own voice and at their own perfect moment of accomplishment.

NOTES

1. Quoted in Dorothy Norman, *Alfred Stieglitz: An American Seer* (New York: Random House, 1973), p. 173.
2. Dorothy Norman, ed., "General Cesnola and the Metropolitan," *Twice a Year*, no. 5/6 (1940–41), pp. 147–49.
3. As Richard Whelan points out in his biography of Stieglitz, Cesnola remained director until his death in November 1904, which calls into question Stieglitz's account of both the agreement and its failure to be realized. See Richard Whelan, *Alfred Stieglitz: A Biography* (Boston: Little, Brown and Co., 1995), p. 186.
4. Stieglitz, letter to Ivins, July 9, 1933, files, Department of Photographs.
5. Weston J. Naef, *The Collection of Alfred Stieglitz: Fifty Pioneers of Modern Photography* (New York: The Metropolitan Museum of Art, 1978). Georgia O'Keeffe, *Georgia O'Keeffe: A Portrait by Alfred Stieglitz* (New York: The Metropolitan Museum of Art, 1978; expanded edition with an afterword by Maria Morris Hambourg, New York: The Metropolitan Museum of Art, 1997). Joel Smith, *Edward Steichen: The Early Years* (Princeton: Princeton University Press, in association with The Metropolitan Museum of Art, 1999). Maria Morris Hambourg, *Paul Strand circa 1916* (New York: The Metropolitan Museum of Art, 1998).
6. Alfred Stieglitz, "A Statement," Anderson Galleries, New York, 1921.
7. Alfred Stieglitz, "Valedictory," *Camera Notes* 4, no. 1 (July 1902), p. 4.
8. Smith, *Steichen: Early Years,* p. 40, n. 5; Norman, *Alfred Stieglitz: An American Seer*, p. 47
9. A gum bichromate print (more properly, but less popularly, called gum dichromate) is made by hand-coating a sheet of paper with a sensitized solution of gum arabic and pigment, placing it in direct contact with a negative, and exposing it to sunlight. Wherever the light passes through the transparent portions of the negative and strikes the coated paper, the pigmented gum solution hardens; where the light is blocked by the dark portions of the negative, the coating remains soluble and floats off the paper when developed in a bath of water. Because the pigment can be any color, and because the print can be manipulated during the developing process, gum bichromate prints often resemble paintings, pastels, or drawings in charcoal or red chalk and are characterized by high contrast and a deliberate lack of detail.
10. Day's exhibition was on view at London's Royal Photographic Society from October 10 to November 8, 1900, and at the Photo-Club de Paris from February 22 to March 10, 1901.
11. Edward Steichen, *A Life in Photography* (Garden City, N.Y.: Doubleday & Company, in collaboration with The Museum of Modern Art, 1963), chap. 3, p. 2.
12. Steichen, *Life in Photography*, chap. 3, p. 1.
13. Alfred Stieglitz, "The Origin of the Photo-Secession and How It Became *291*," *Twice a Year*, no. 8/9 (1942), p. 117.
14. Steichen's work appeared in *Camera Work*, nos. 2 (April 1903; 11 photographs), 7 (July 1904; 1 photograph), 9 (January 1905; 1 photograph), 11 (July 1905; 2 photographs), 13 (January 1906; 1 photograph and a Photo-Secession poster), 14 (April 1906; 9 photographs), Special Steichen Supplement (April 1906; 16 photographs), 15 (July 1906; 1 photograph), 19 (July 1907; 1 photograph), 22 (April 1908; 3 photographs), 34/35 (April–July 1911; 4 photographs), 42/43 (April–July 1913, pub. November; 14 photographs and 3 paintings), and 44 (October 1913, pub. March 1914; 1 photograph).
15. Sidney Allan [Sadakichi Hartmann], "A Visit to Steichen's Studio," *Camera Work*, no. 2 (April 1903), p. 28.
16. *Camera Work*, no. 14 (April 1906), p. 48.
17. The other exhibitions were: 1908 (included prints of *After the Grand Prix—Paris* and *Steeplechase Day, Paris—The Grandstand* [plates 84, 85] and the Autochrome *Rodin—The Eve* [plate 82]); 1909 (featuring photographs of Rodin's *Balzac* [plates 79–81]); and 1910 (a show of color photographs).
18. Allan, "Visit to Steichen's Studio," p. 28.
19. Alfred Stieglitz, "Photograph the Flat-Iron Building, 1902–03," *Twice a Year*, no. 14/15 (1946), pp. 188–90; quoted in Whelan, *Stieglitz: A Biography*, p. 161.
20. The brown version of *The Flatiron* (33.43.44) is inscribed "STEICHEN MDCCCCV," presumably indicating a print date of 1905. The blue-green version (33.43.39) retains the original exhibition label indicating its presence in the 1910 Buffalo show, where it was described in the catalogue as being from a negative of 1904 printed in 1909. Naef (*Collection of Stieglitz*, p. 455) dated the green version (33.43.43) to 1909 because of its similarity to the blue-green version; two factors, however, argue in favor of a 1904 or 1905 date for this print: the green hue of the color reproduction of *The Flatiron* in *Camera Work,* no. 14 (April 1906) and the fact that the print visible in the installation view of the inaugural show at the Little Galleries (fig. 4) appears to have greater contrast than the brown version printed in 1905.
21. Steichen, *Life in Photography*, chap. 3, pp. 2–3. Smith (*Steichen: Early Years*, p. 45, n. 93) notes that the Metropolitan's print is a replacement for the one presented to Stieglitz in 1904, which had faded after frequent exhibition.
22. Steichen, *Life in Photography*, chap. 4, p. 1.
23. Steichen, "Color Photography," in *Camera Work*, no. 22 (April 1908), p. 24.
24. Steichen, *Life in Photography*, chap. 4, p. 1.
25. Ibid., p. 2.

26. Smith (*Steichen: Early Years*, p. 35) writes beautifully of Stieglitz's reaction: "Portraits-once-removed of Rodin and, of course, of Balzac, they surely spoke to Stieglitz of himself, too, a perpetually wronged genius staring down the void, feeling kinship with the moon but gazing in troubled love at civilization slumbering below."
27. Steichen, *Life in Photography*, chap. 4, p. 3.
28. For a full account of Stieglitz's exhibition, promotion, and collection of modern art, see Sarah Greenough, ed., *Modern Art and America: Alfred Stieglitz and His New York Galleries*, exh. cat. (Washington, D.C.: National Gallery of Art; Boston: Bulfinch Press, 2000).
29. Whelan (*Stieglitz: A Biography*, p. 309) writes that Arthur Davies "almost certainly asked Stieglitz to help [organize the Armory Show], but the latter declined to become directly involved. . . . He did, however, promise to loan some works and to give his blessing for 291 artists to participate. He also agreed to be listed as an honorary vice president of the exhibition, along with Claude Monet, Odilon Redon, Mrs. Jack Gardner of Boston, and Mabel Dodge."
30. Steichen, *Life in Photography*, chap. 5, p. 2.
31. Steichen was hired by Condé Nast in 1923 as chief photographer for *Vogue* and *Vanity Fair*.
32. Calvin Tompkins, "Profiles: Paul Strand; Look to Things around You," *New Yorker*, September 16, 1974, p. 51; quoted in Hambourg, *Strand circa 1916*, p. 24.
33. Calvin Tompkins, interview with Paul Strand, June 30, 1973, typescript, pp. 2–3, Joyce F. Menschel Photography Library, The Metropolitan Museum of Art; quoted in Hambourg, *Strand circa 1916*, p. 26.
34. William Innes Homer, interview with Paul Strand, June 25, 1974, typescript, p. 5, Joyce F. Menschel Photography Library, The Metropolitan Museum of Art; quoted in Hambourg, *Strand circa 1916*, p. 34.
35. Tompkins, interview with Strand, June 30, 1973, typescript, p. 6; quoted in Hambourg, *Paul Strand circa 1916*, p. 35.
36. Alfred Stieglitz, "Our Illustrations," *Camera Work*, no. 49/50 (June 1917), p. 36.
37. *Manhatta* was the first of five films Strand filmed or directed; the others were *The Live Wire* (1925), *The Plow that Broke the Plains* (1936), *The Wave* (1936), and *Native Land* (1942).
38. For a full account of Strand's time in Mexico and of the publication of the portfolio *Photographs of Mexico*, see James Krippner et al., *Paul Strand in Mexico* (New York: Aperture, 2010). Strand's later books were *Time in New England* (1950), *La France de profil* (1952), *Un paese* (1955), *Tir a'Mhurain / Outer Hebrides* (1962), *Living Egypt* (1969), and *Ghana: An African Portrait* (1976). *Photographs of Mexico* was reprinted in 1967 under the title *The Mexican Portfolio.*
39. Whelan, *Stieglitz: A Biography*, p. 279, quoting Edward Abrahams, "Alfred Stieglitz and The Metropolitan Museum of Art," *Arts*, June 1979, p. 88 (quotation from *Outlook*, February 20, 1924).
40. *O'Keeffe: A Portrait*, pp. 2–3.
41. Sarah Greenough's monumental catalogue raisonné of the National Gallery of Art's "key set" provides the best narrative of Stieglitz's photographic career and is the essential reference for dating and titling his photographs: Sarah Greenough, *Alfred Stieglitz: The Key Set. The Alfred Stieglitz Collection of Photographs* (Washington, D.C.: National Gallery of Art; New York: Harry N. Abrams, 2002). Of the 1,642 photographs that Stieglitz (and later O'Keeffe) selected to represent his career from 1886 to 1937 (the key set), 1,190 date to the period from 1917 forward.
42. Unsigned and undated memo to William Ivins, files, Department of Photographs. In 1929, 154 visitors came to see Stieglitz's photographs; 84 came to see works by Dürer, 109 for Rembrandt, 39 for Whistler, and 45 for Blake.
43. Stieglitz's account of the gift, written in a letter to assistant curator Olivia Paine, who received his phone call offering it, is transcribed in full in Naef, *Collection of Stieglitz*, pp. 9–10.
44. Stieglitz, letter to Ivins, July 9, 1933, files, Department of Photographs.

PLATES

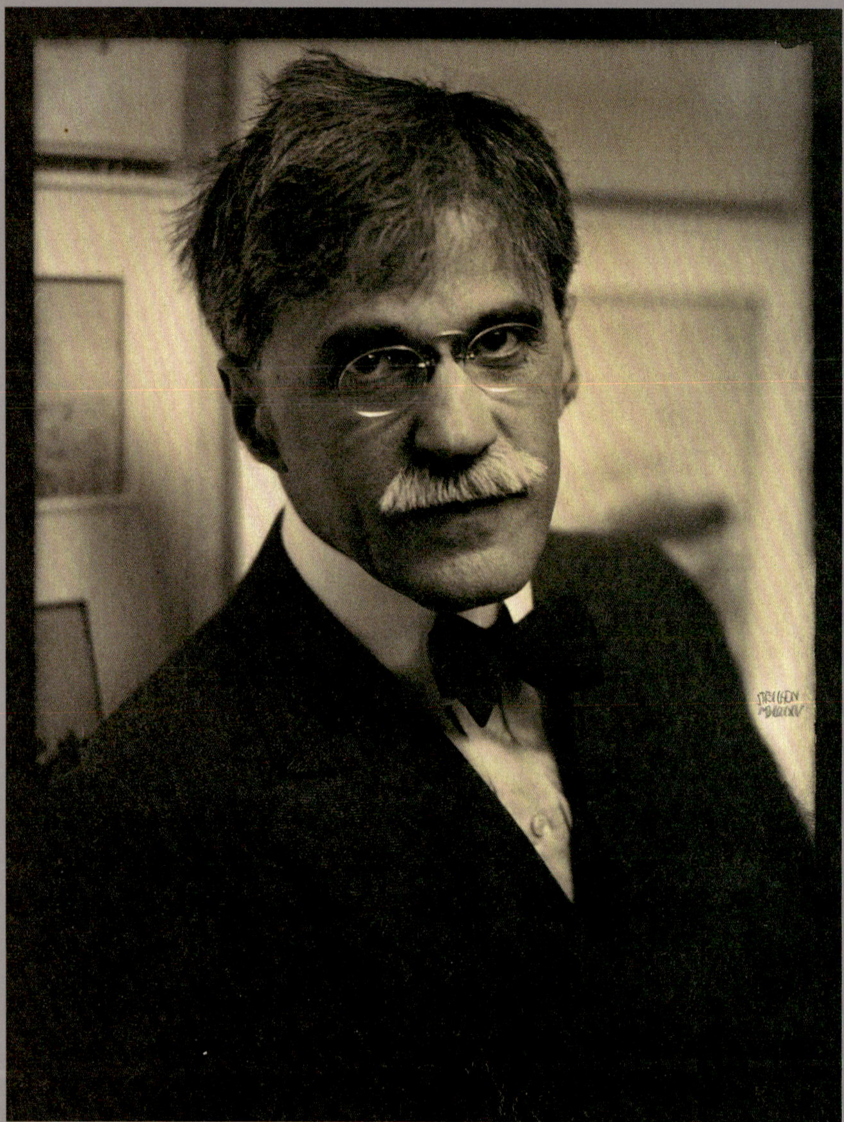

Edward Steichen
Alfred Stieglitz at 291
1915
Gum bichromate over platinum print
11 5/16 x 9½ in. (28.8 x 24.2 cm)
The Metropolitan Museum of Art, New York
Alfred Stieglitz Collection, 1933
33.43.29

ALFRED STIEGLITZ

1. ***Spring Showers, the Coach***
1899–1900

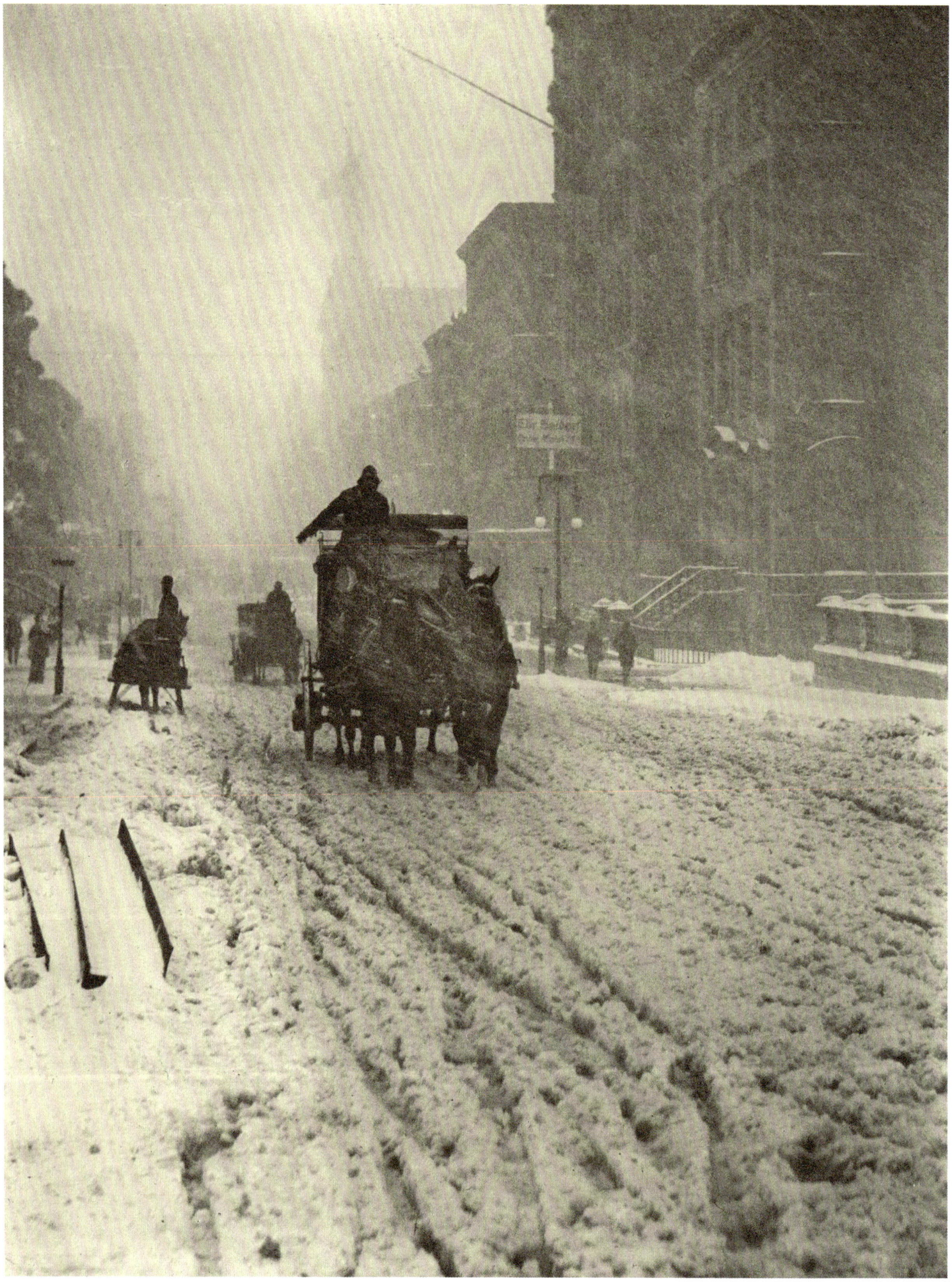

2. *Winter, Fifth Avenue*
1893, printed 1897

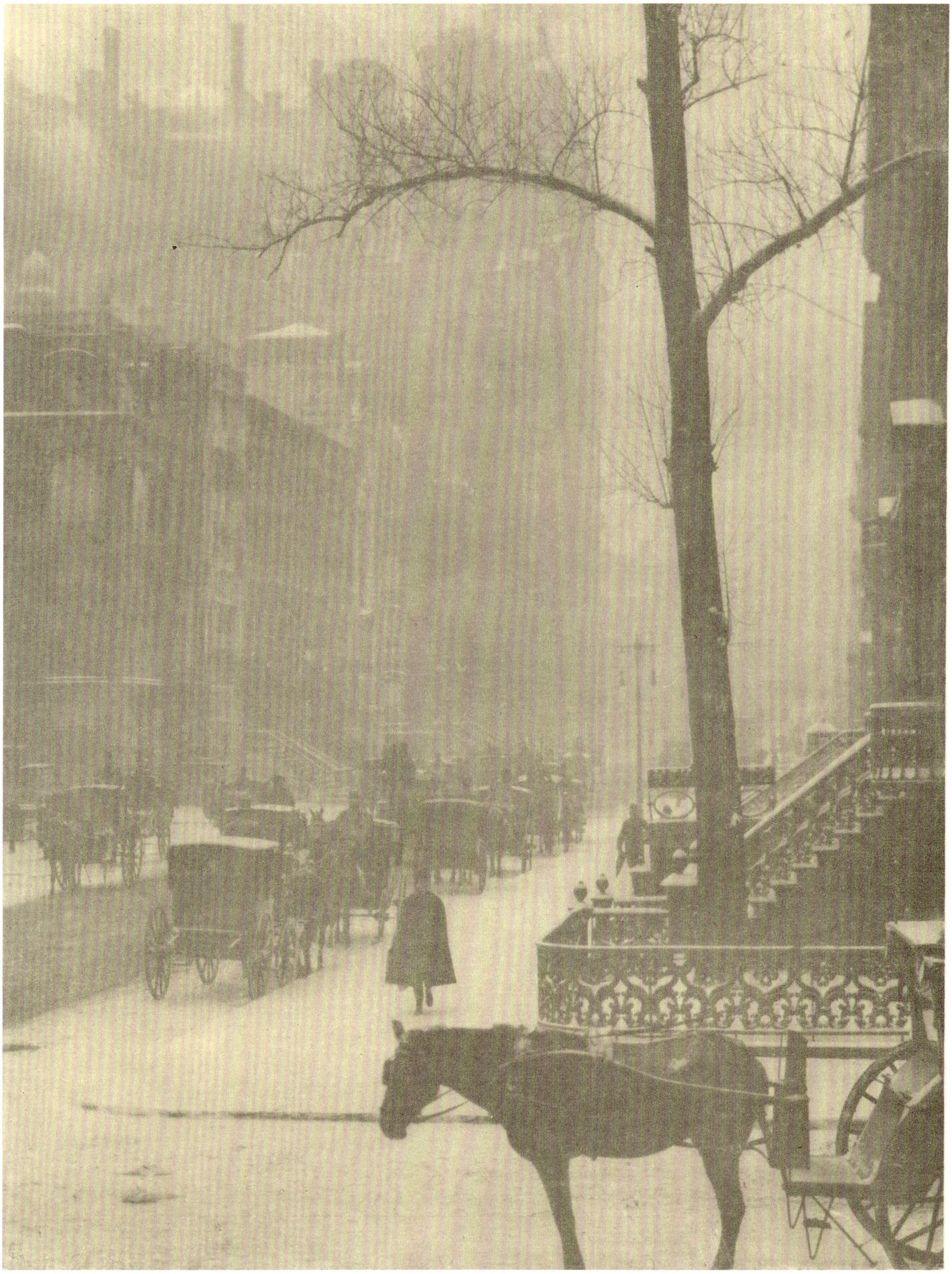

3. *The Street—Fifth Avenue*
1900–1901, printed 1903–4

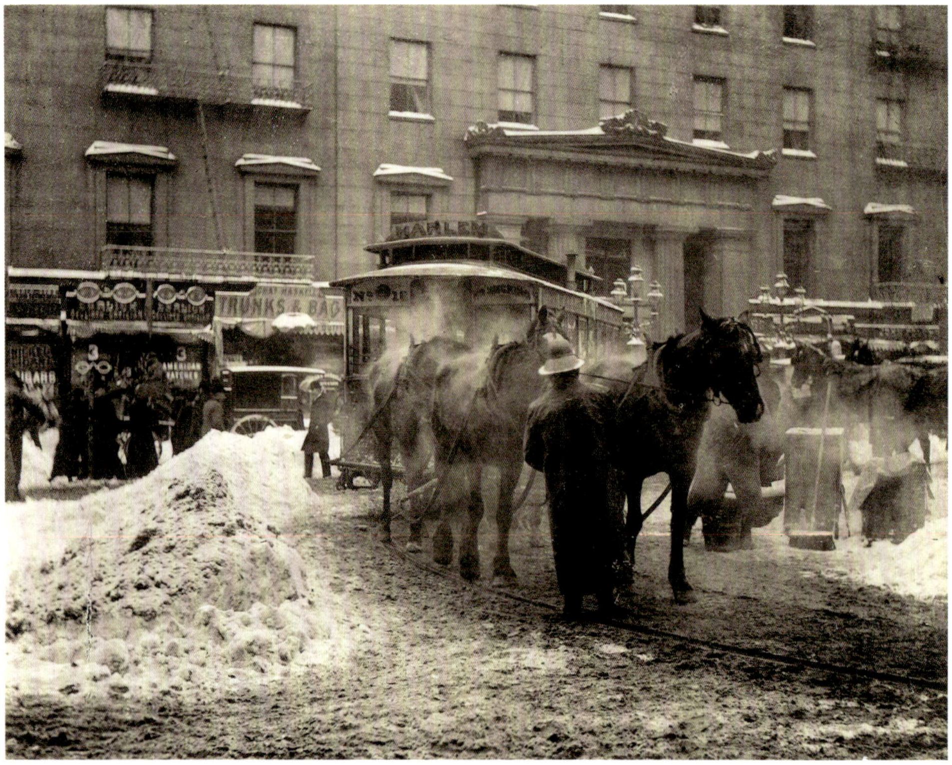

4. *The Terminal*
1893, printed 1920s–1930s

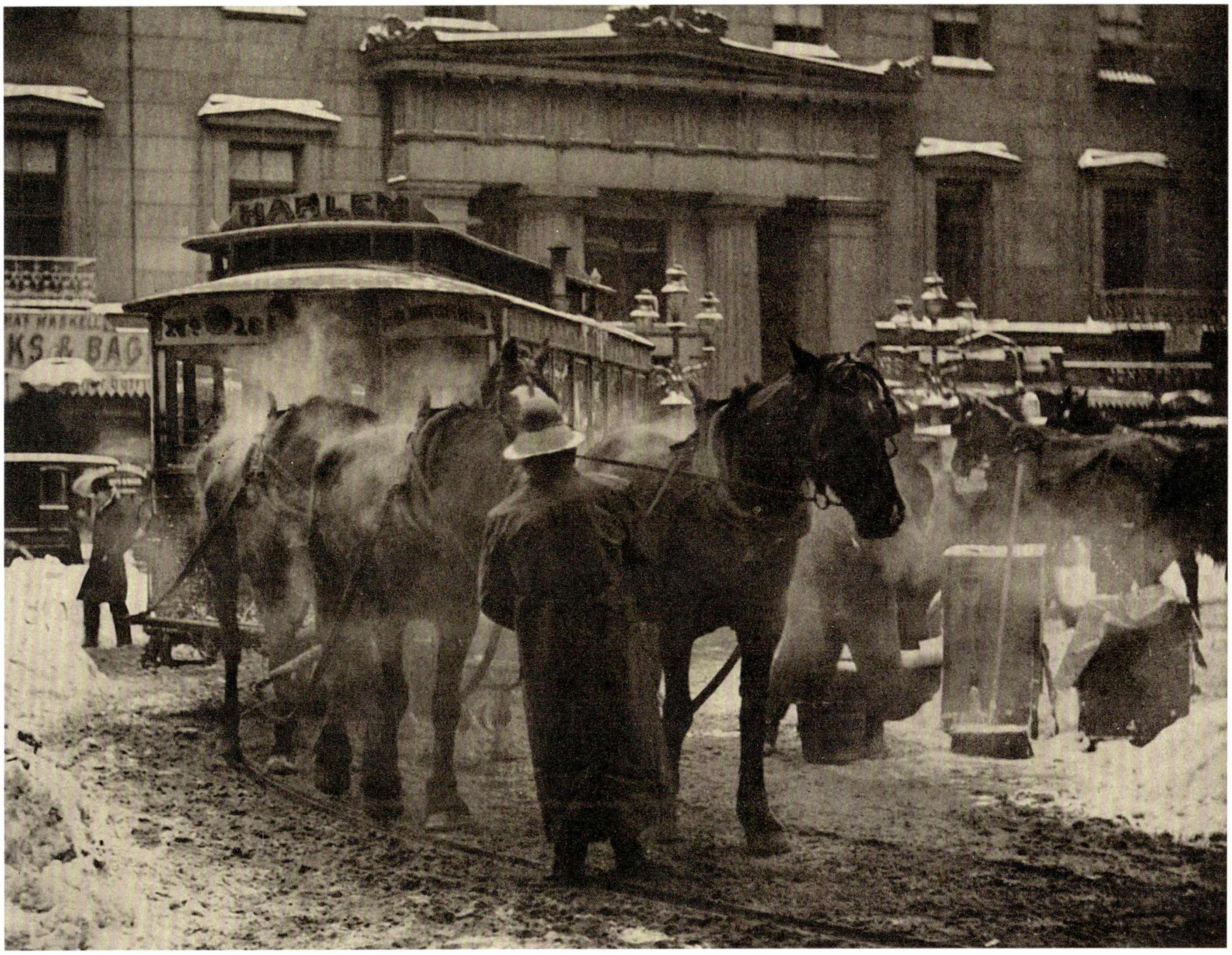

5. ***The Terminal***
1893, printed 1913 or earlier

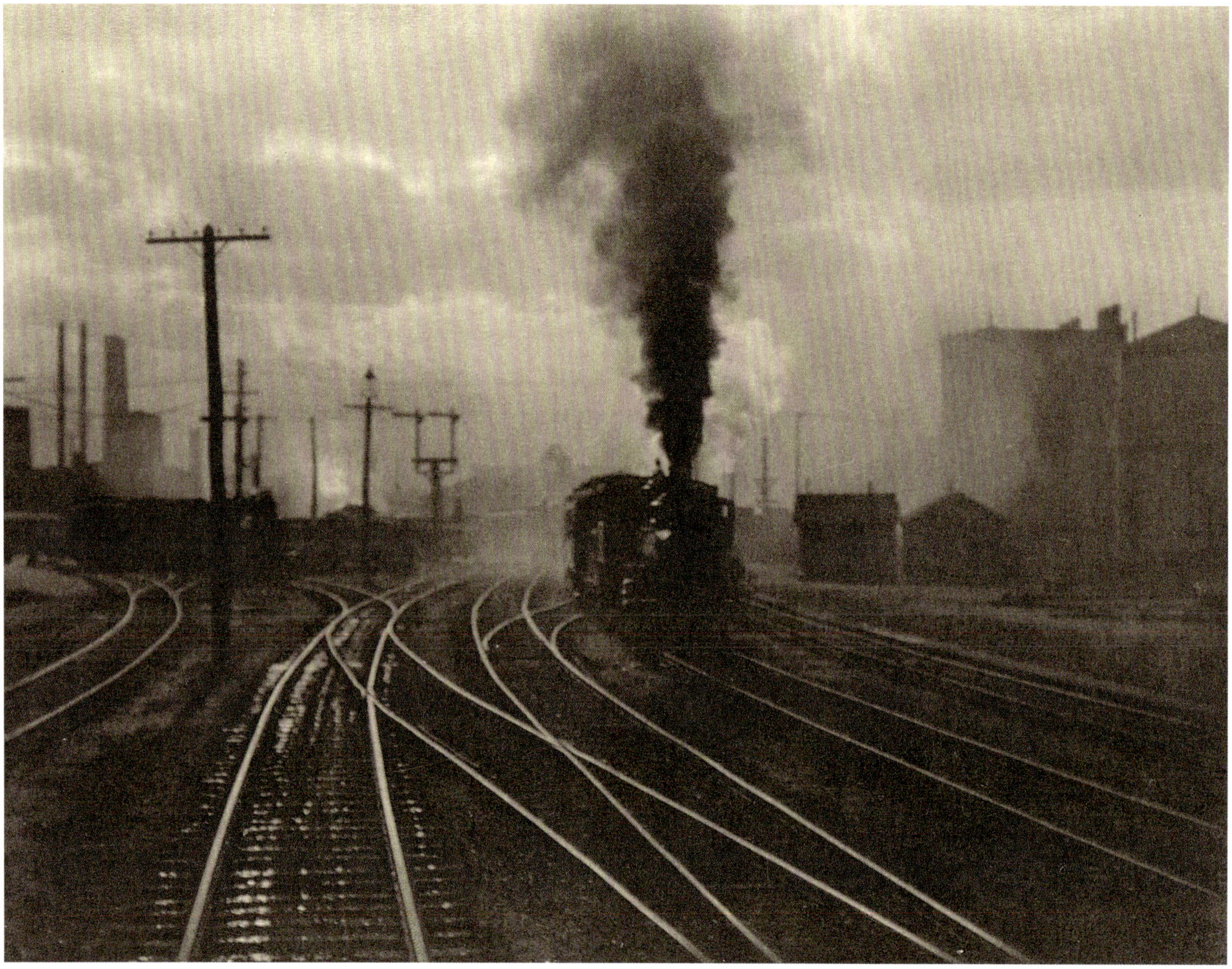

6. ***The Hand of Man***
1902, printed 1910

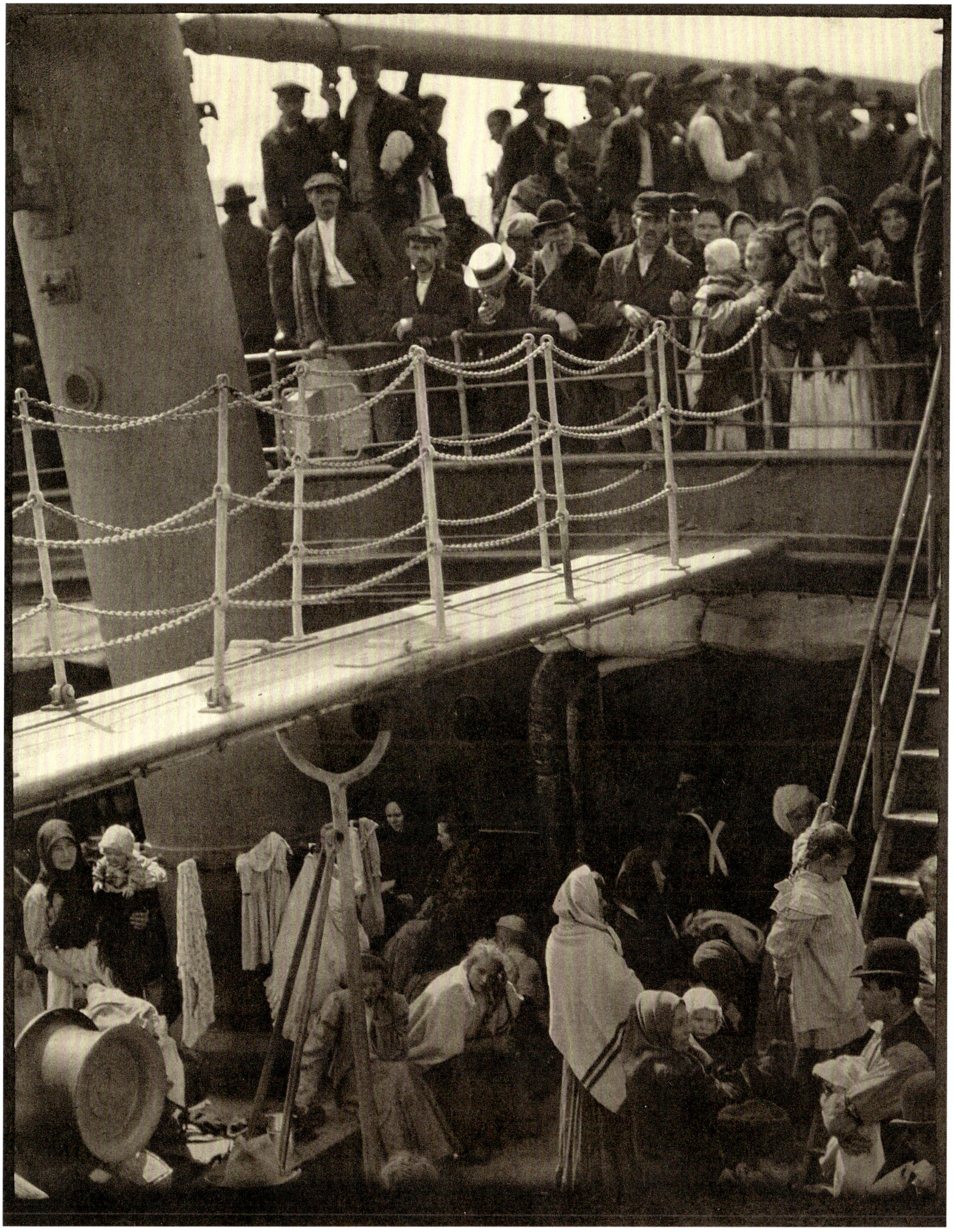

7. *The Steerage*
1907, printed 1913 or earlier

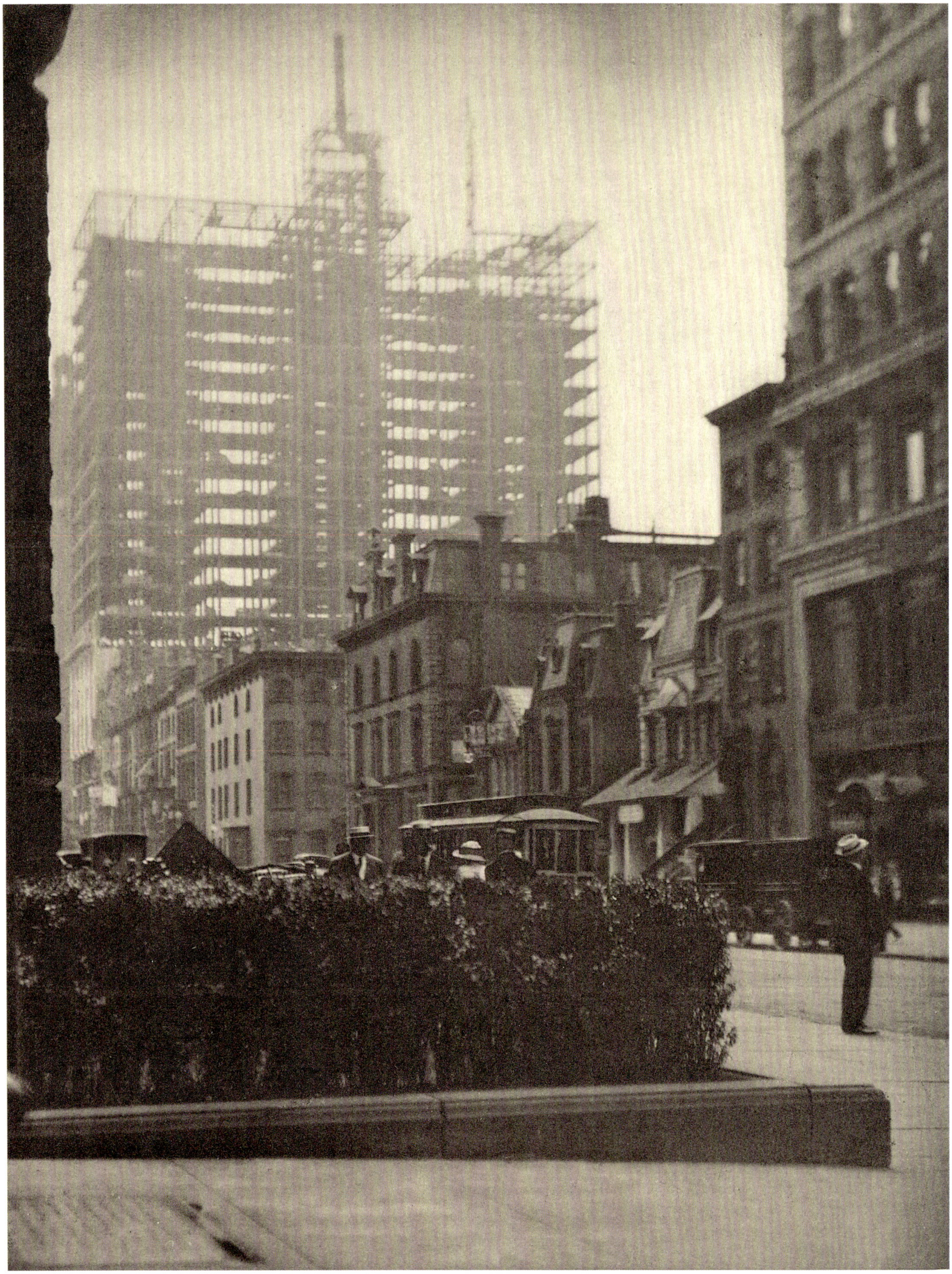

8. ***Old and New New York***
1910, printed 1913 or earlier

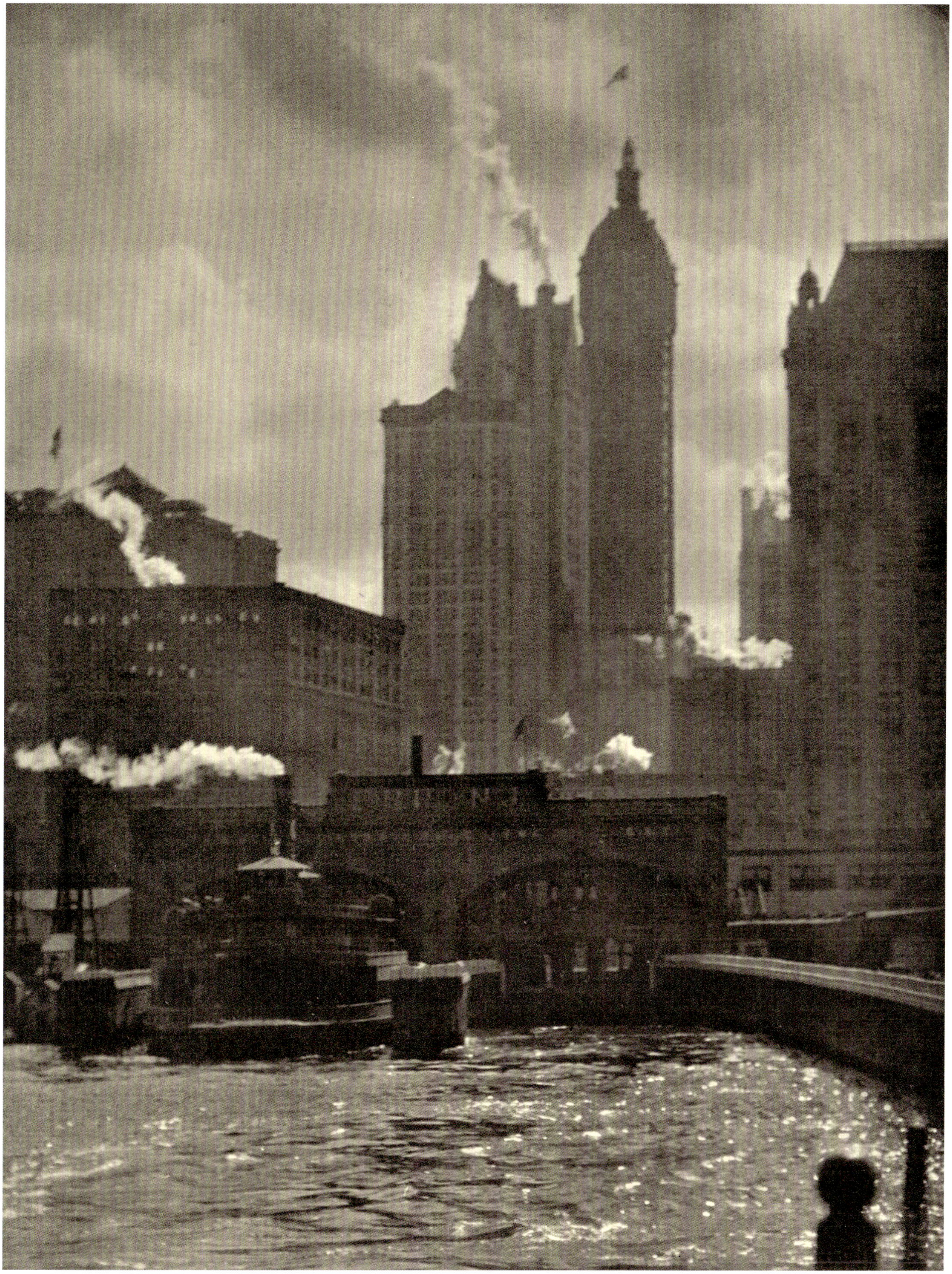

9. ***The City of Ambition***
1910, printed 1913 or earlier

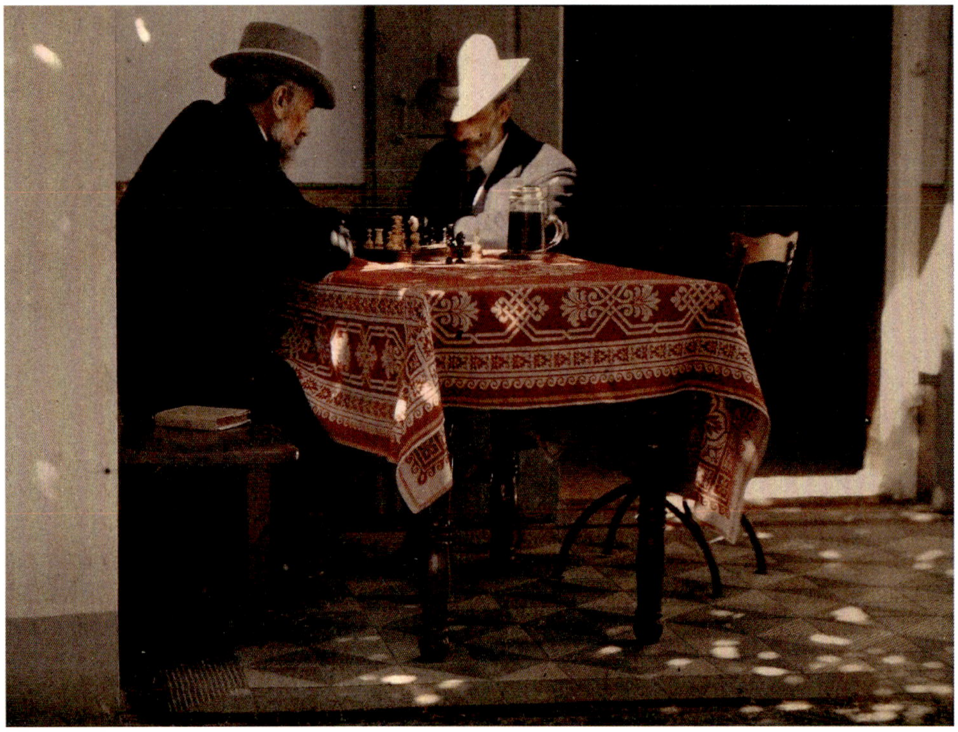

10. *[Two Men Playing Chess]*
1907

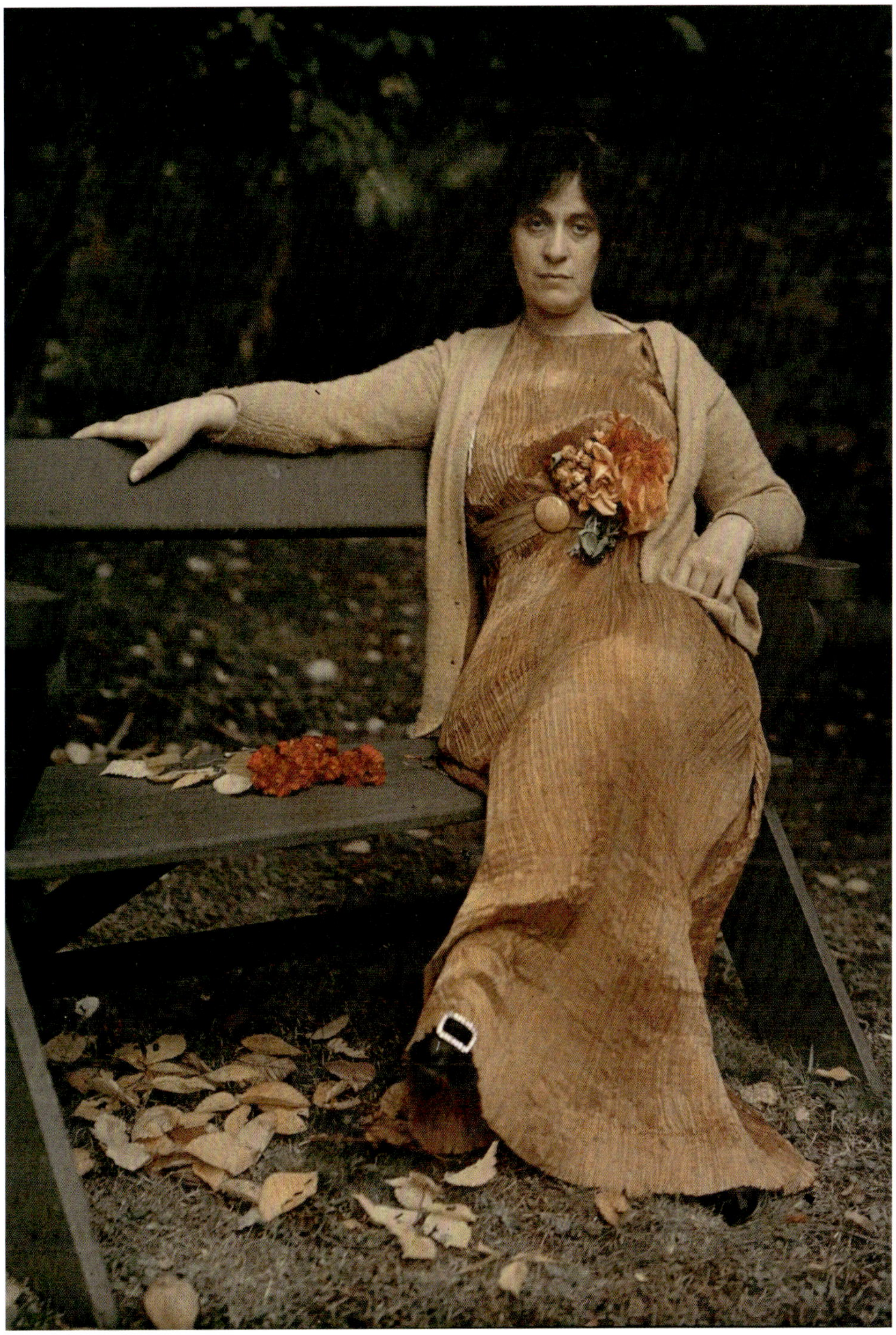

11. ***Mrs. Selma Schubart***
1907

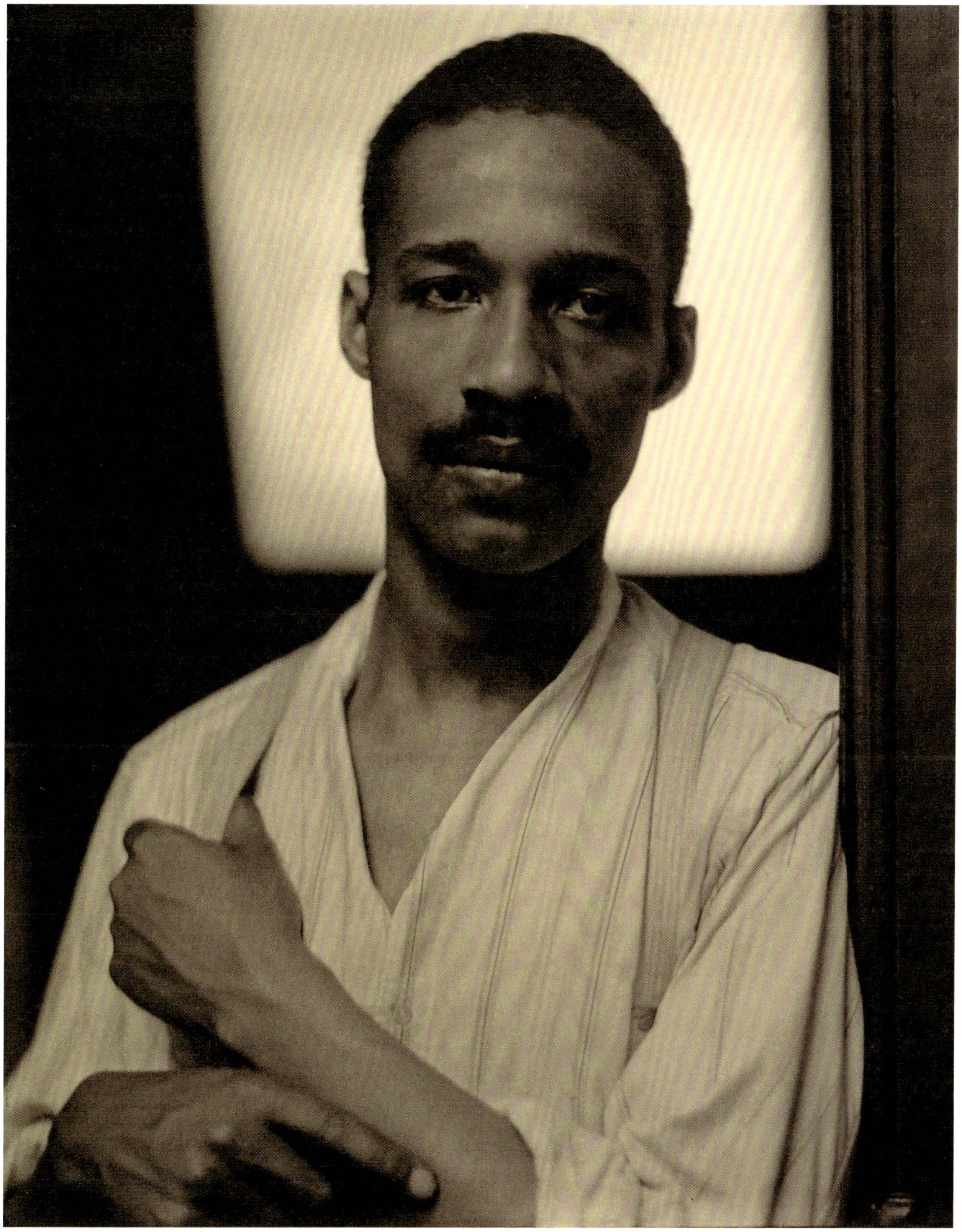

12. ***Hodge Kirnon***
1917

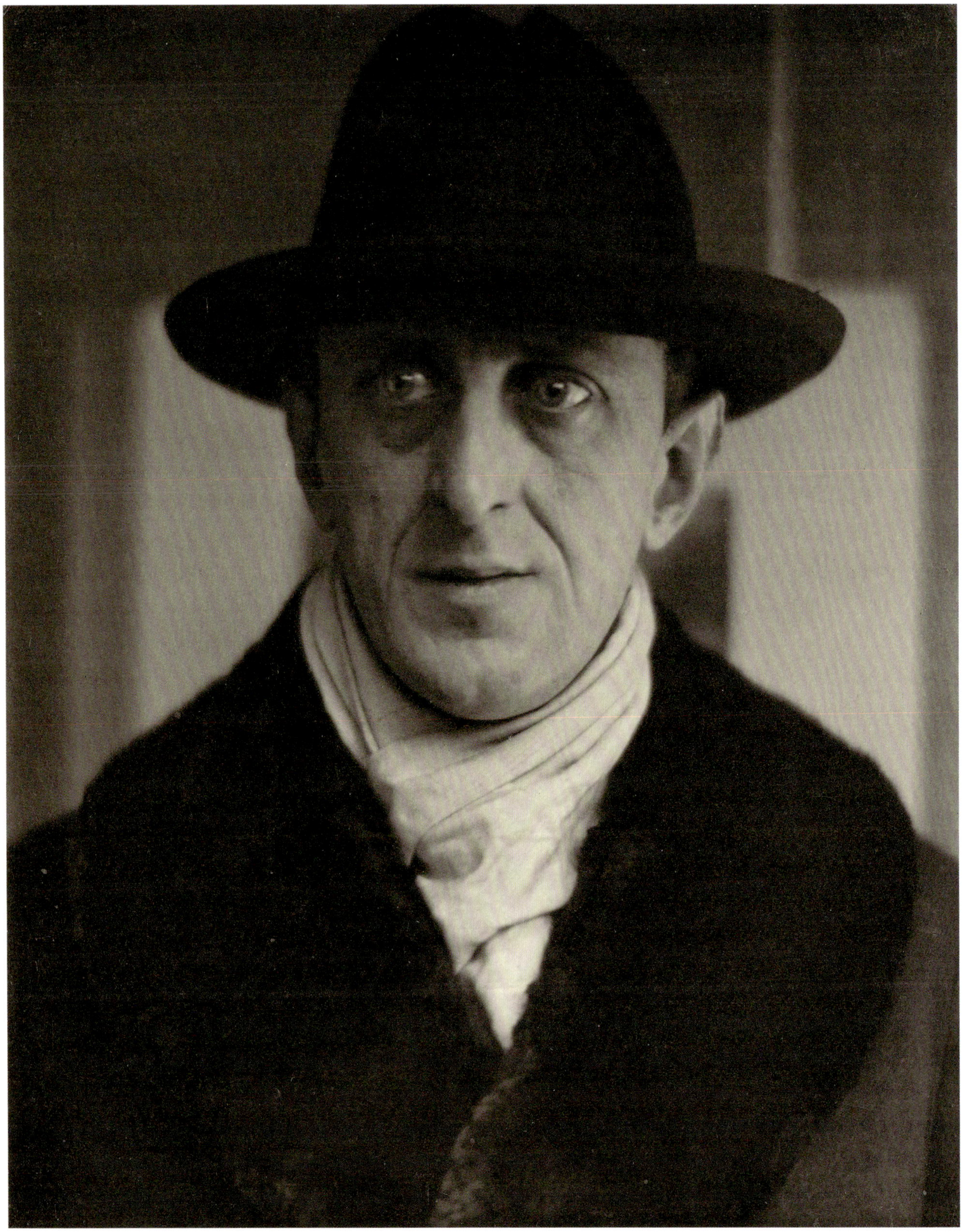

13. ***Marsden Hartley***
1916

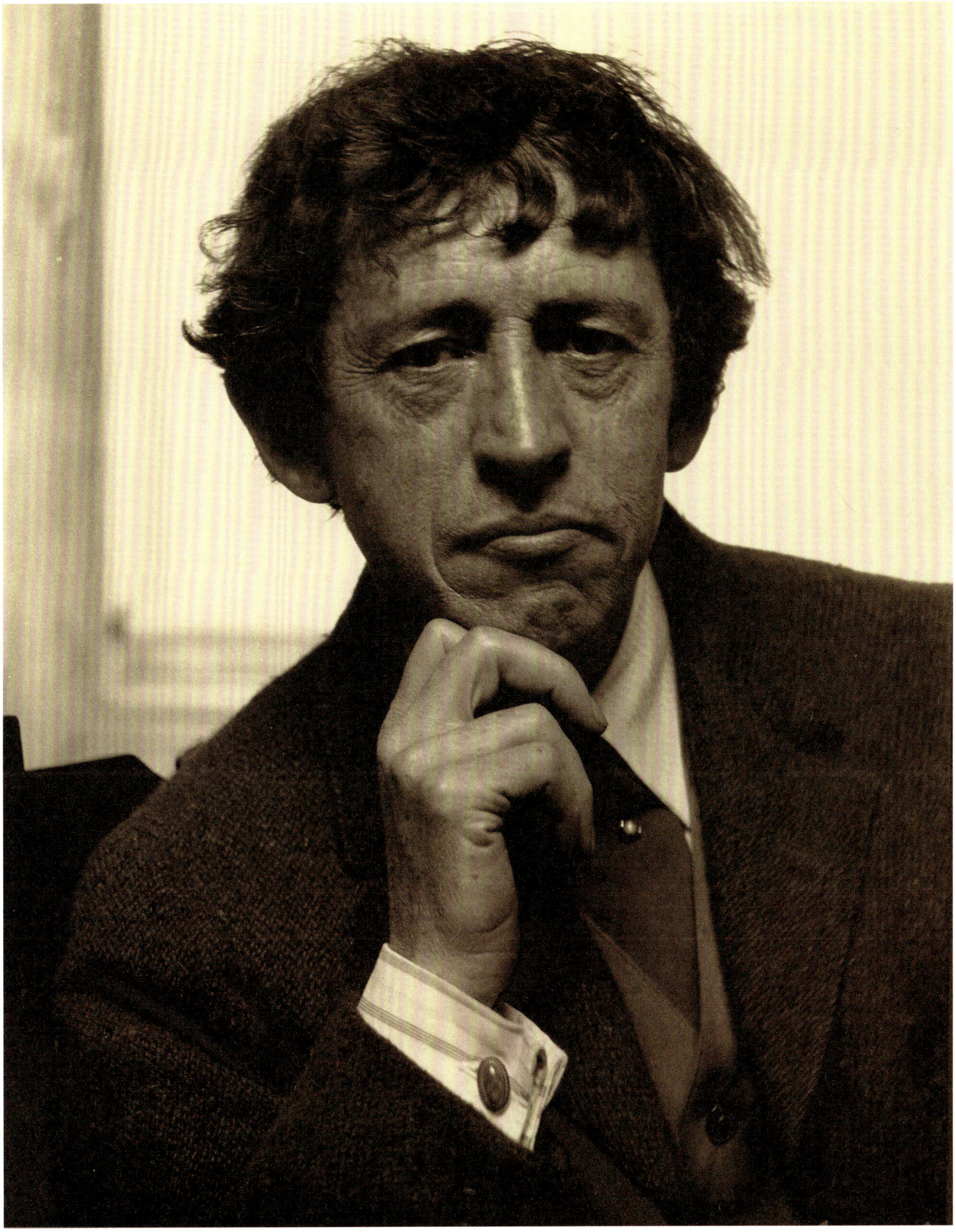

14. ***John Marin***
1921–22

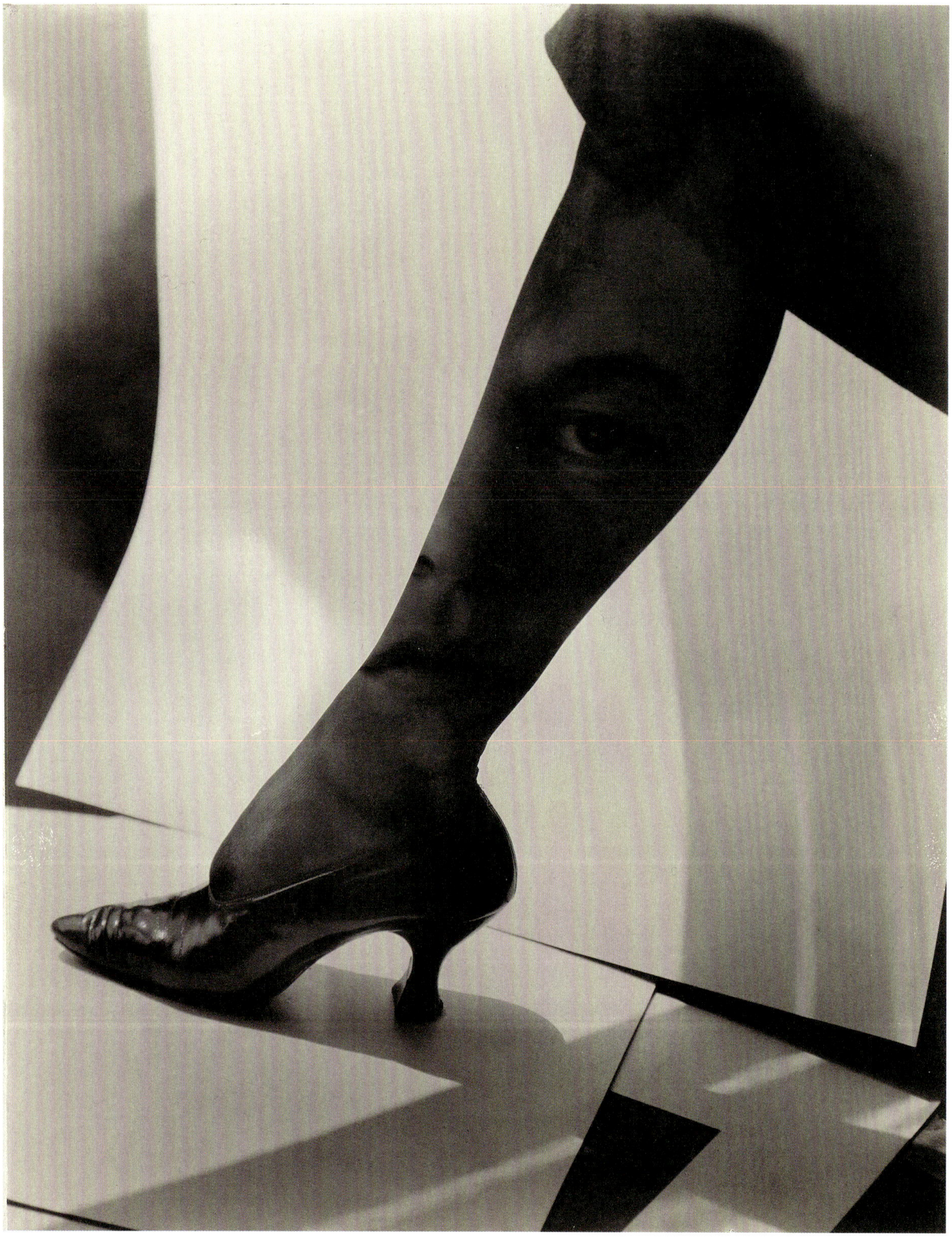

15. ***Dorothy True***
1919

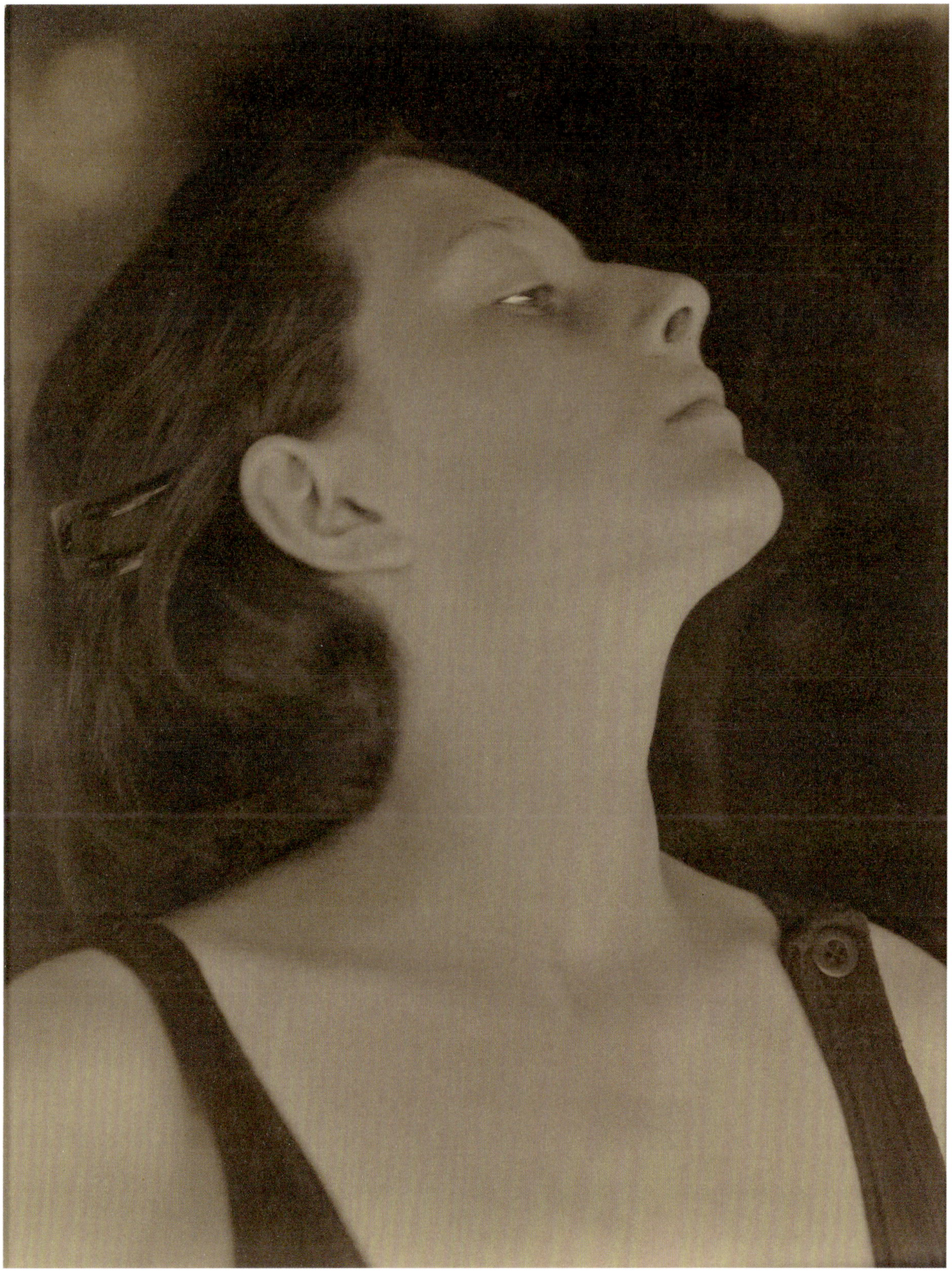

16. ***Margaret Treadwell***
1921

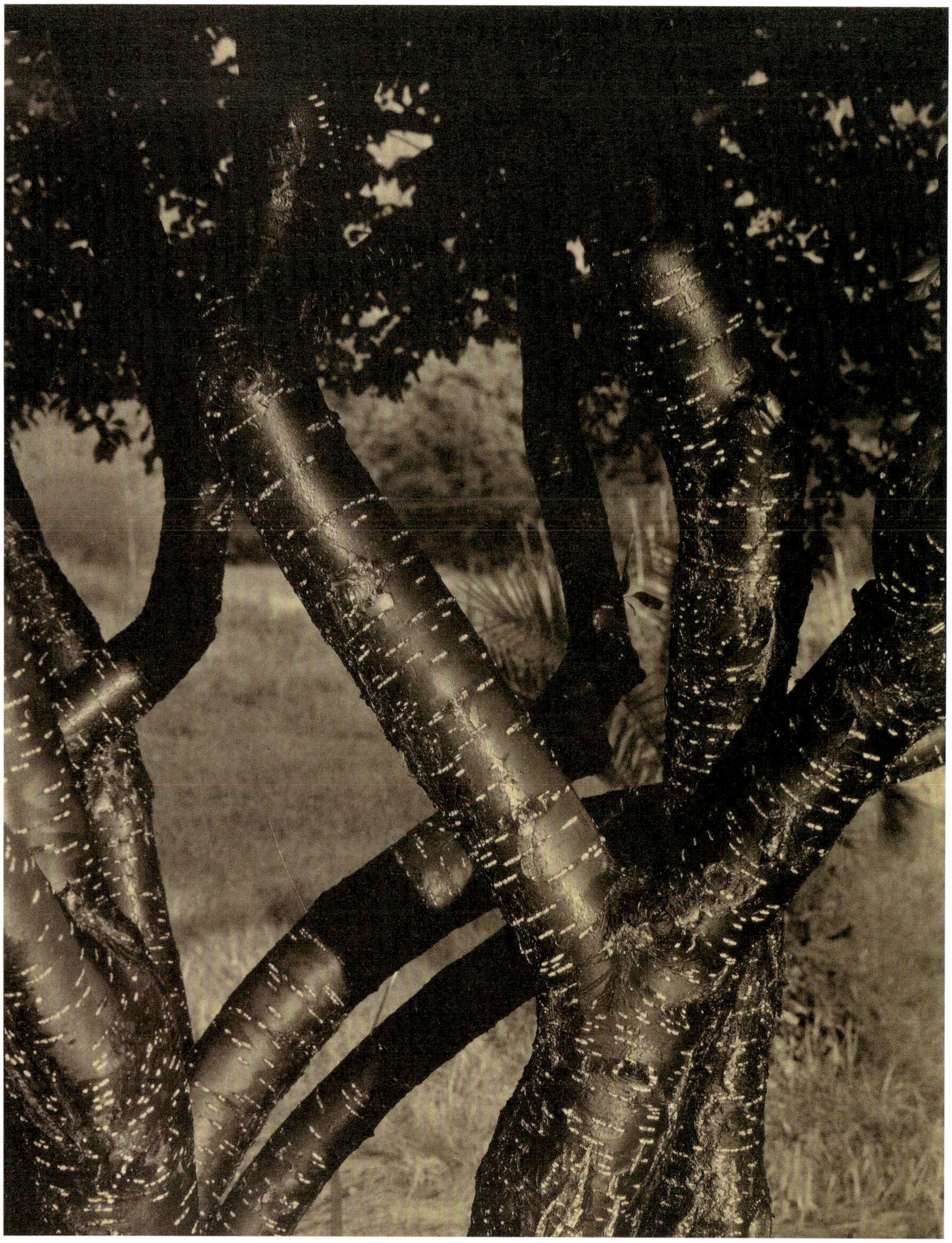

17. ***Dancing Trees***
1921–22

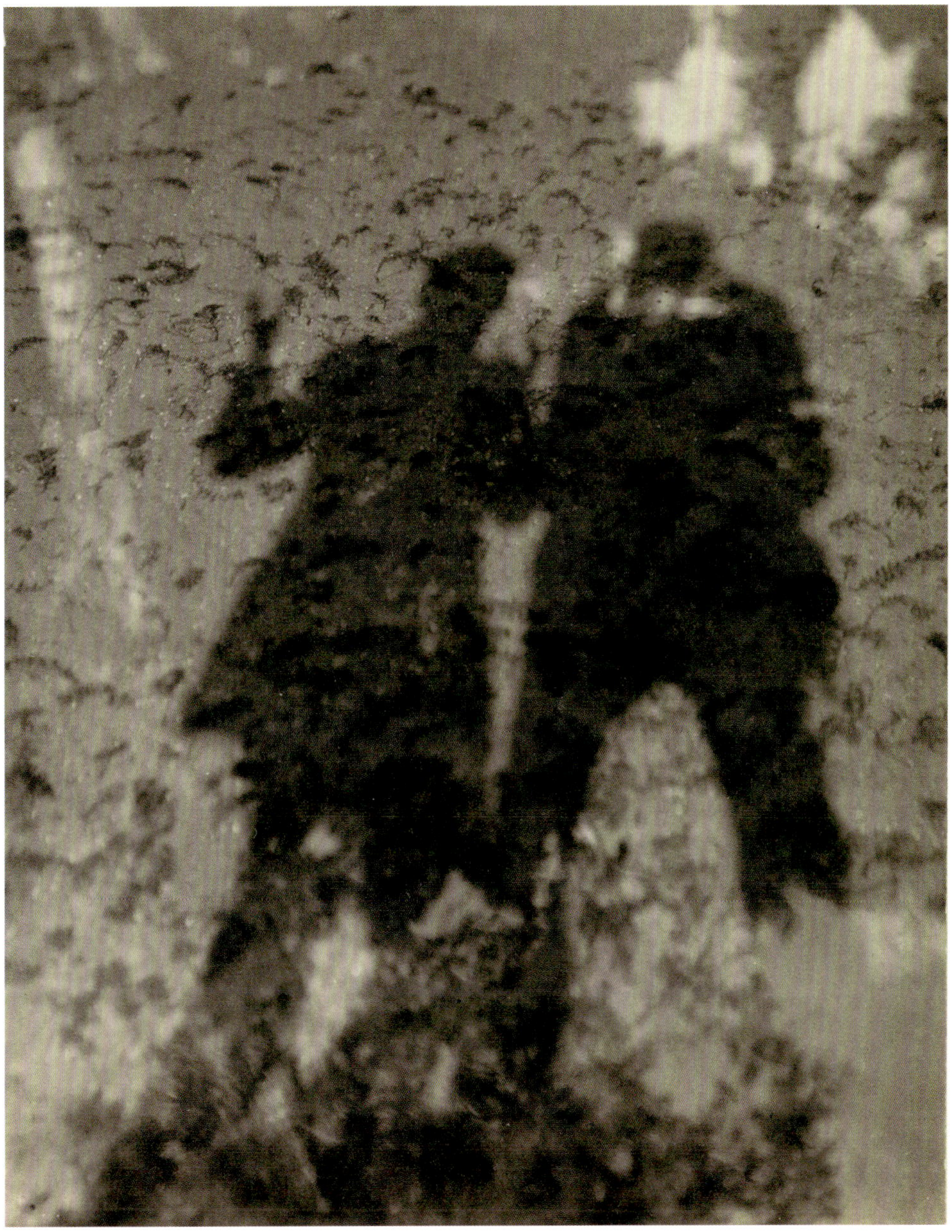

18. ***Shadows in Lake***
1916

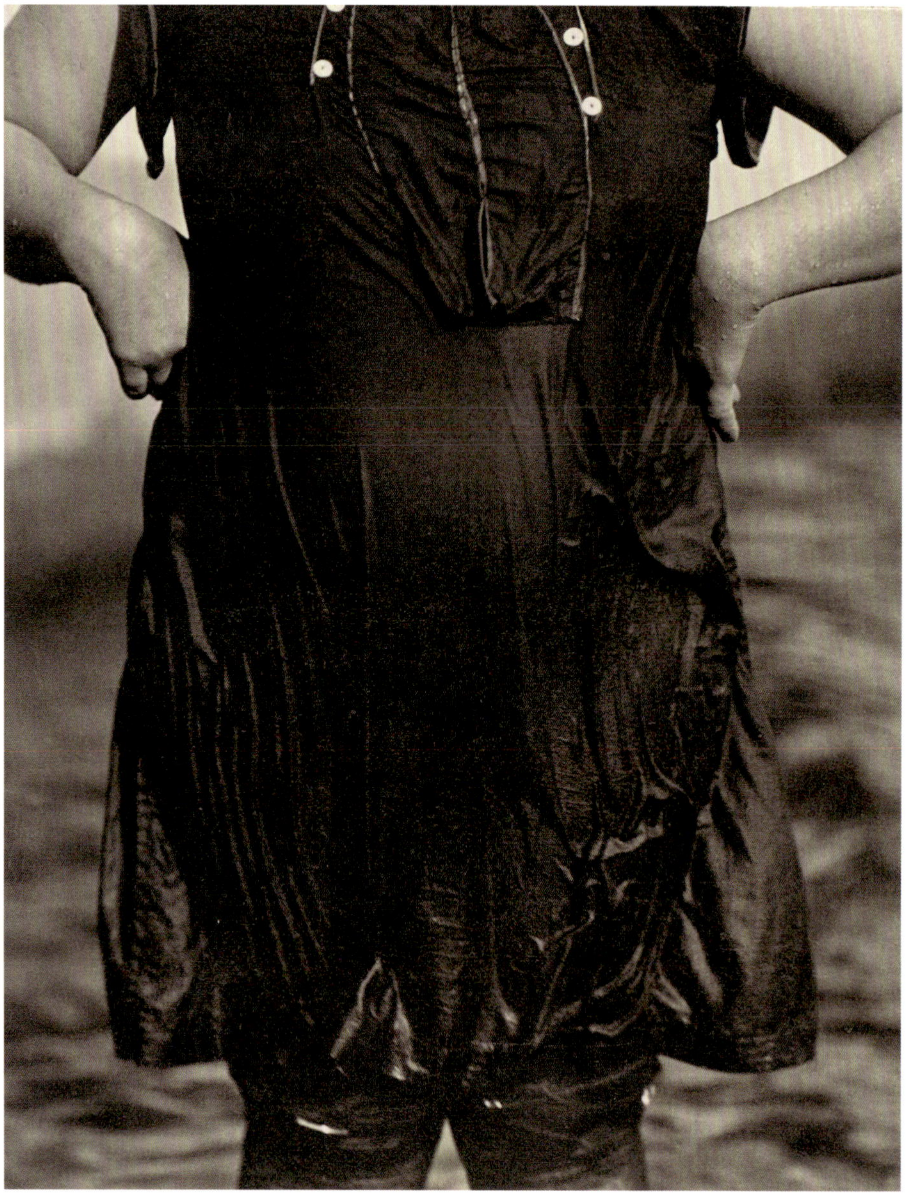

19. *Katherine*
1921

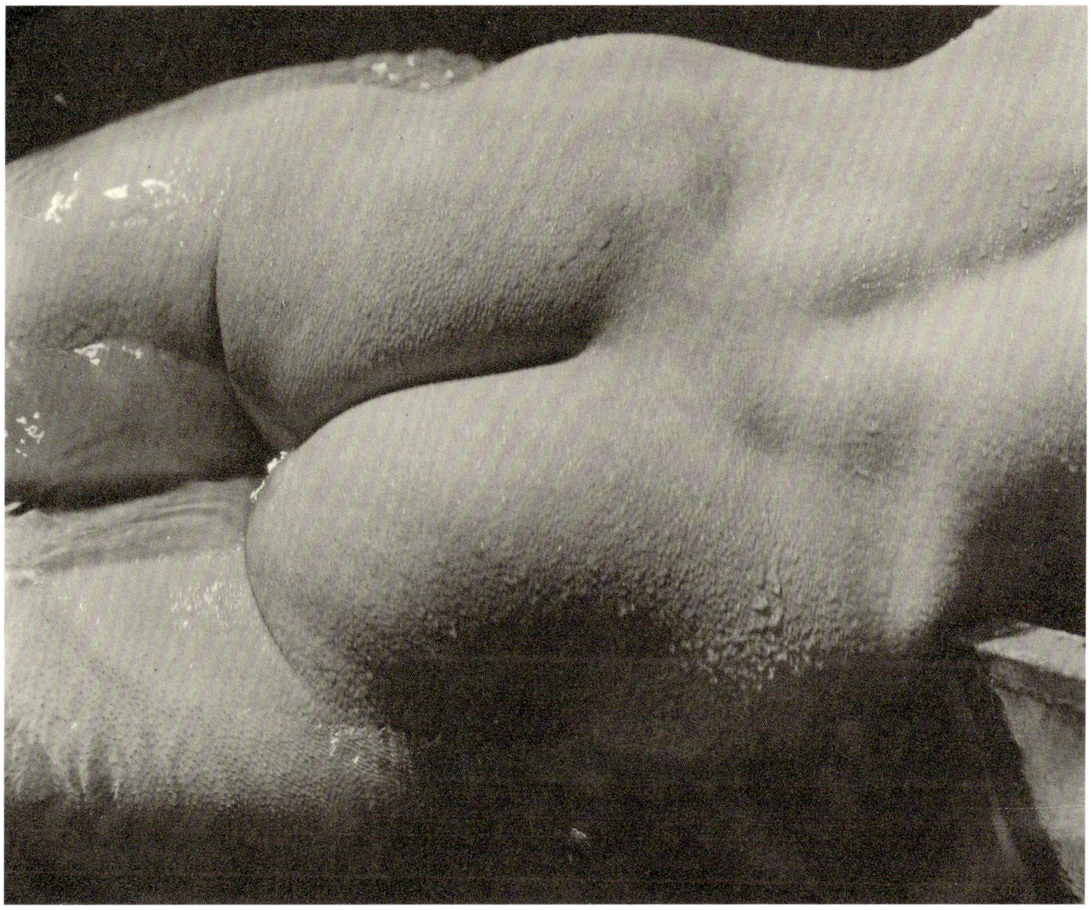

20. *Rebecca Salsbury Strand*
1922

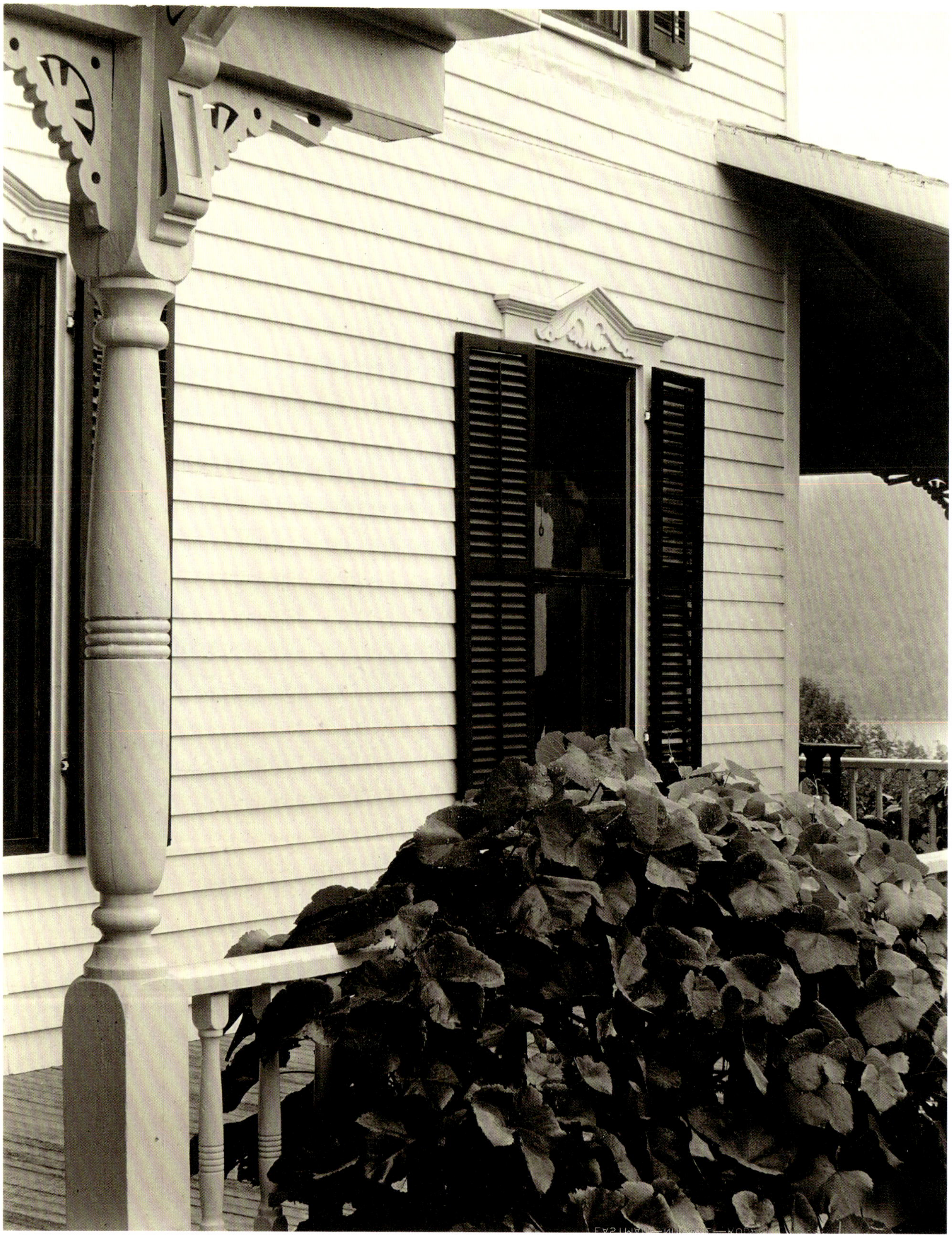

21. ***House and Grape Leaves***
1934

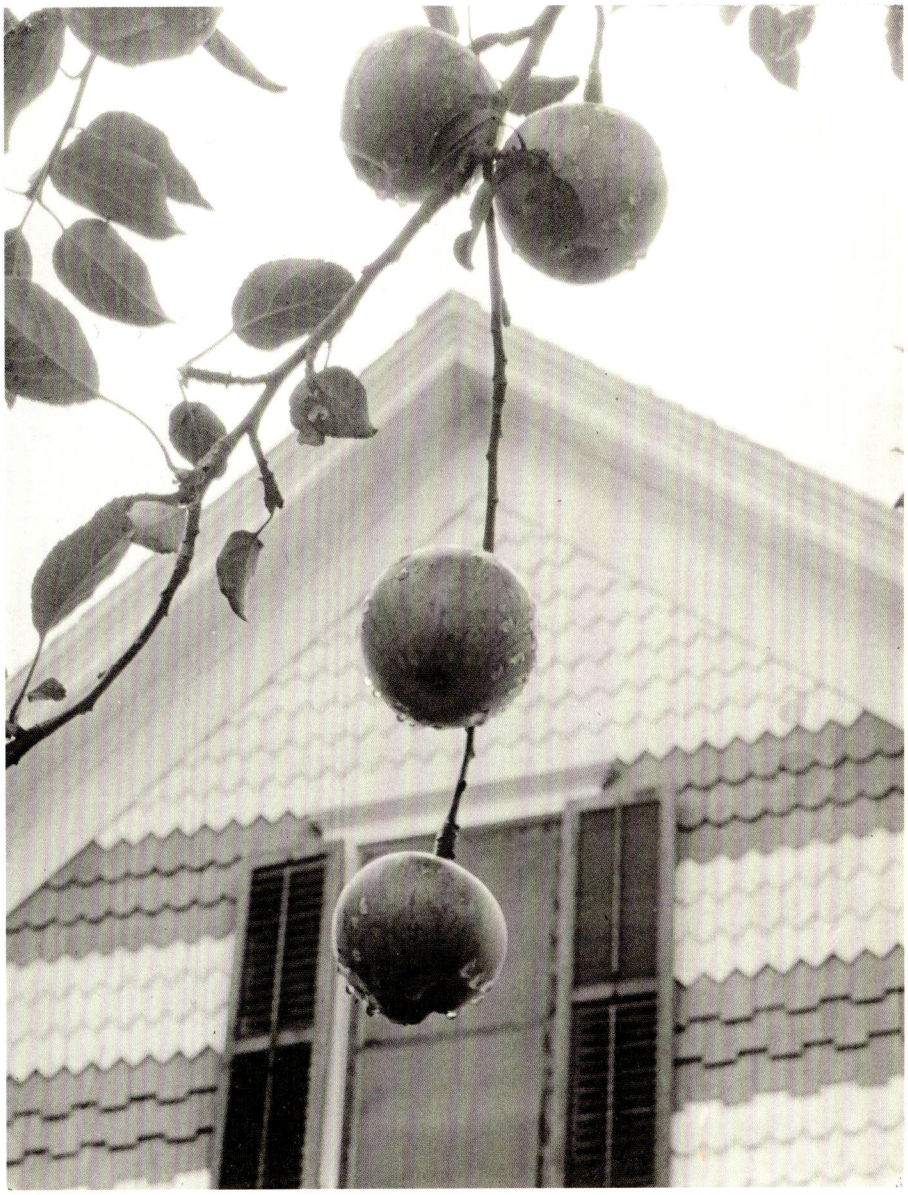

22. ***Gable and Apples***
1922

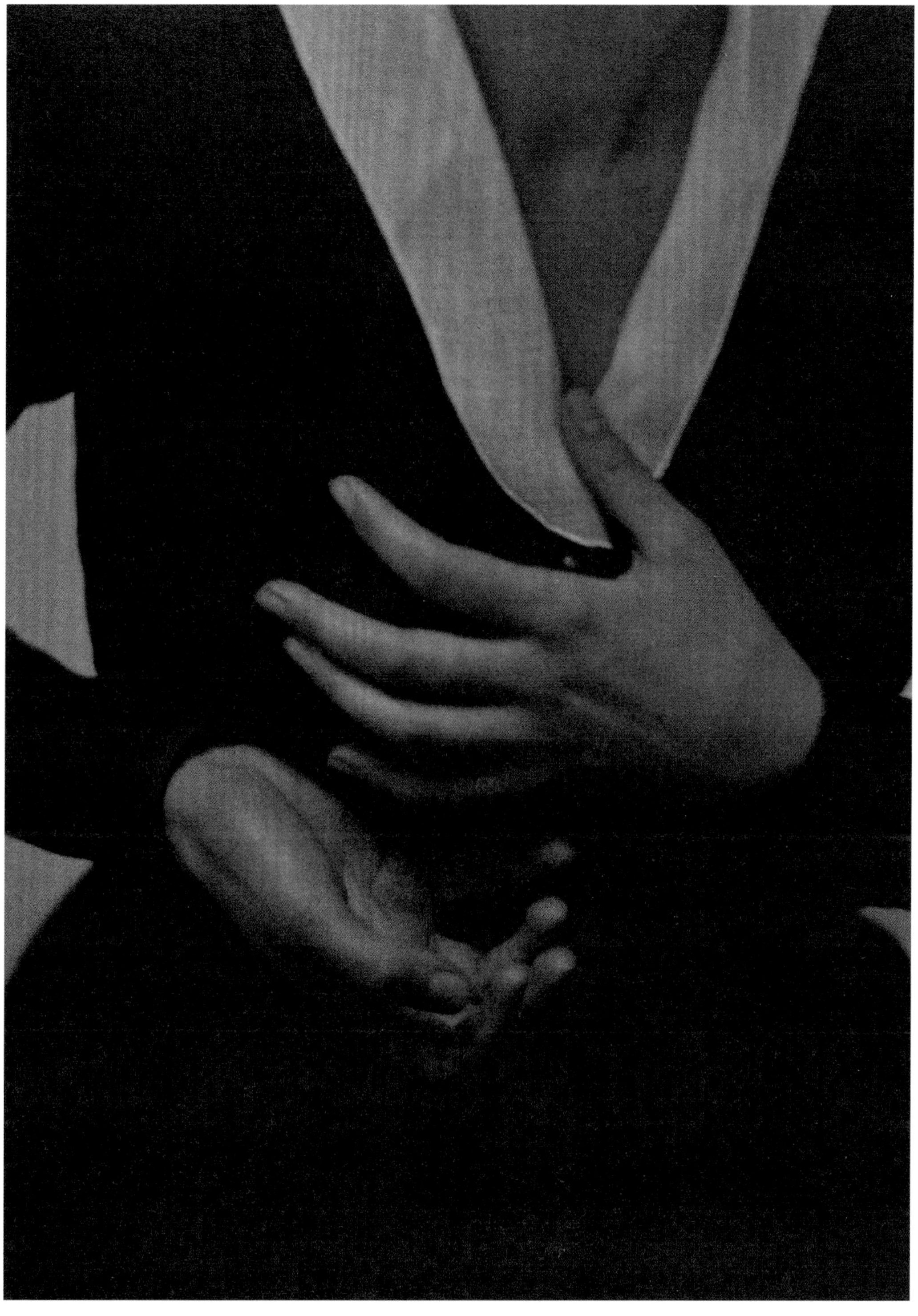

23. ***Georgia O'Keeffe—Hands***
1917

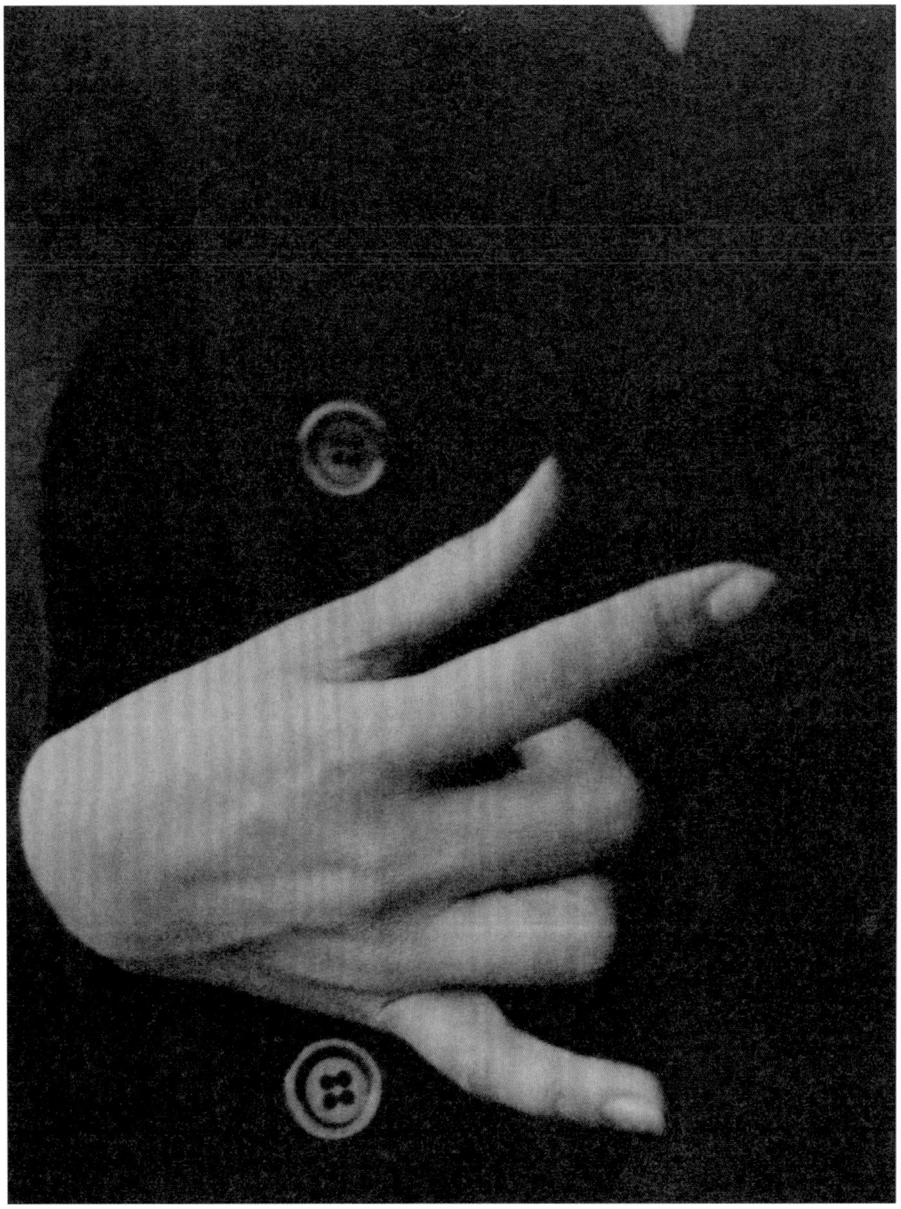

24. ***Georgia O'Keeffe—Hand***
1918

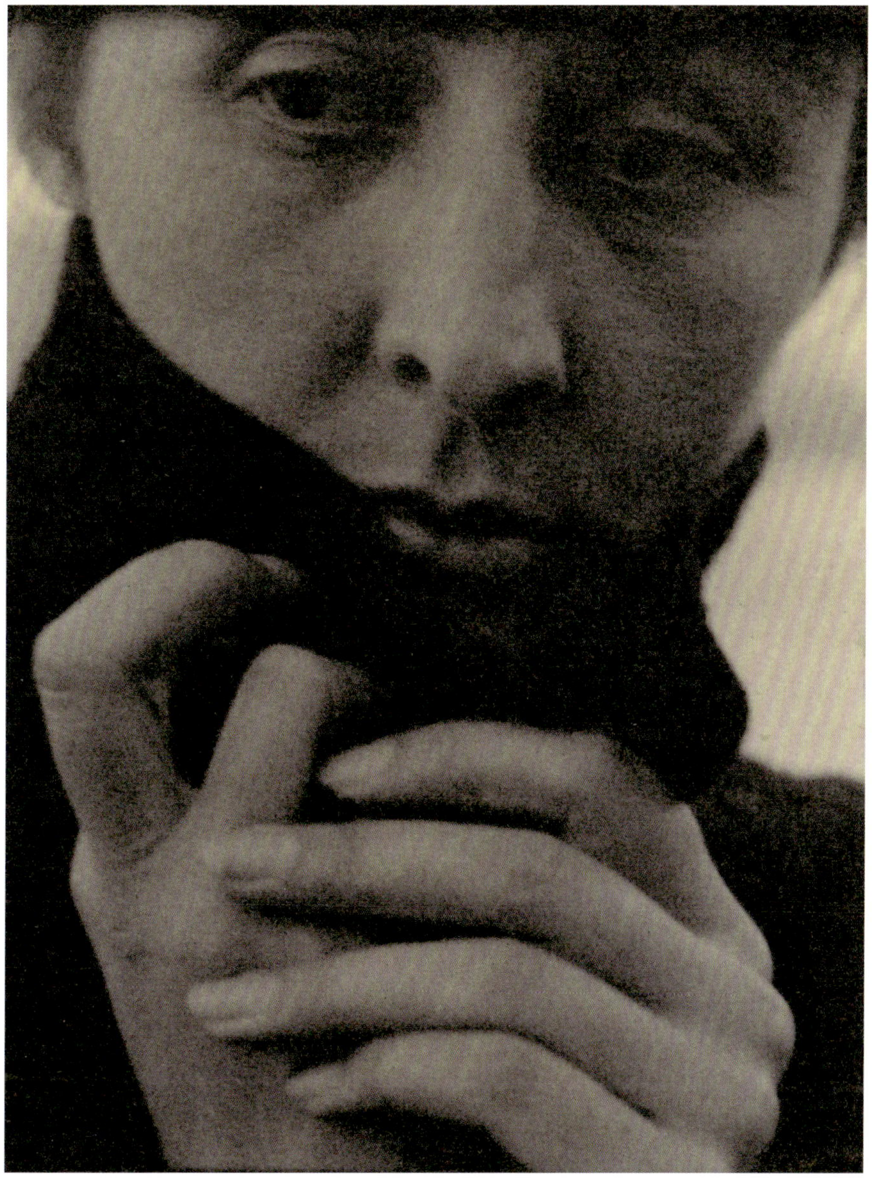

25. *Georgia O'Keeffe*
1918

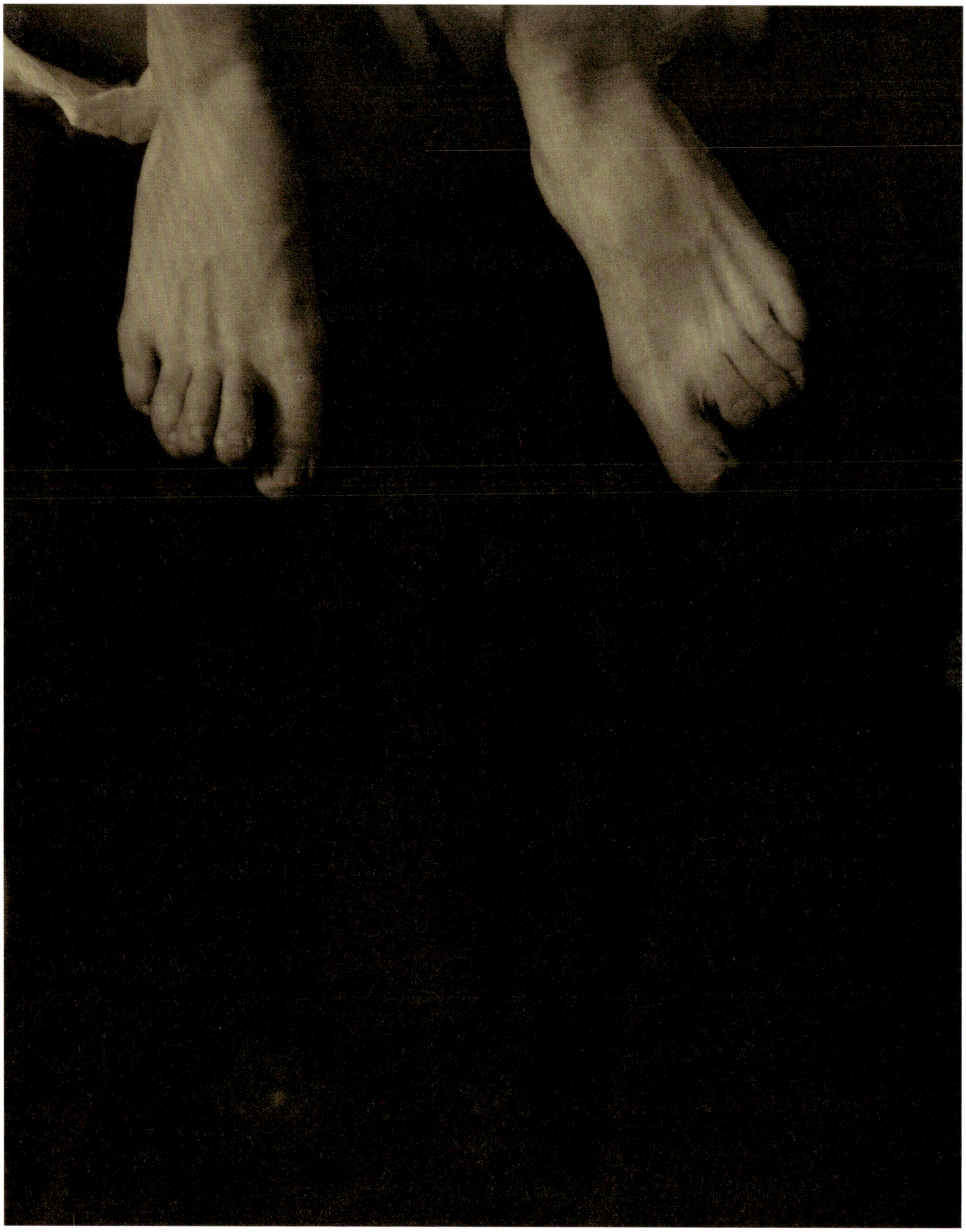

26. *Georgia O'Keeffe—Feet*
1918

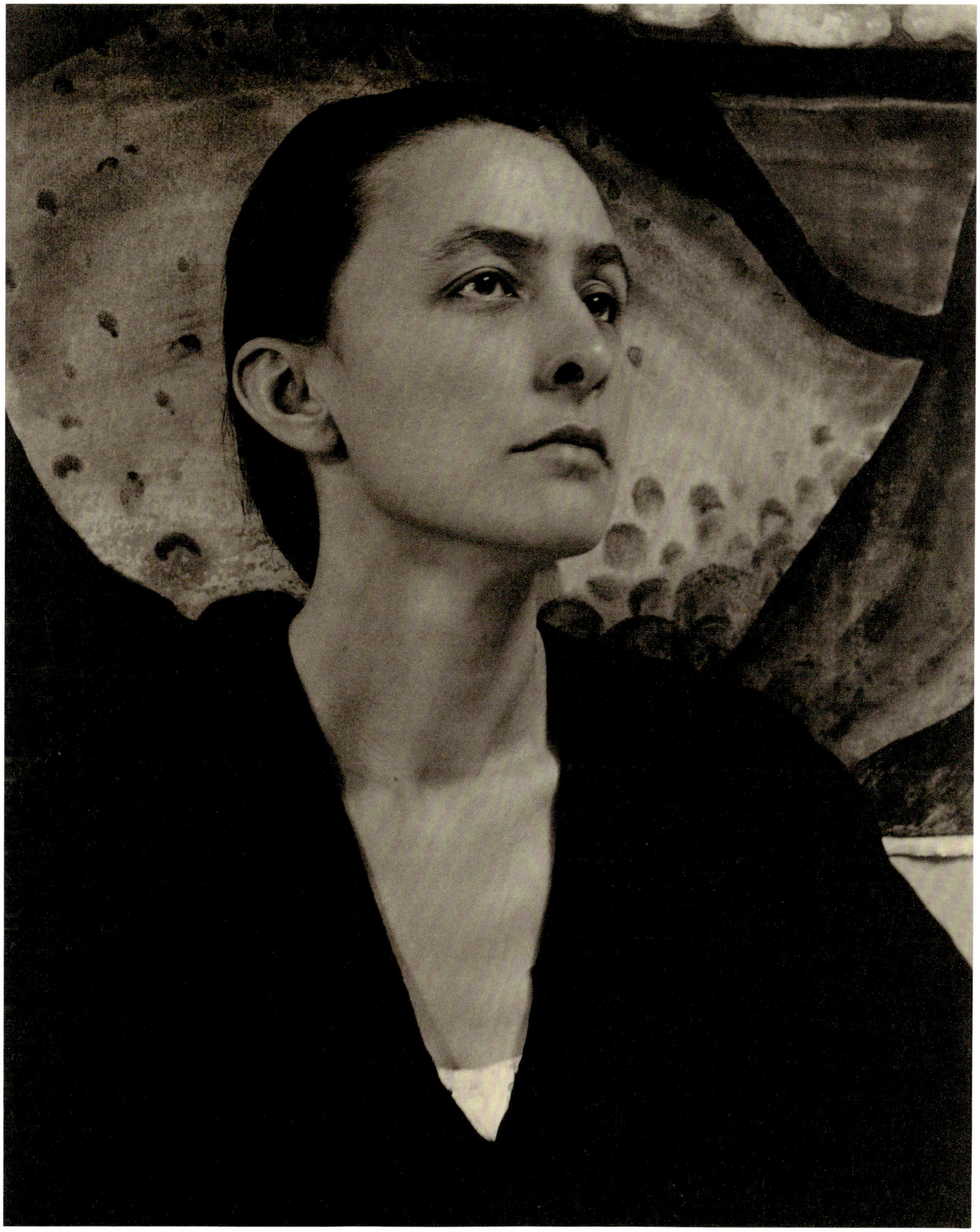

27. ***Georgia O'Keeffe***
1918

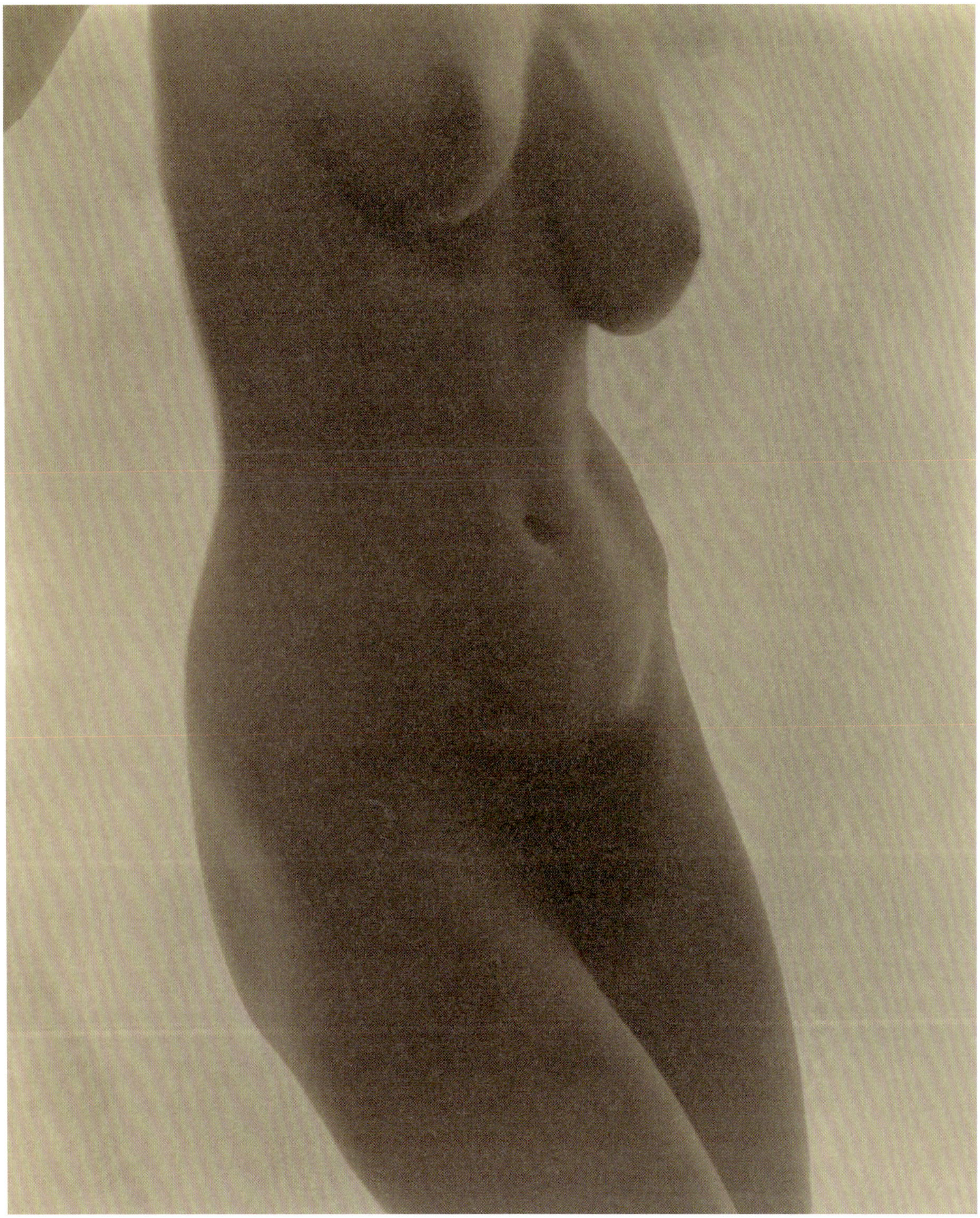

28. ***Georgia O'Keeffe***
1918

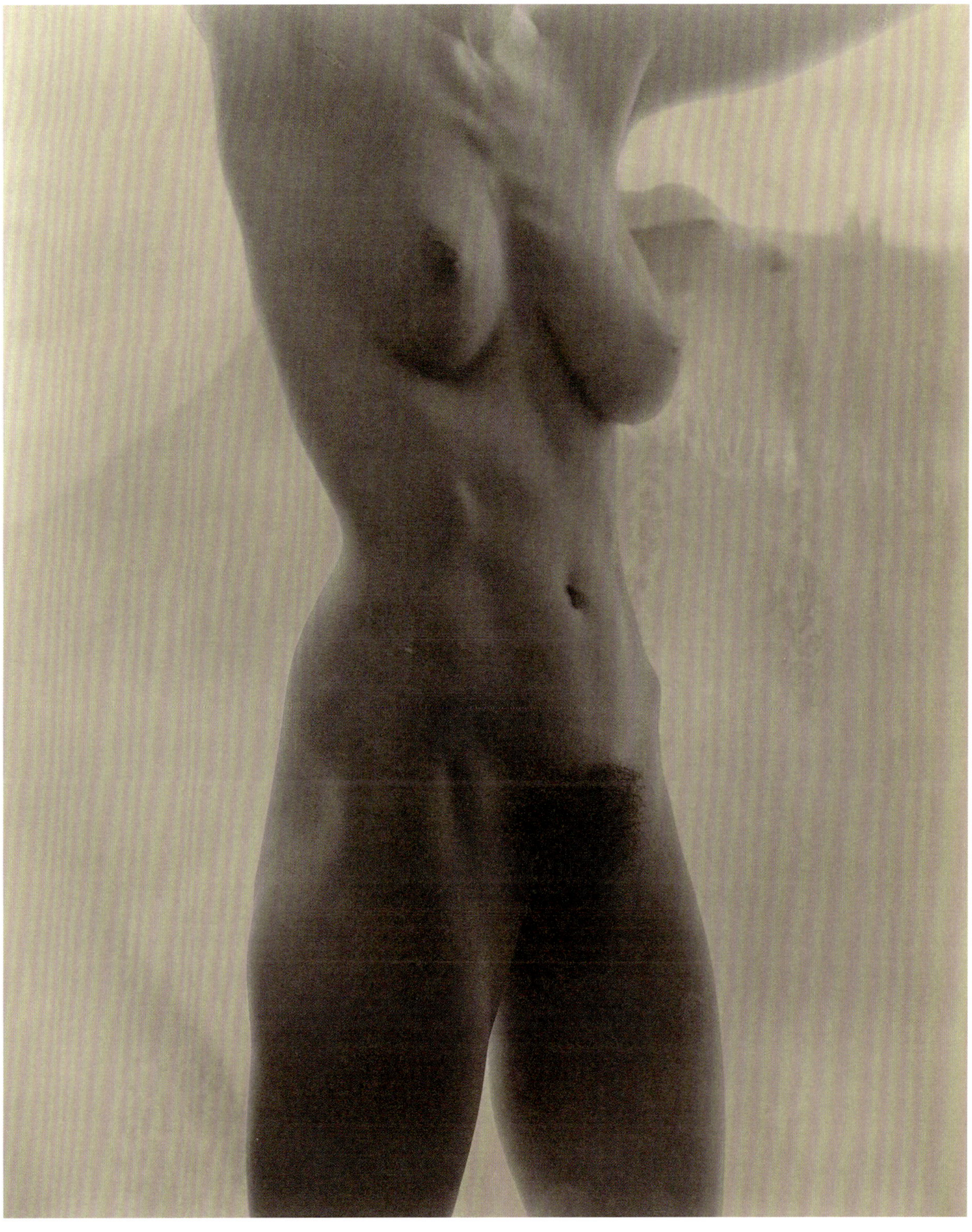

29. *Georgia O'Keeffe—Torso*
1918

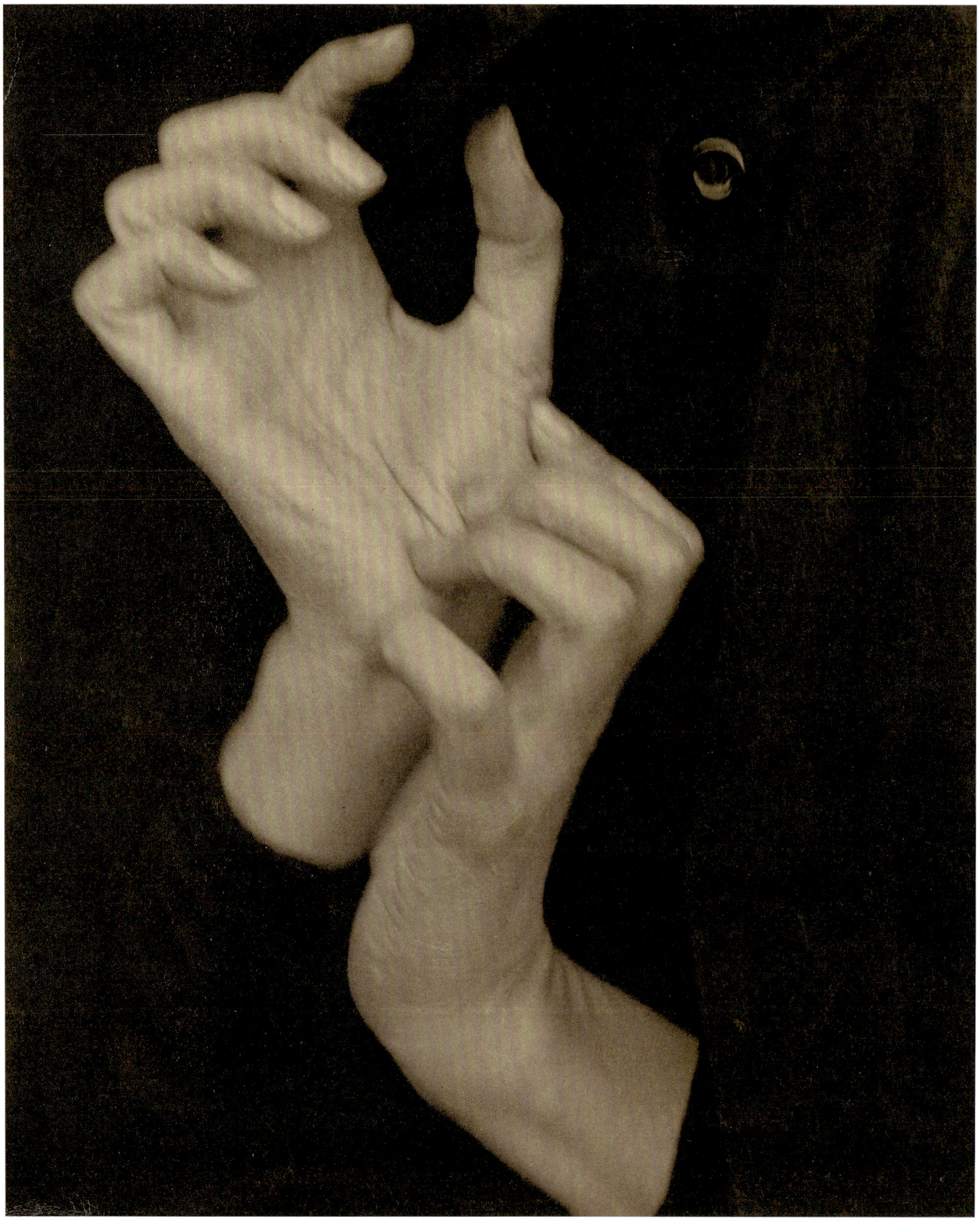

30. ***Georgia O'Keeffe—Hands***
1919

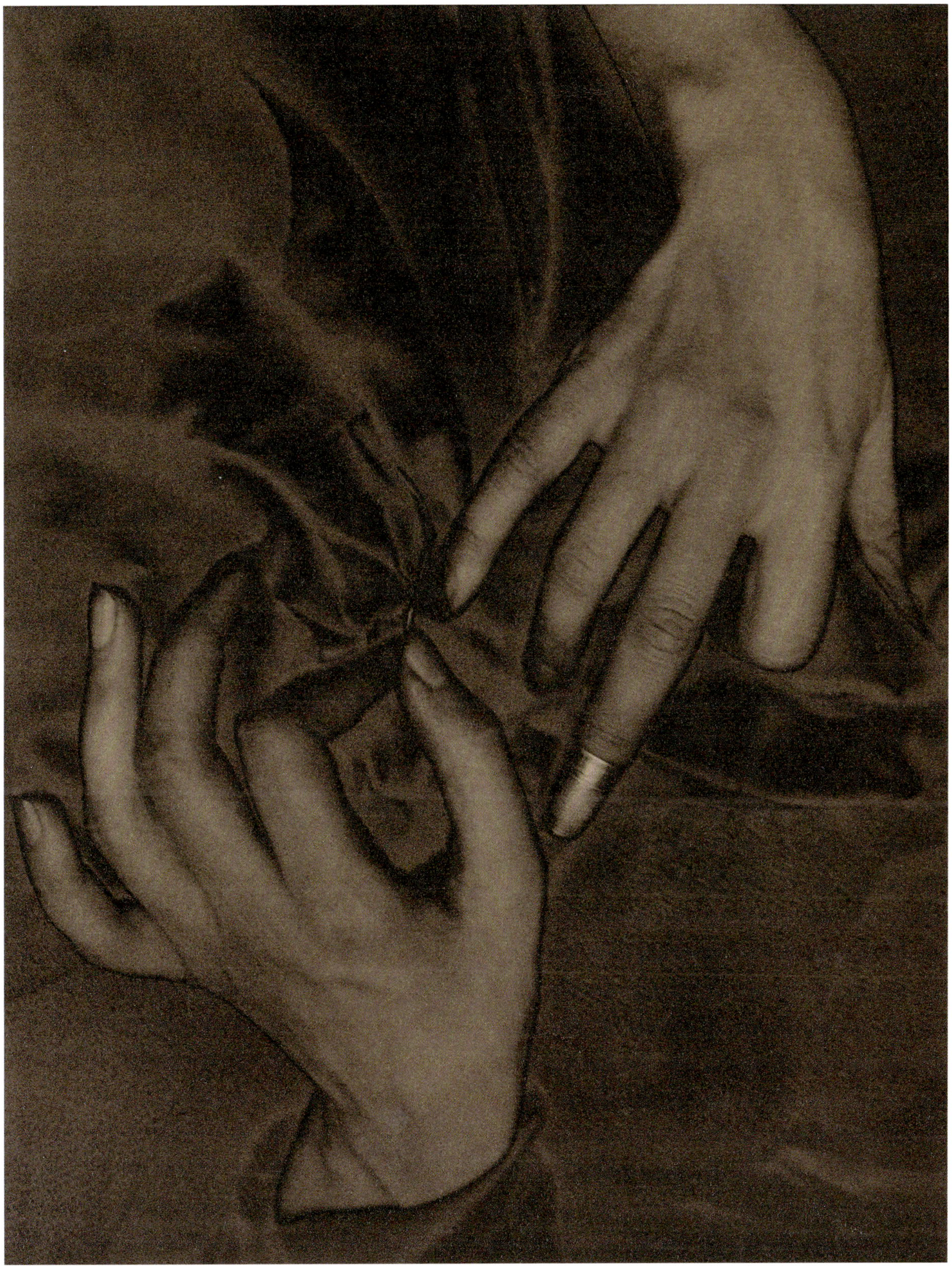

31. ***Georgia O'Keeffe***
1919

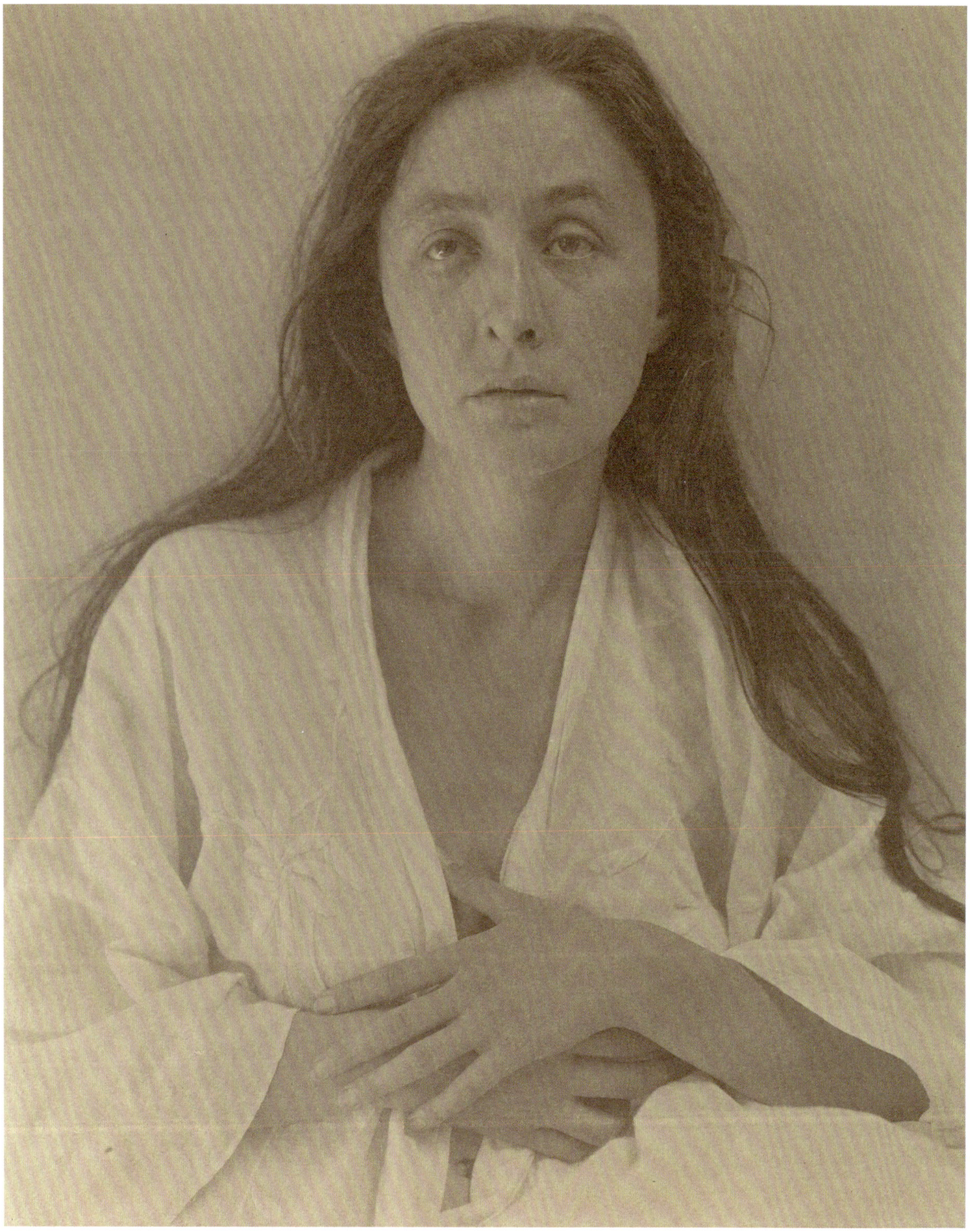

32. ***Georgia O'Keeffe***
1918

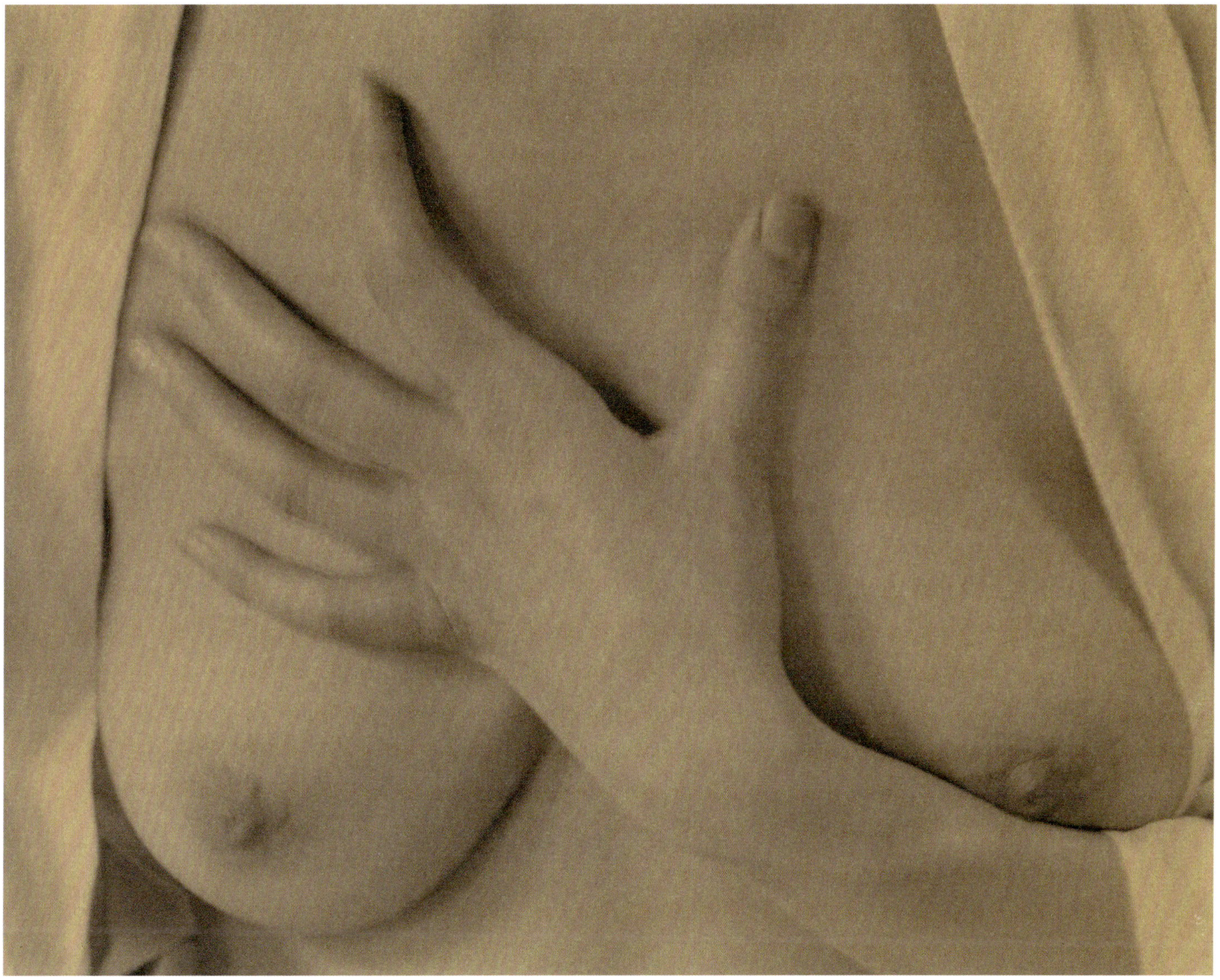

33. *Georgia O'Keeffe—Hand and Breasts*
1919

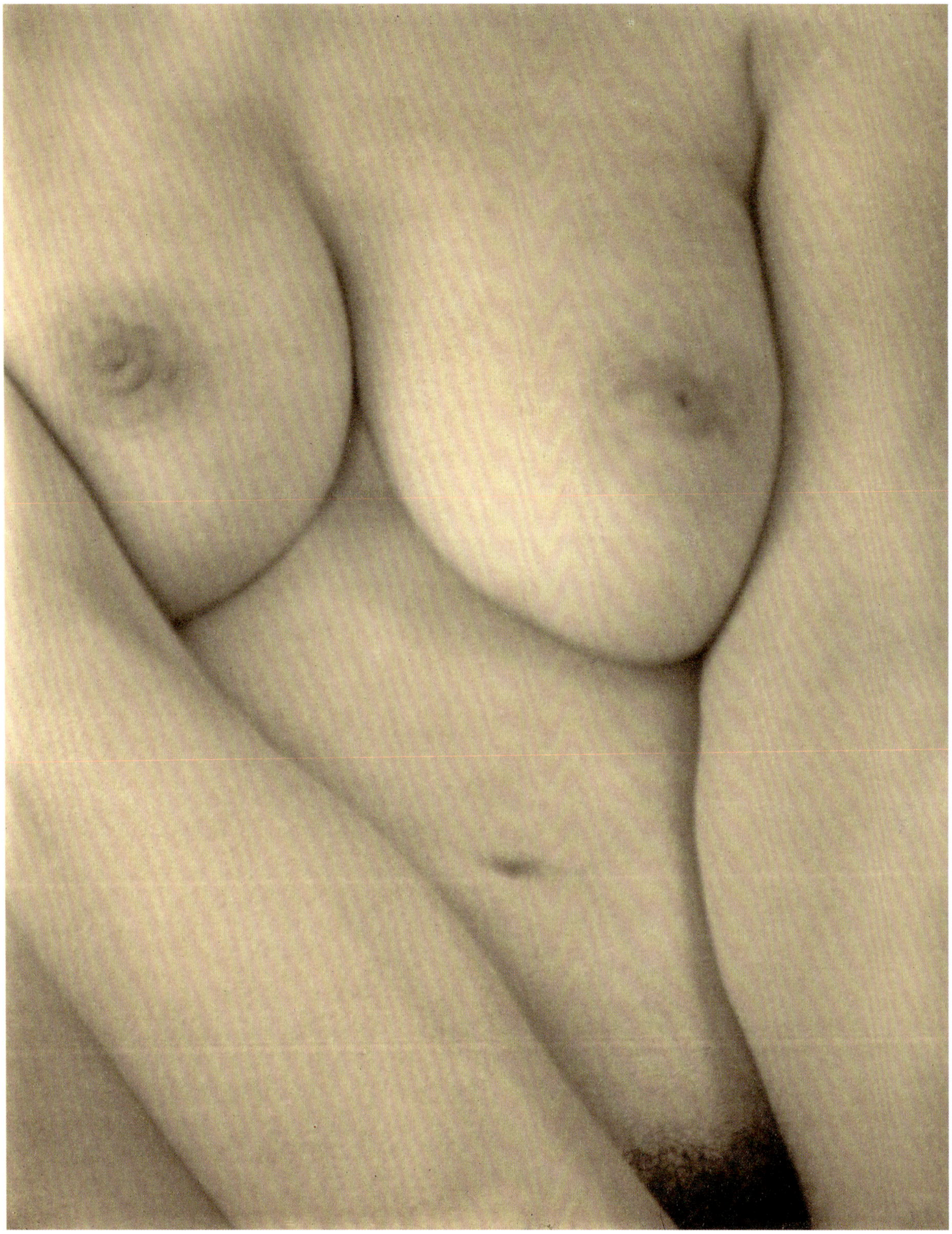

34. ***Georgia O'Keeffe—Breasts***
1919

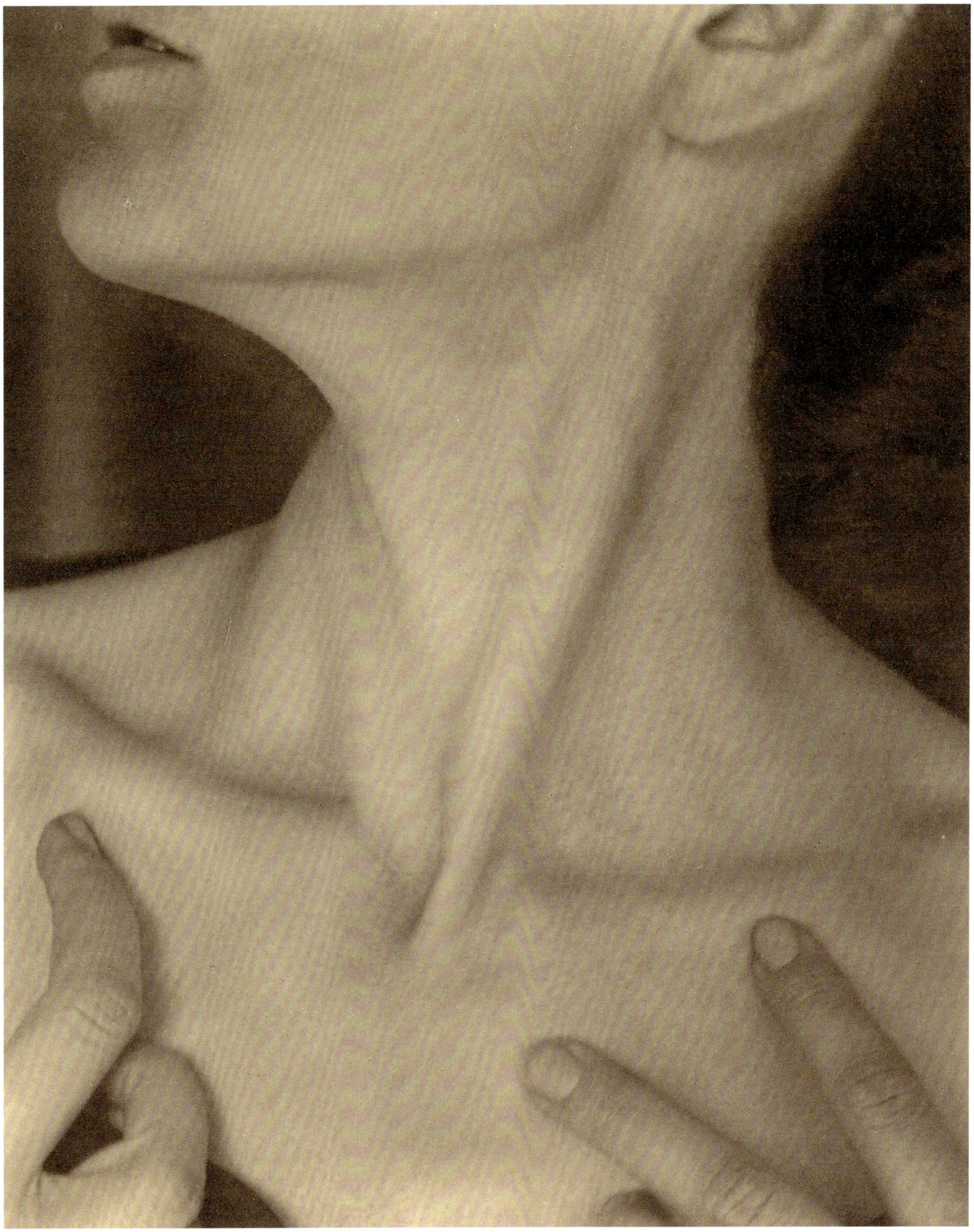

35. ***Georgia O'Keeffe—Neck***
1921

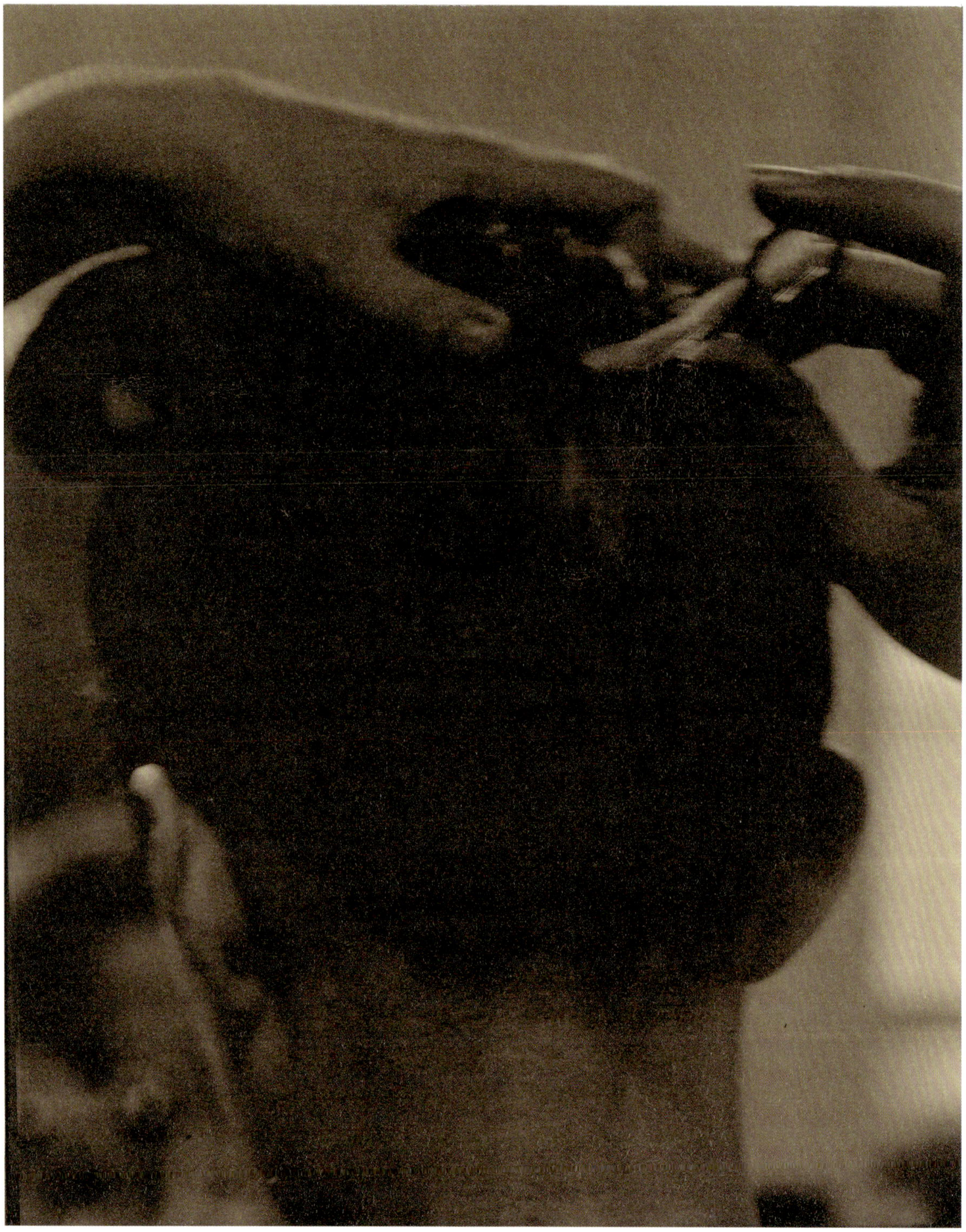

36. *Georgia O'Keeffe*
1919–21

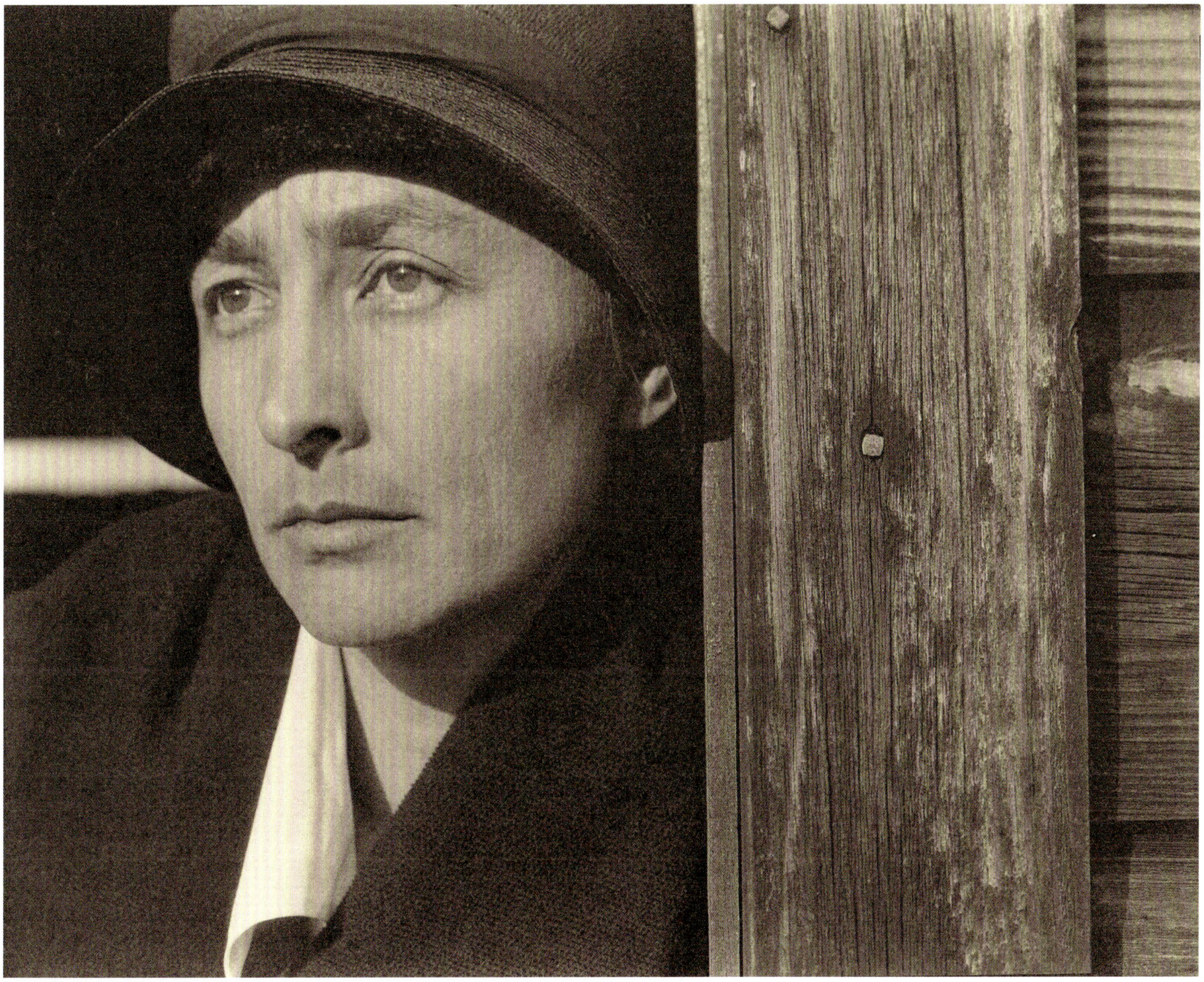

37. ***Georgia O'Keeffe***
1922

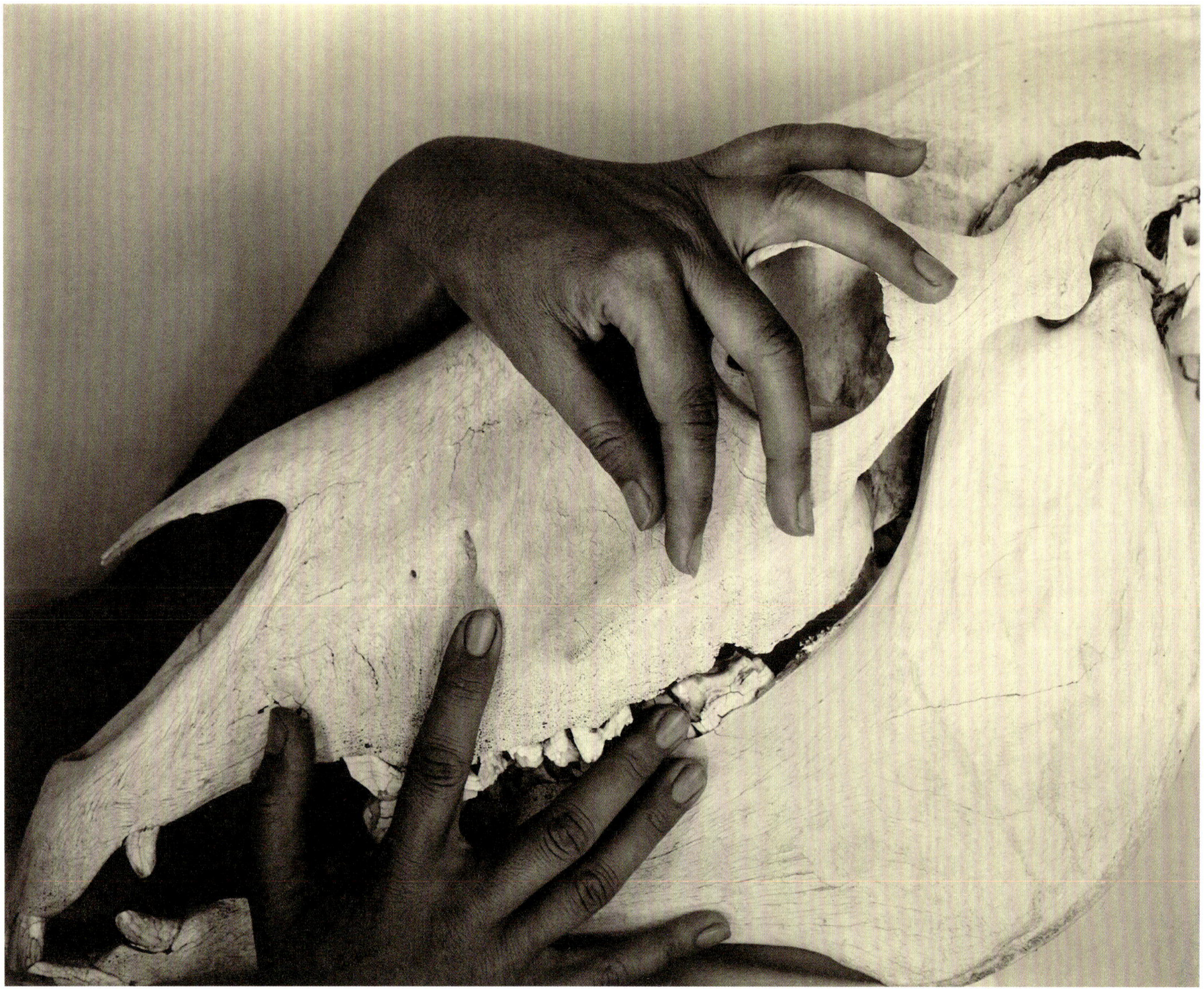

38. ***Georgia O'Keeffe—Hands and Horse Skull***
1931

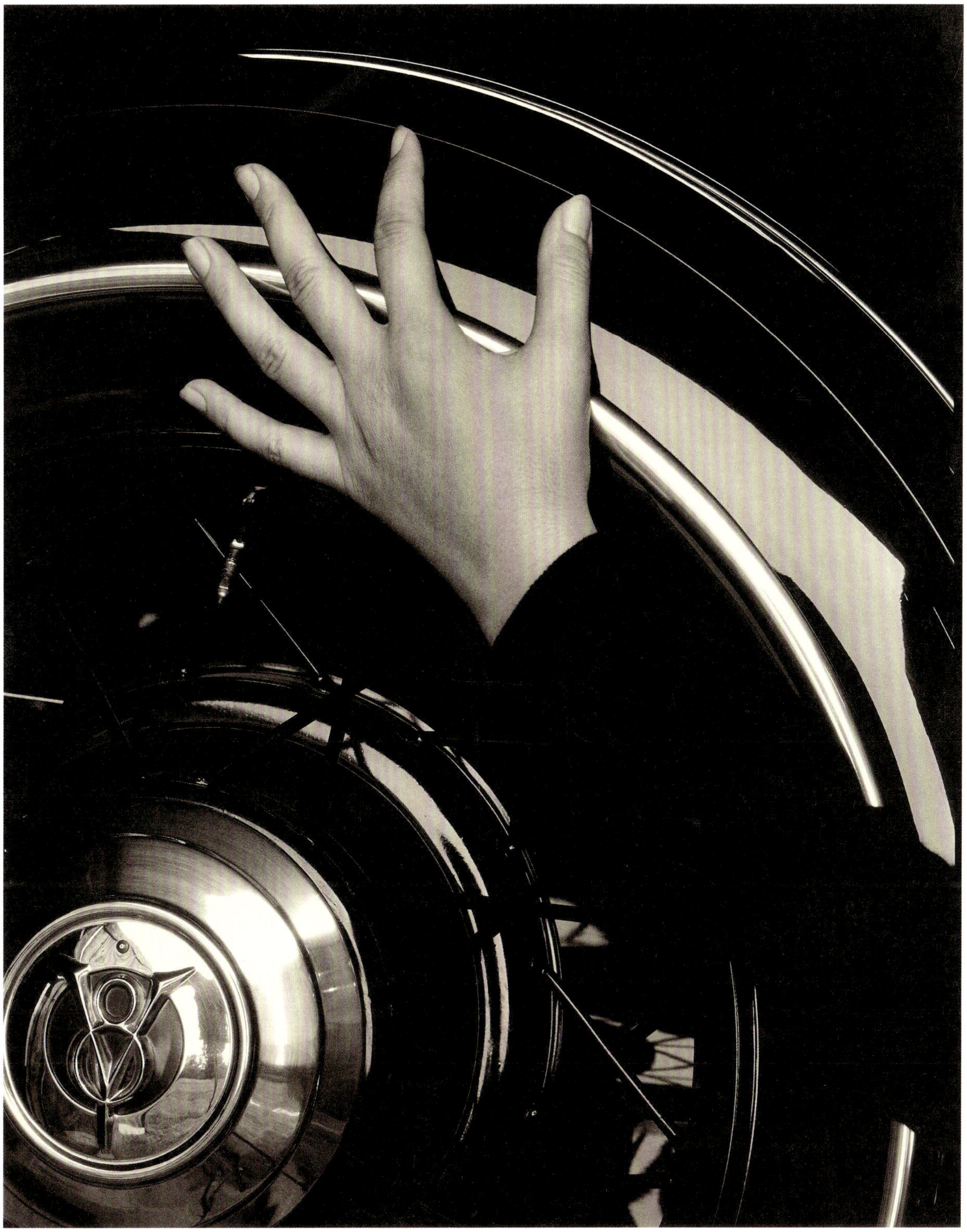

39. ***Georgia O'Keeffe—Hand and Wheel***
1933

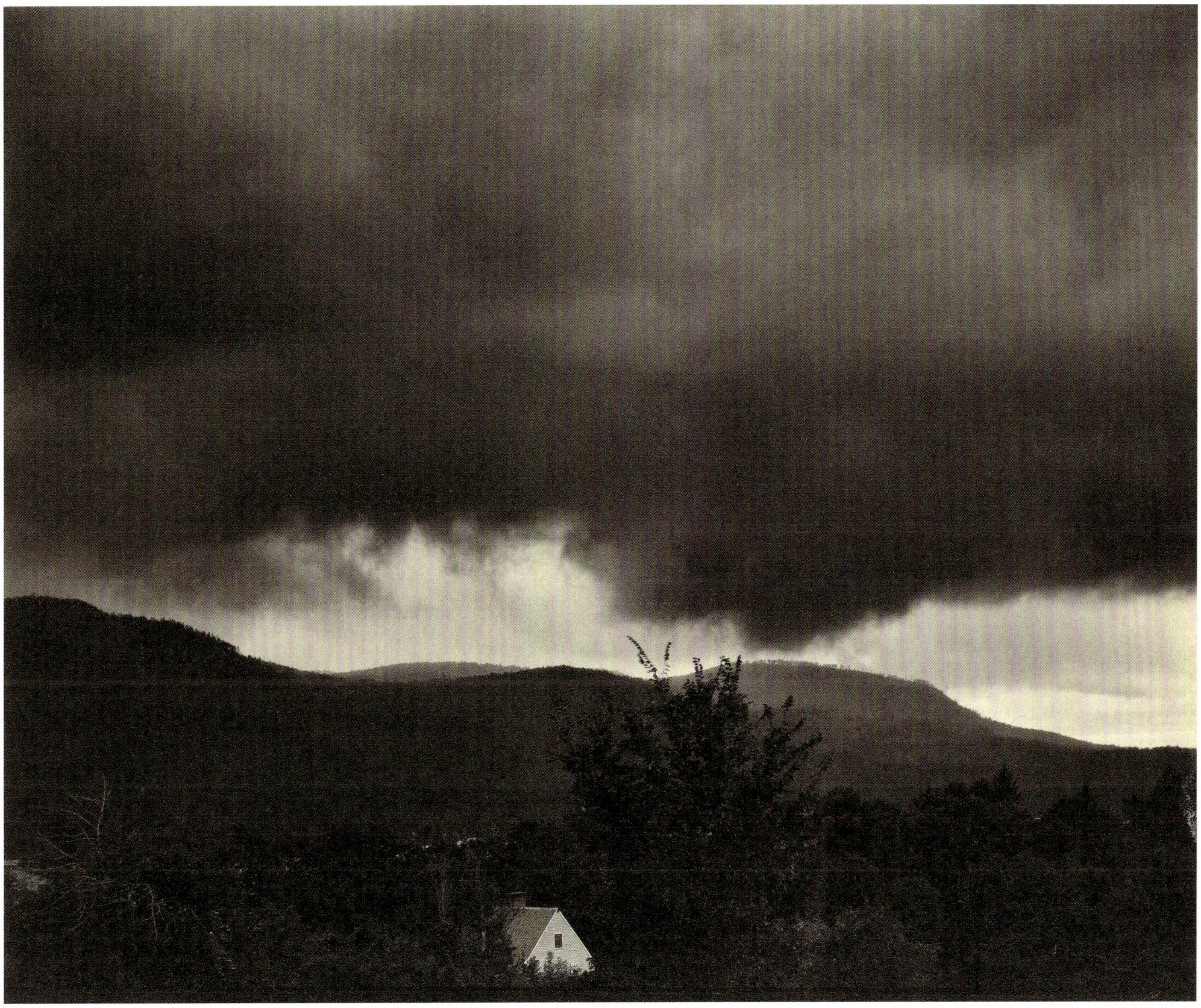

40. *Music No. 1*
1922

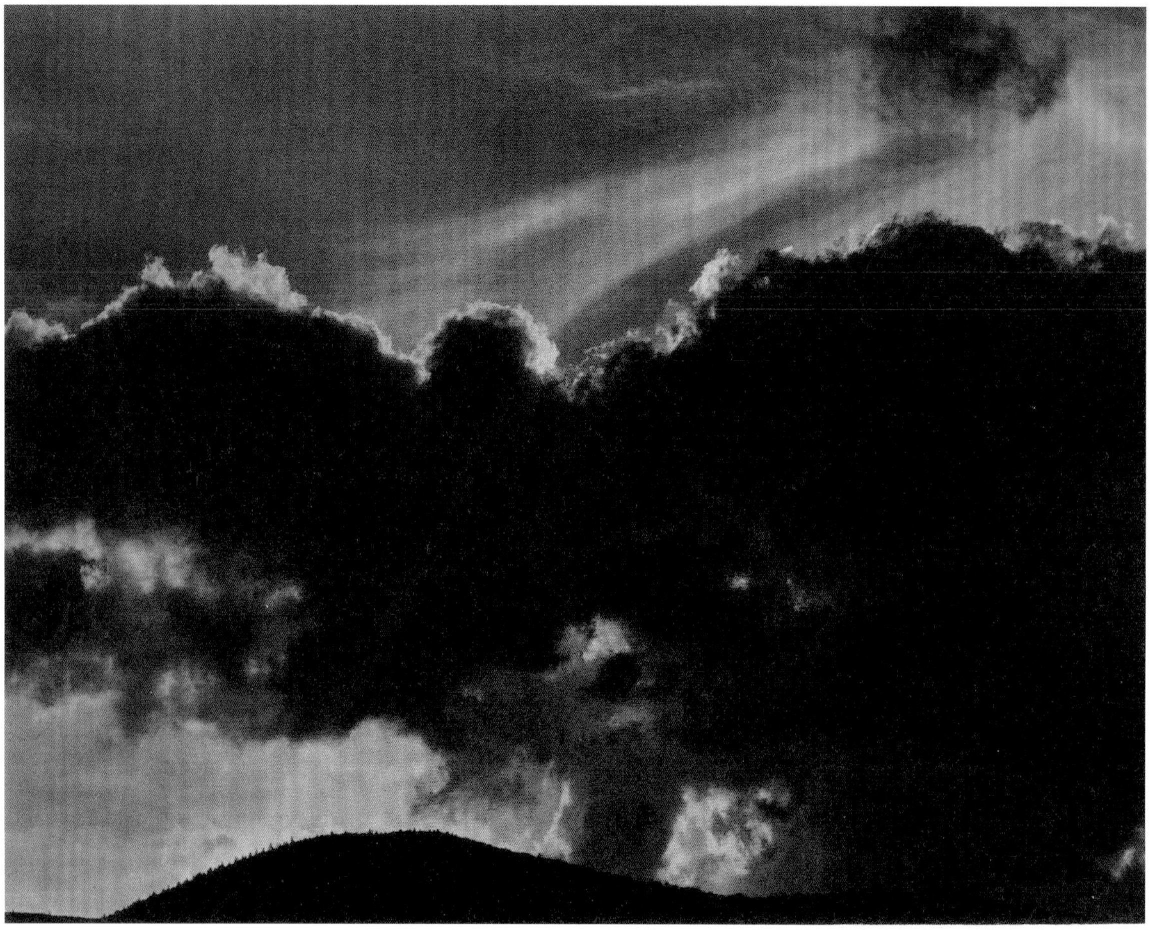

41. ***Equivalent***
1924

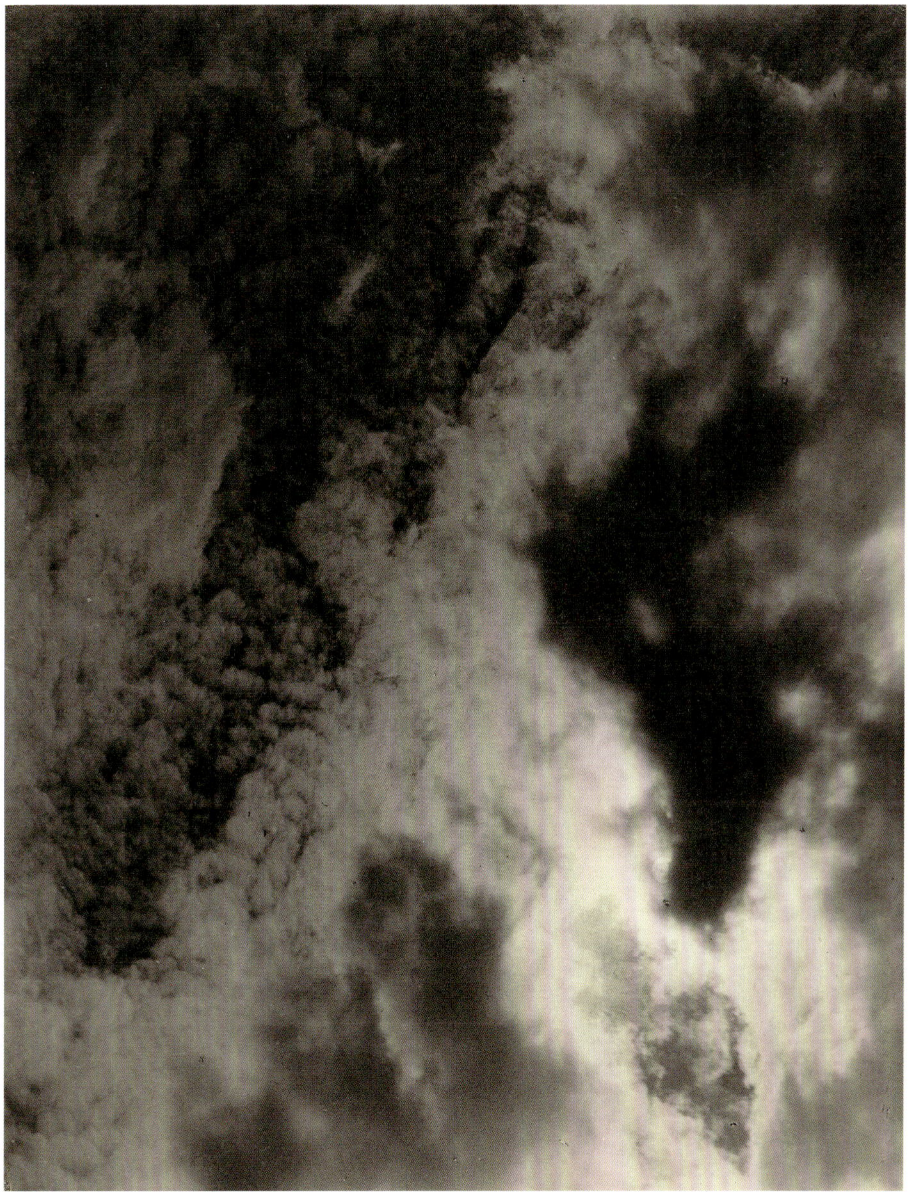

42. ***Equivalent***
1925

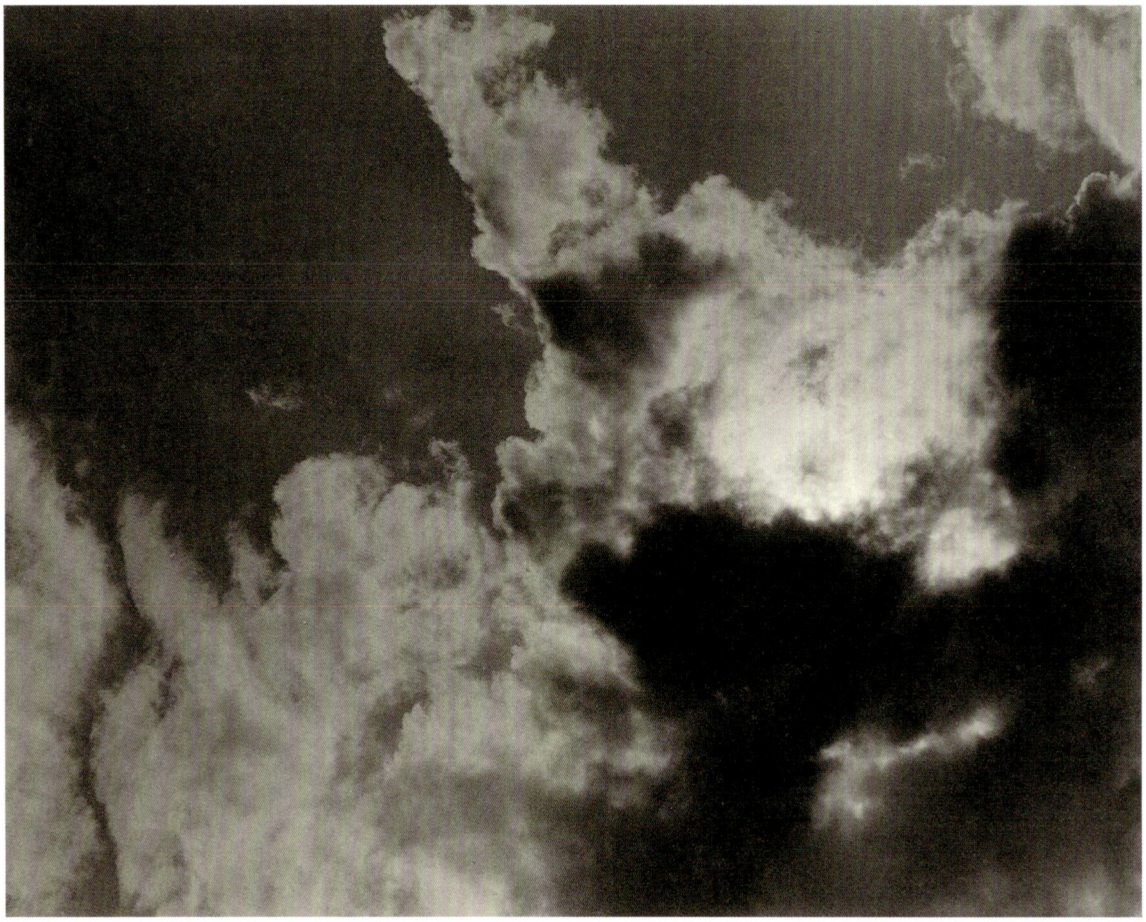

43. ***Equivalent***
1925

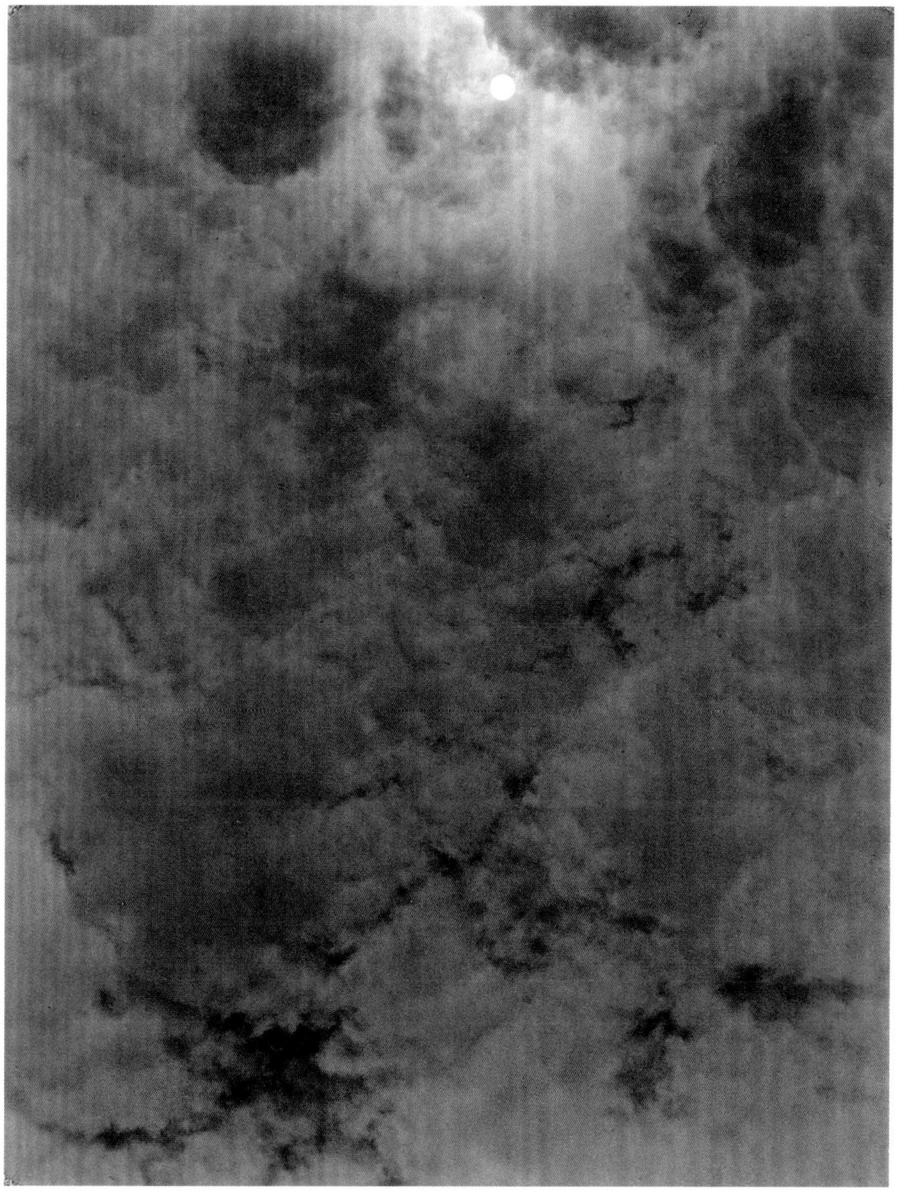

44. ***Equivalent***
1925

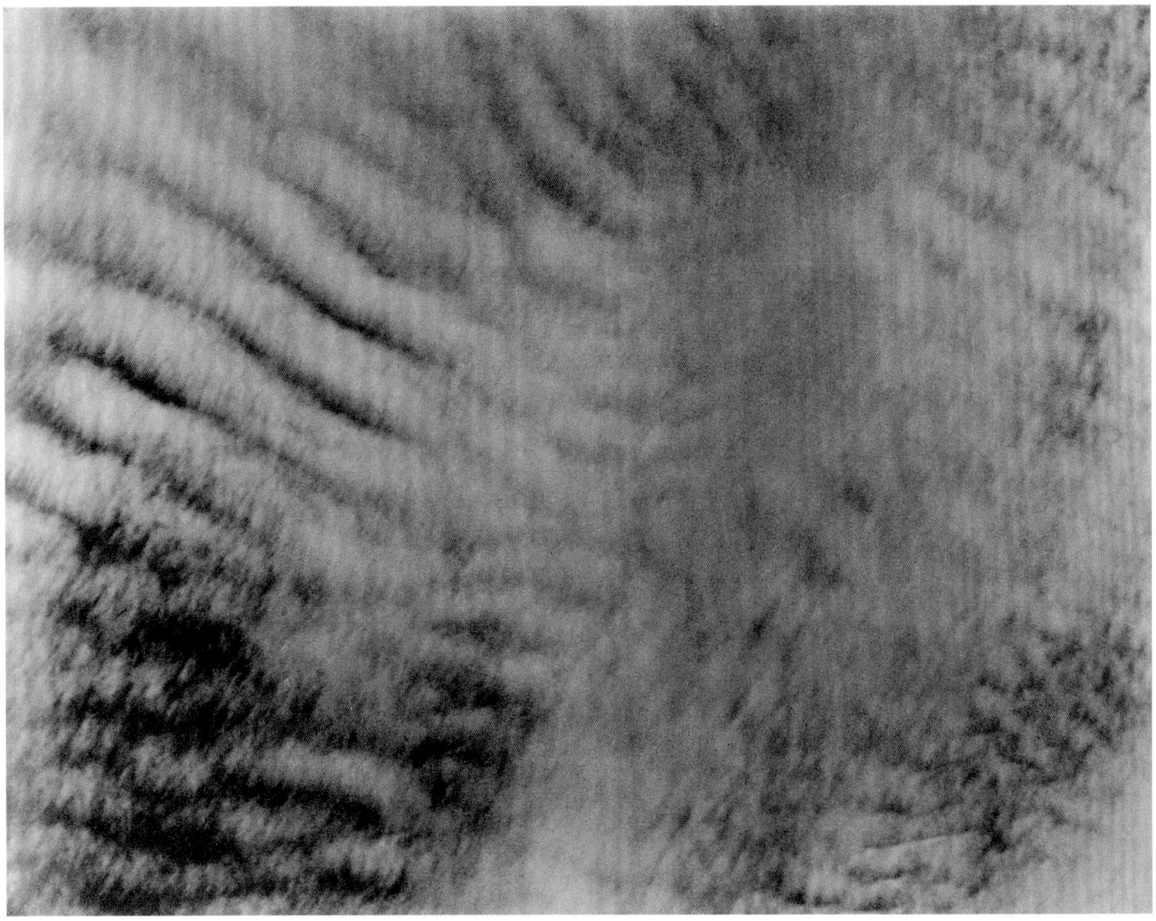

45. ***Equivalent***
1927

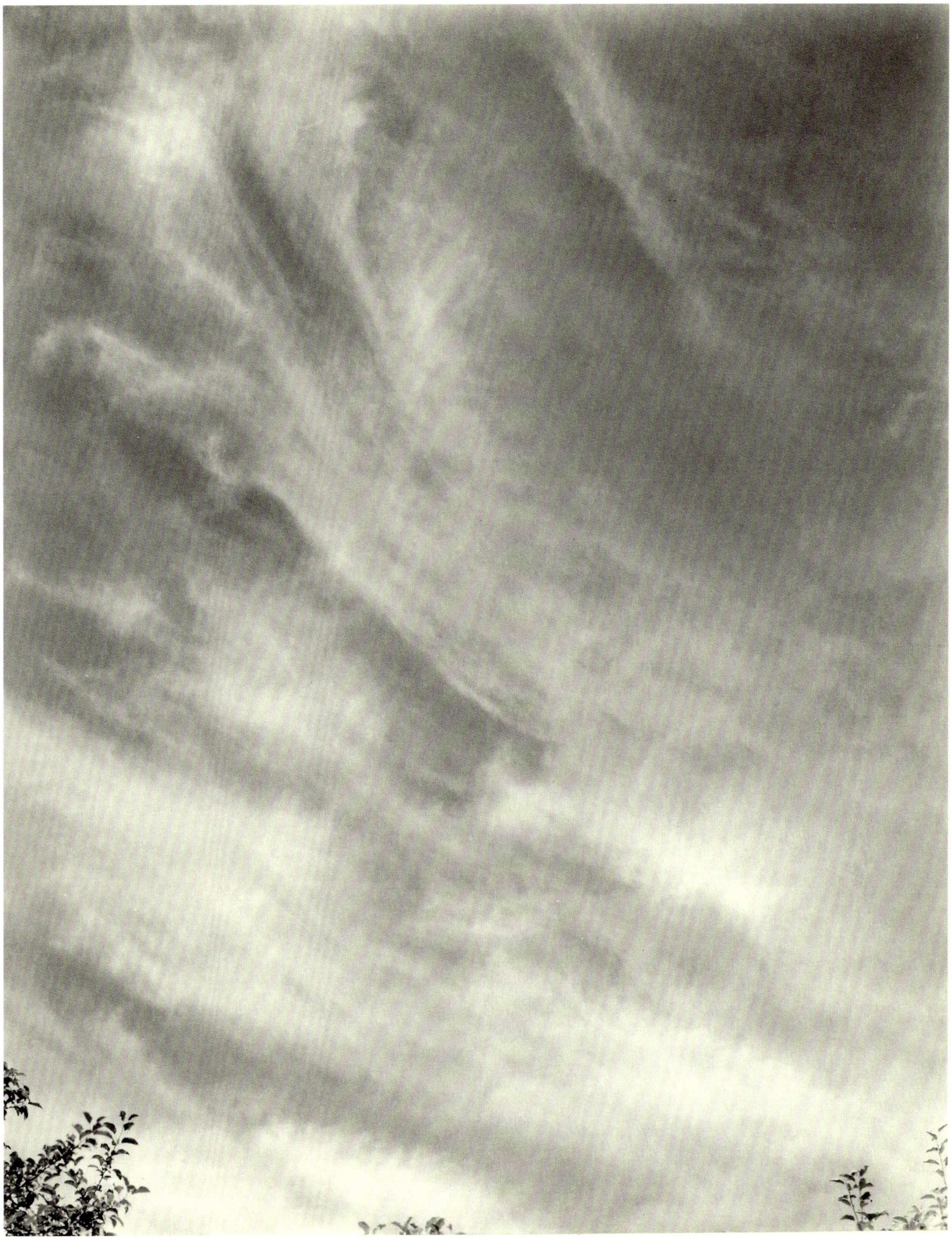

46. ***Equivalent***
1935

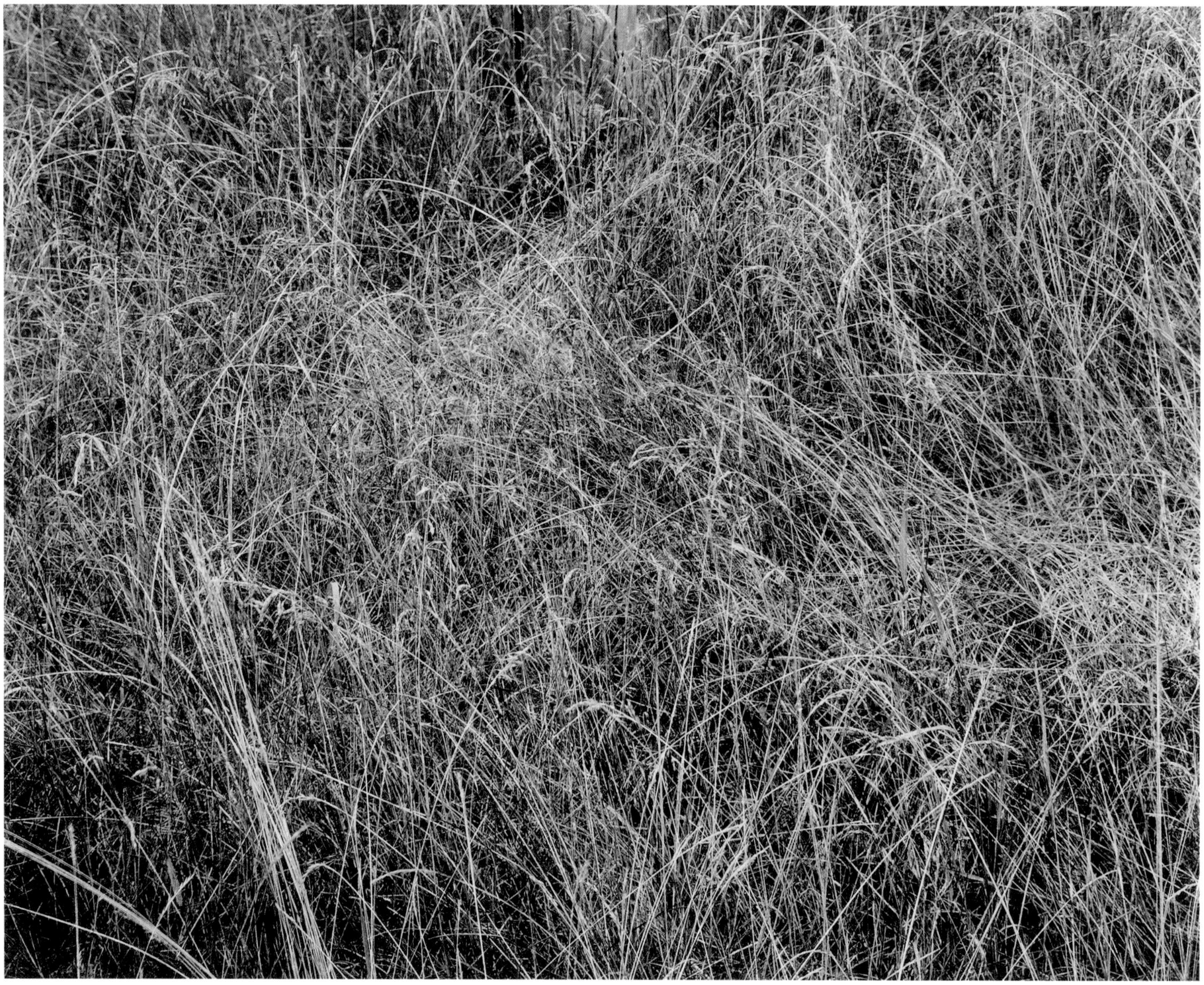

47. *Grass*
1933

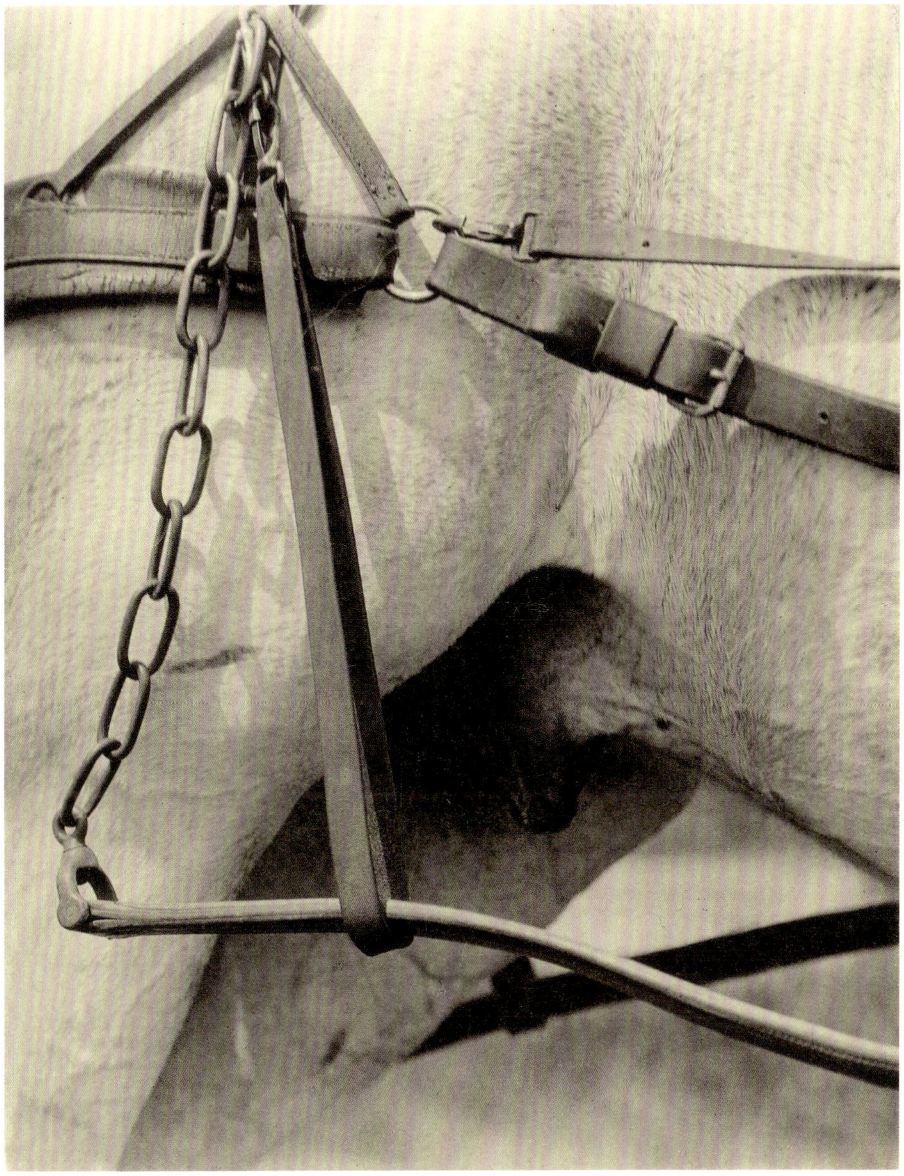

48. *Spiritual America*
1923

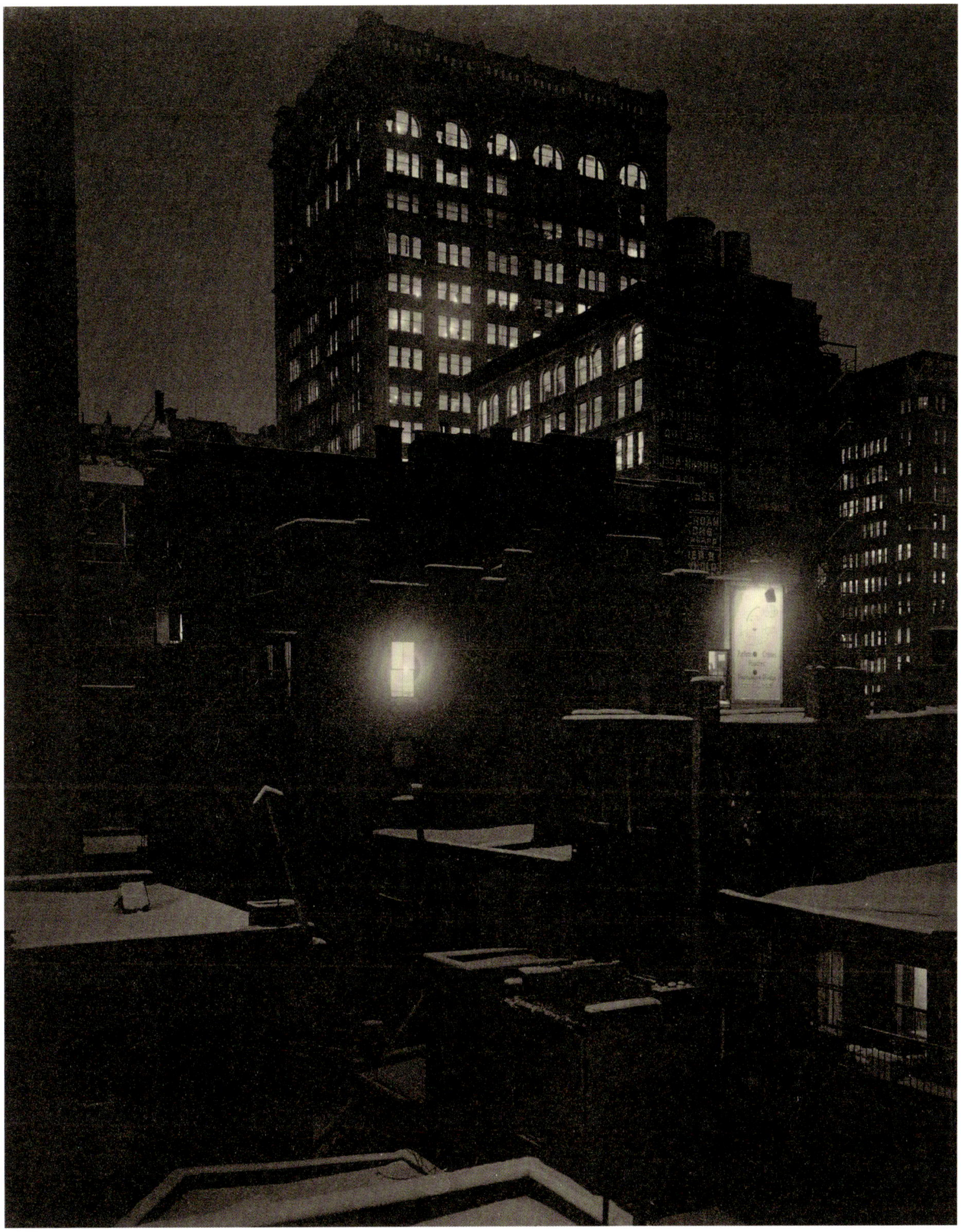

49. ***From the Back Window, 291***
1915

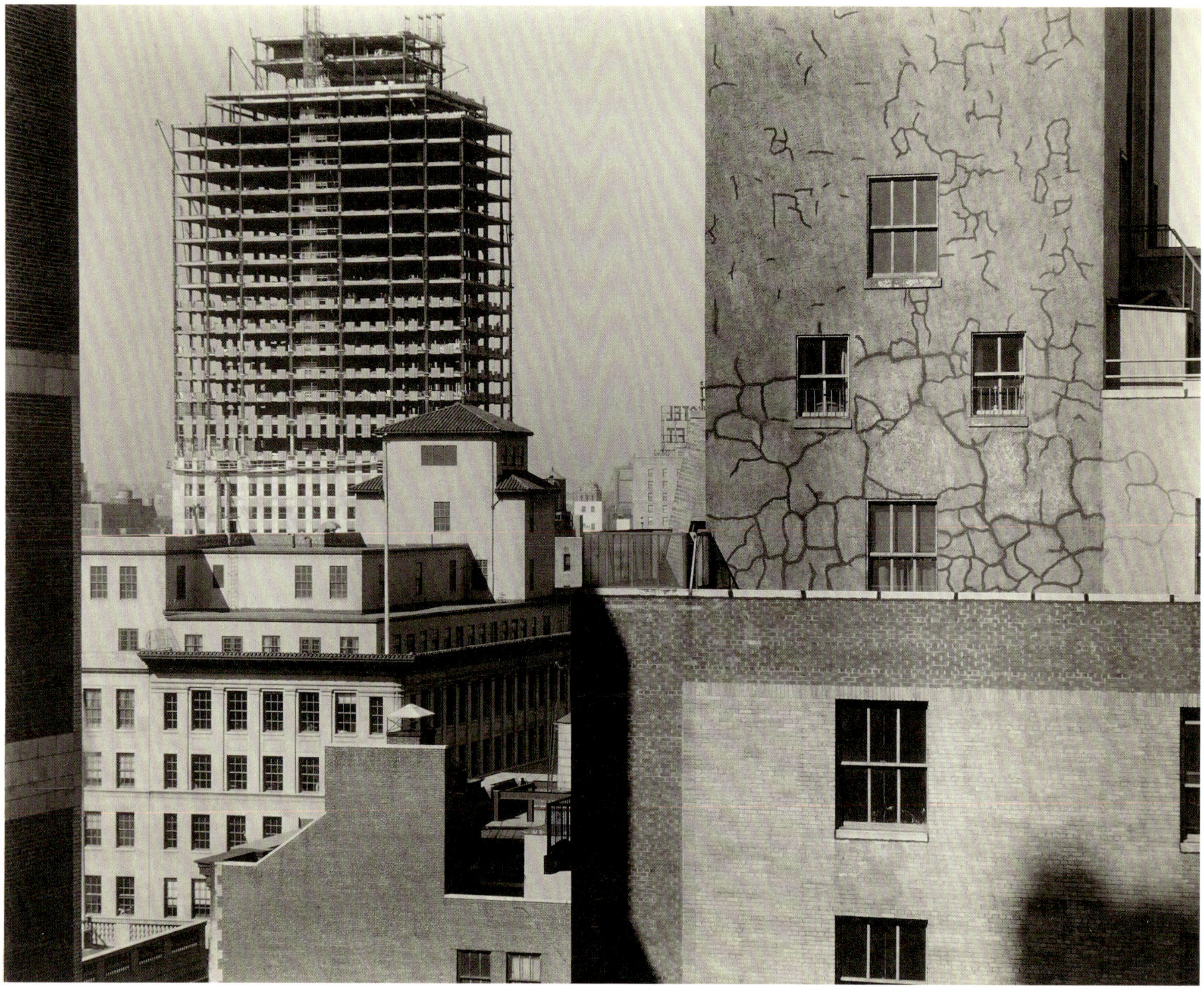

50. ***From My Window at An American Place, Southwest***
1932

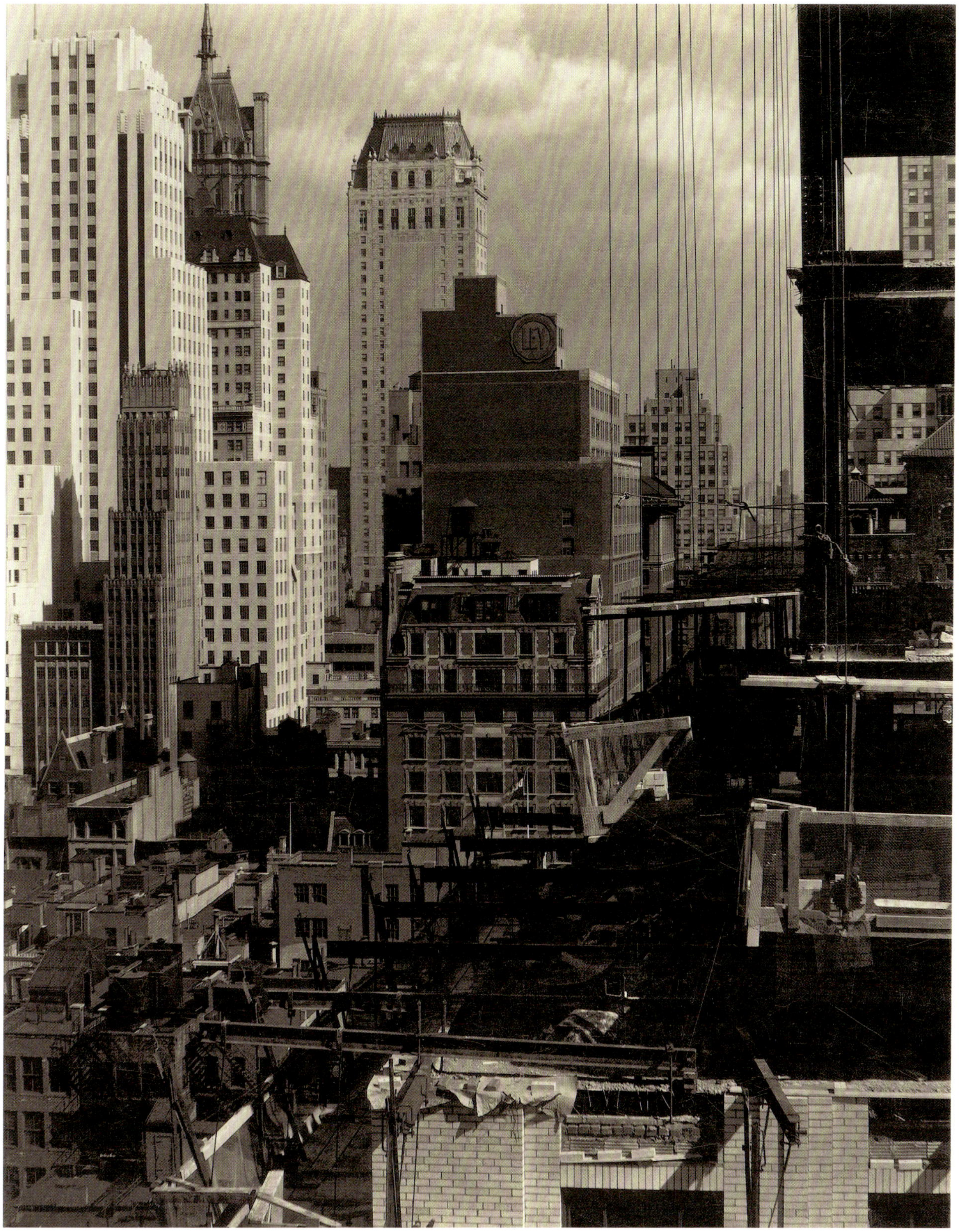

51. *From My Window at An American Place, North*
1931

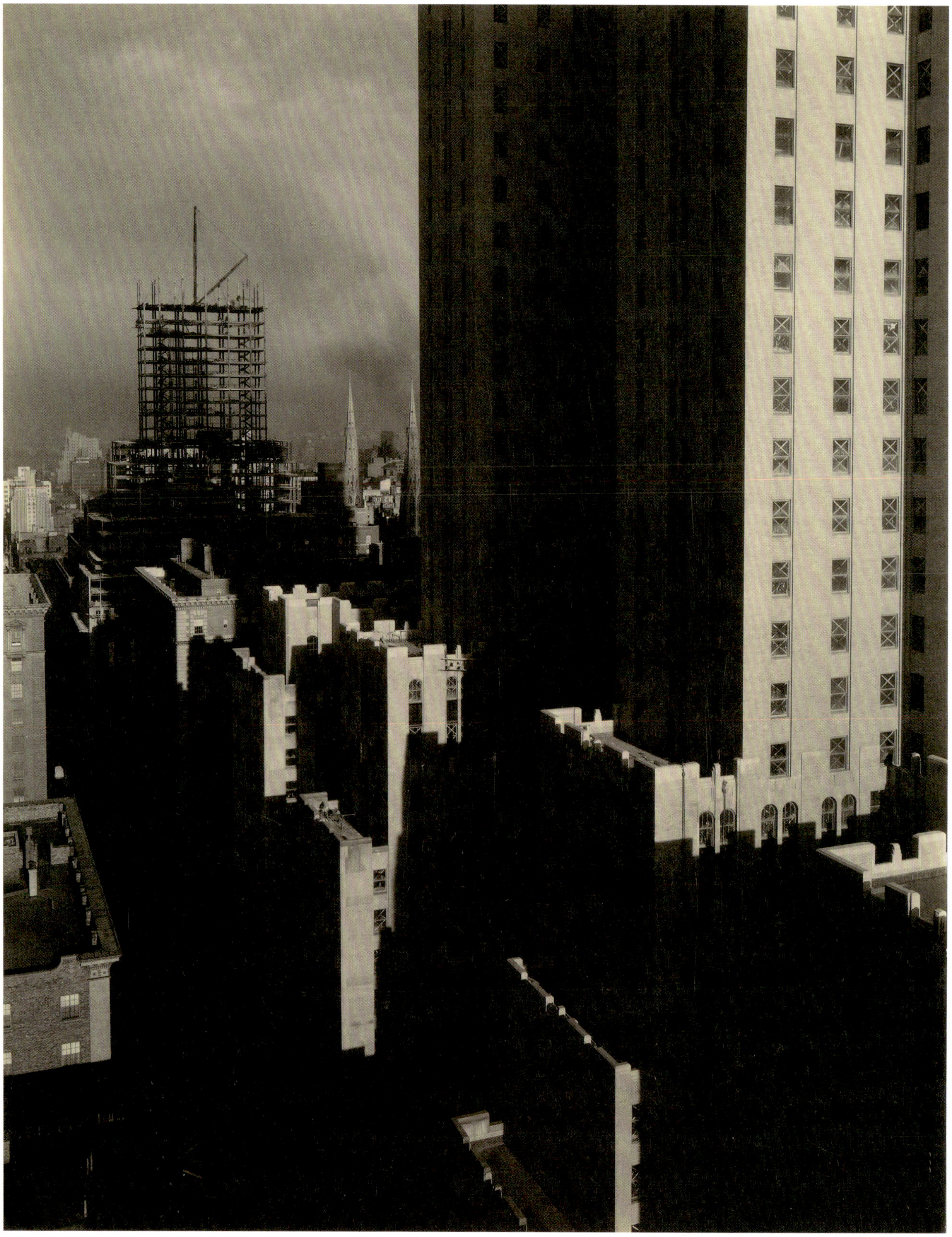

52. *From My Window at the Shelton, West*
1931

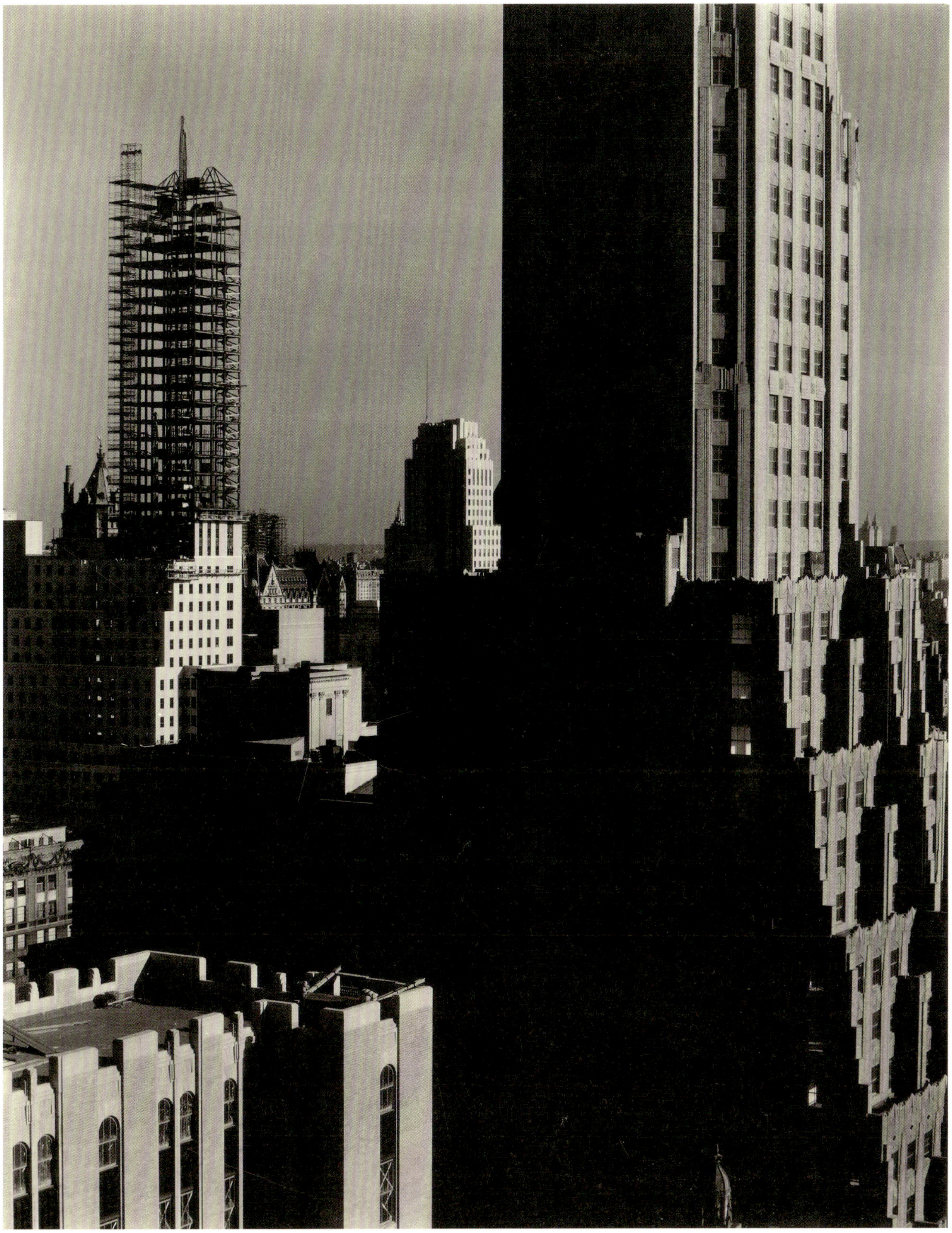

53. *Looking Northwest from the Shelton, New York*
1932

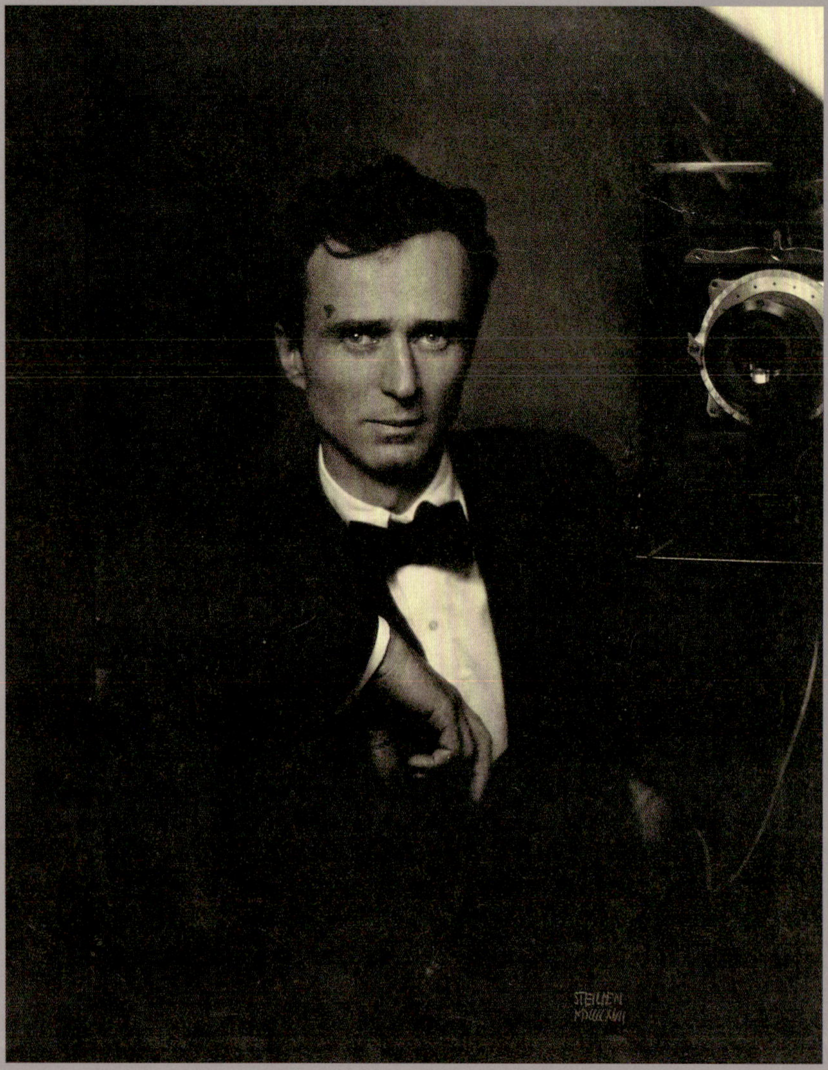

Edward Steichen
Self-Portrait
1917
Platinum print
9⅝ x 7¹³⁄₁₆ in. (24.5 x 19.8 cm)
The Metropolitan Museum of Art, New York
Gilman Collection, Purchase, Harriette and
Noel Levine Gift, 2005
2005.100.156

EDWARD STEICHEN

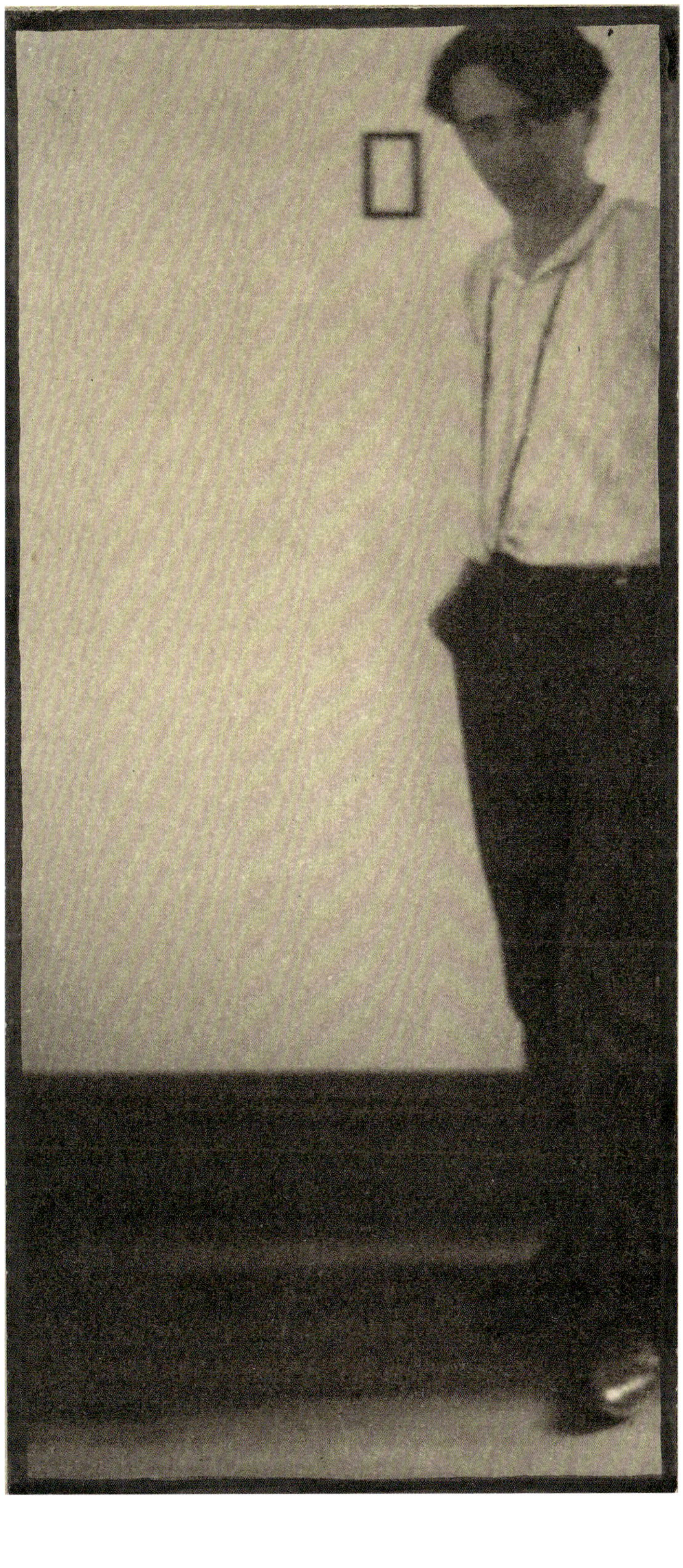

54. ***Self-Portrait***
1899

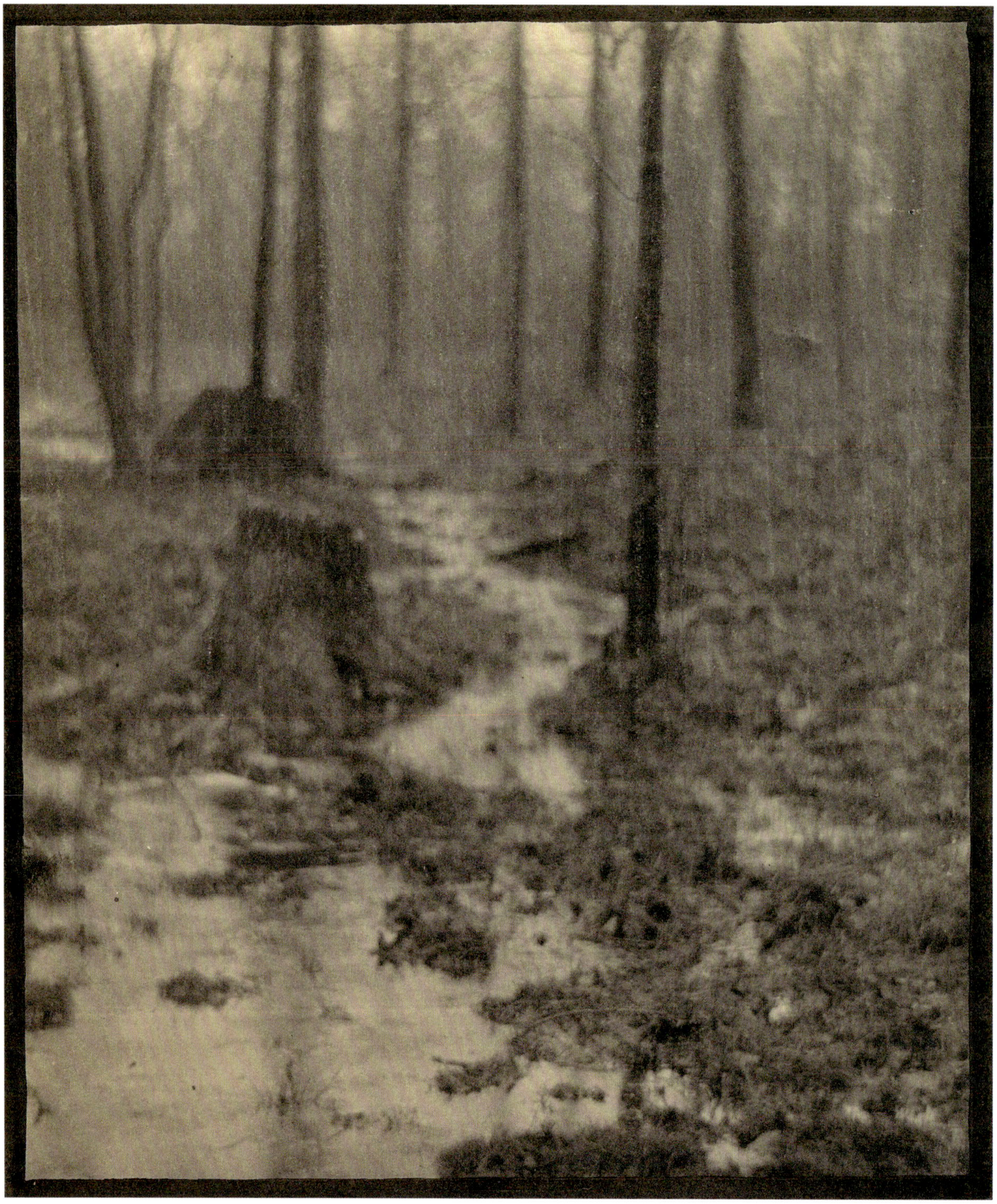

55. ***Woods Interior***
1899

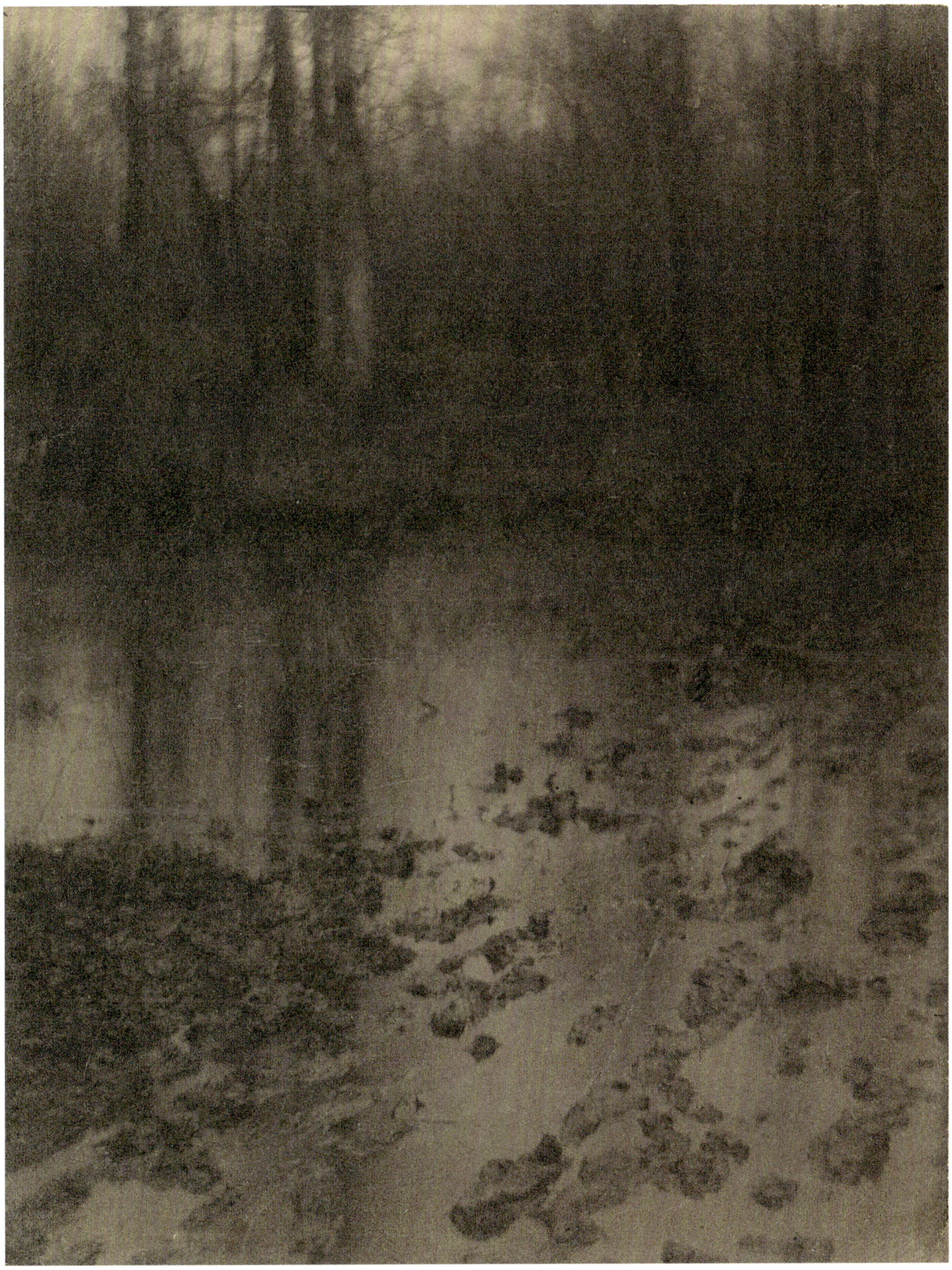

56. ***The Pool—Evening***
1899

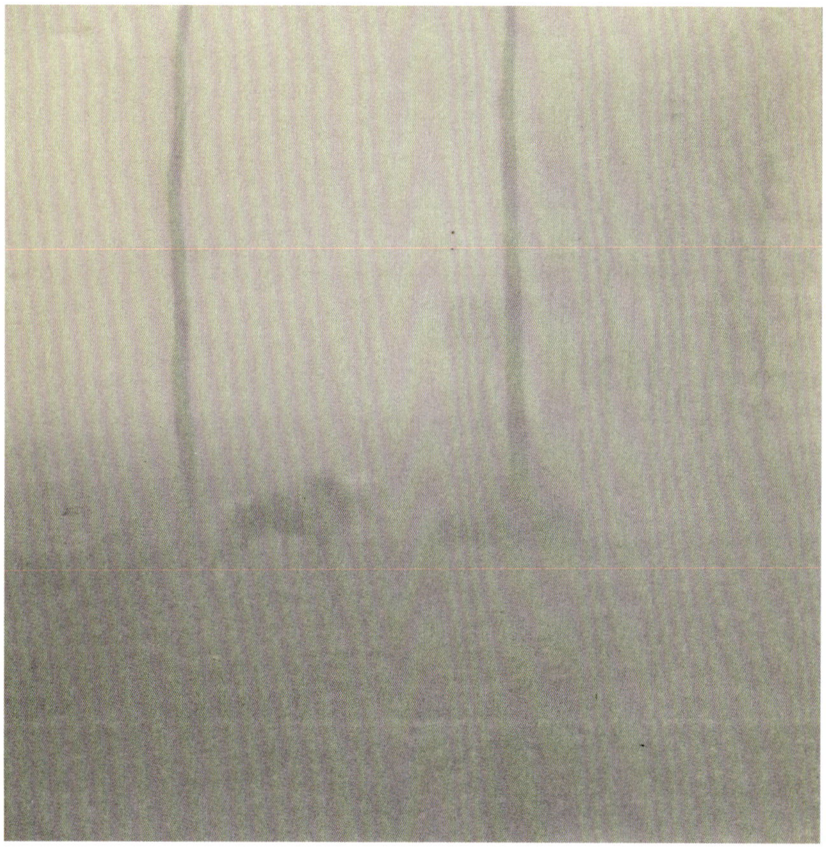

57. ***Voulangis***
1900–1902

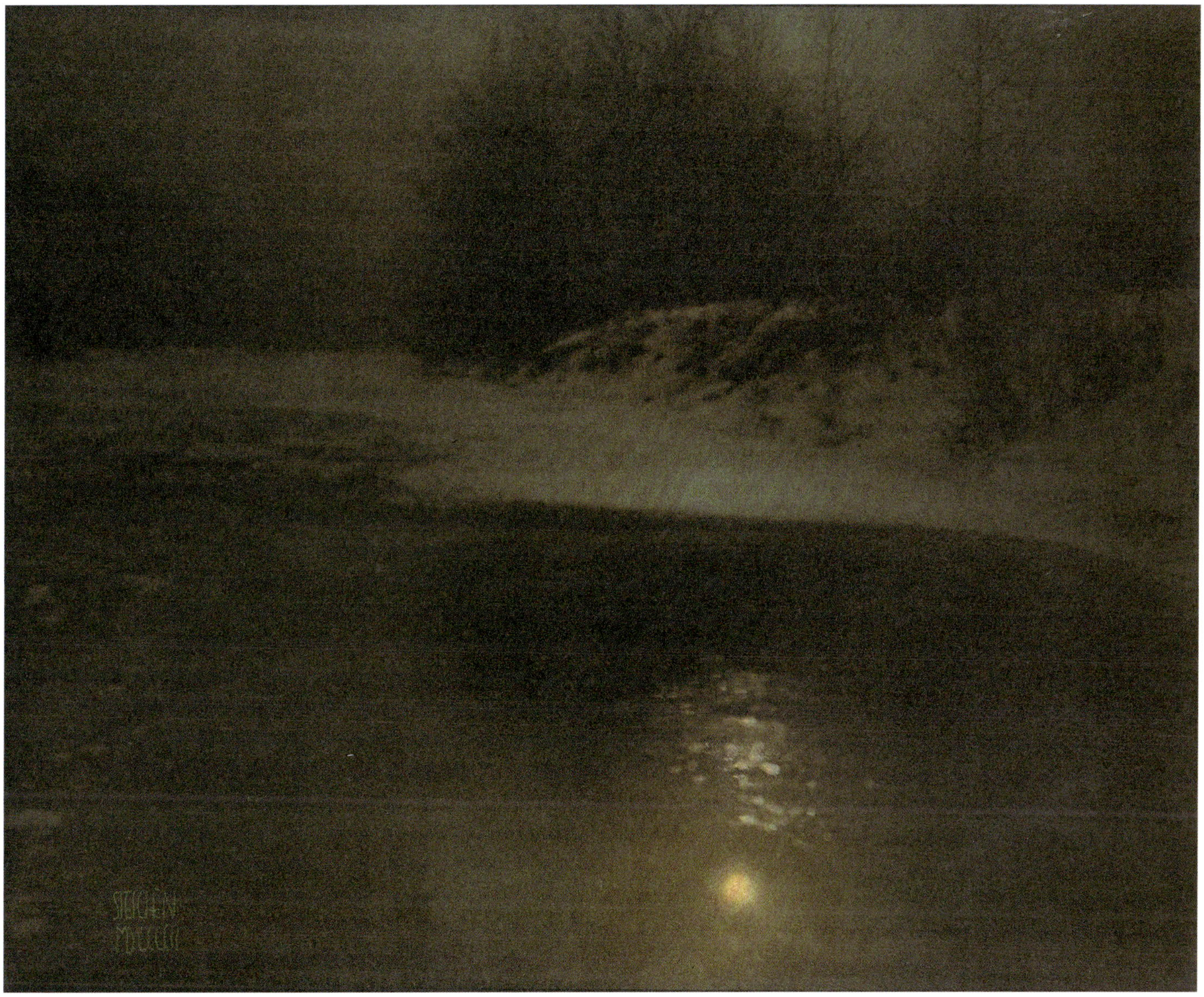

58. ***Moonlight—Winter***
1902

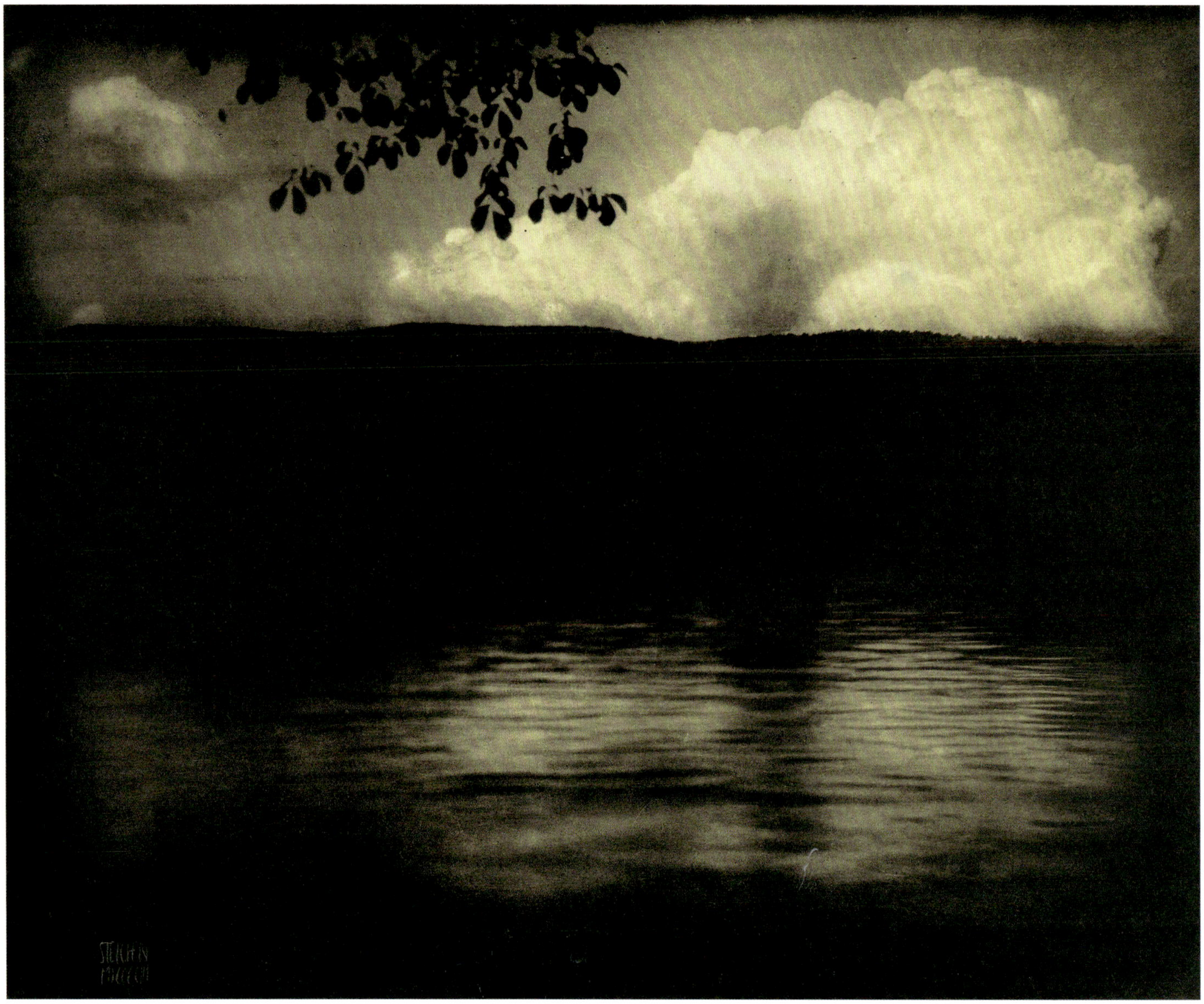

59. *The Big Cloud, Lake George*
1903, printed 1904

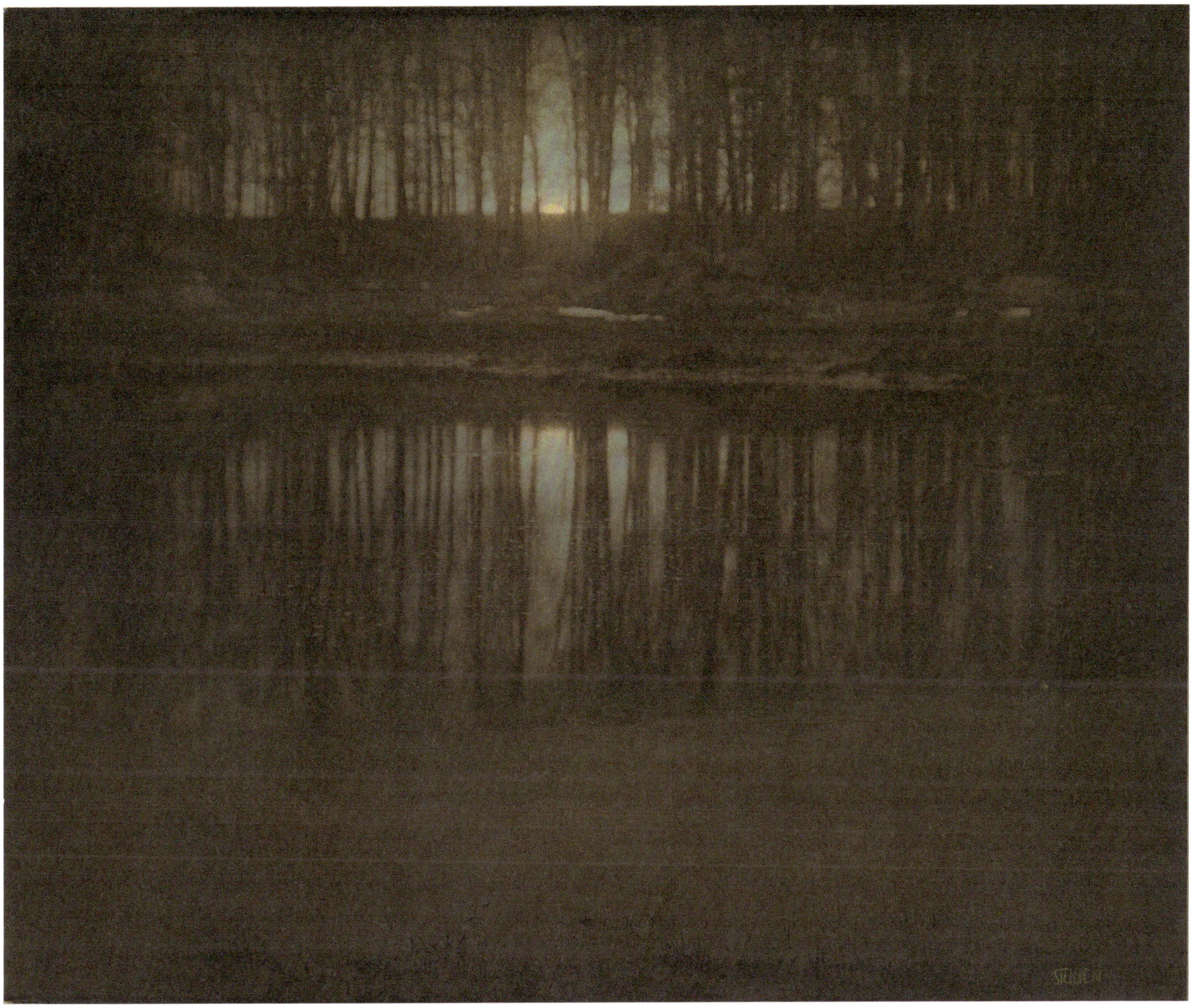

60. *The Pond—Moonrise*
1904

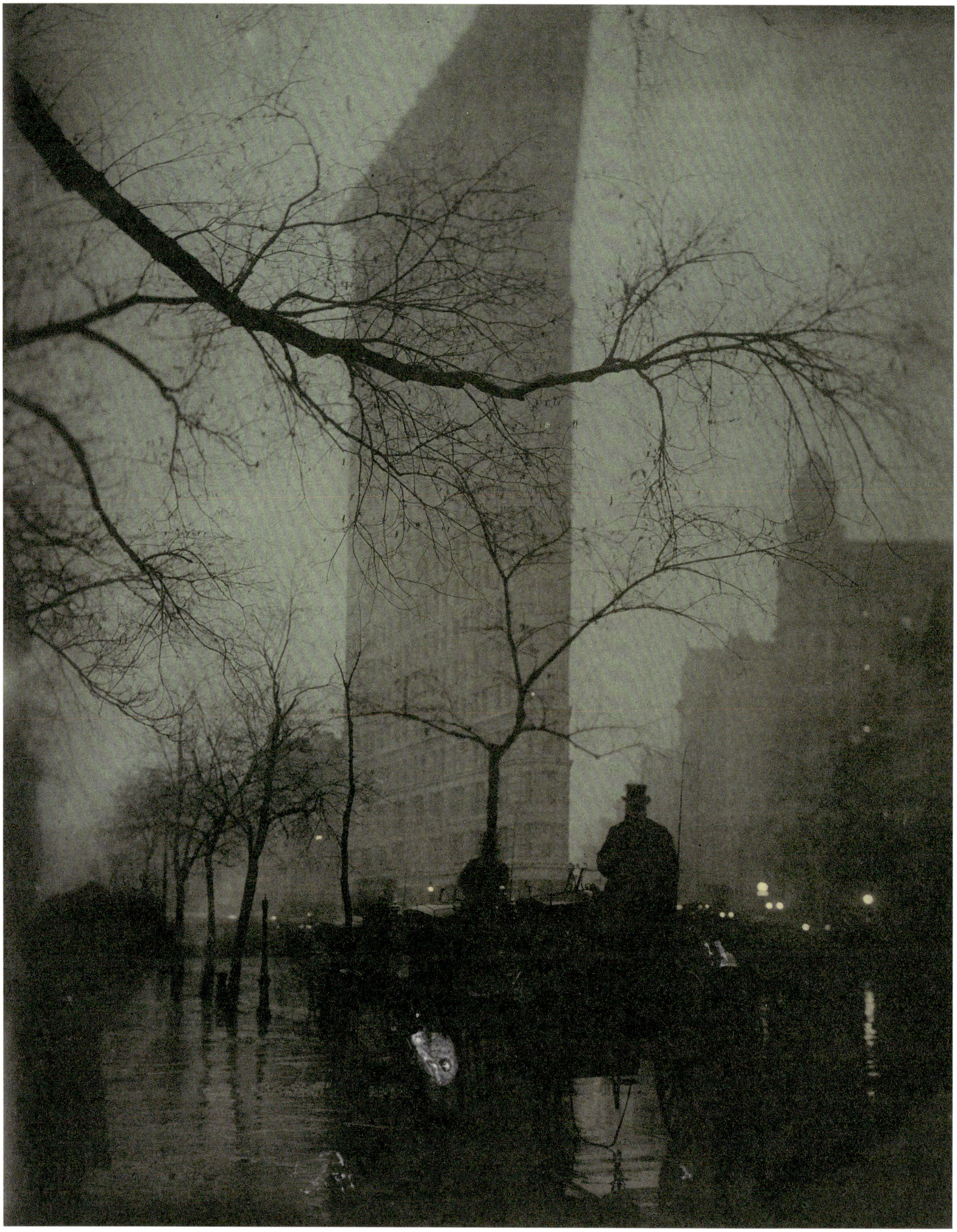

61. ***The Flatiron***
1904

62. ***The Flatiron***
1904, printed 1909

63. ***The Flatiron***
1904, printed 1905

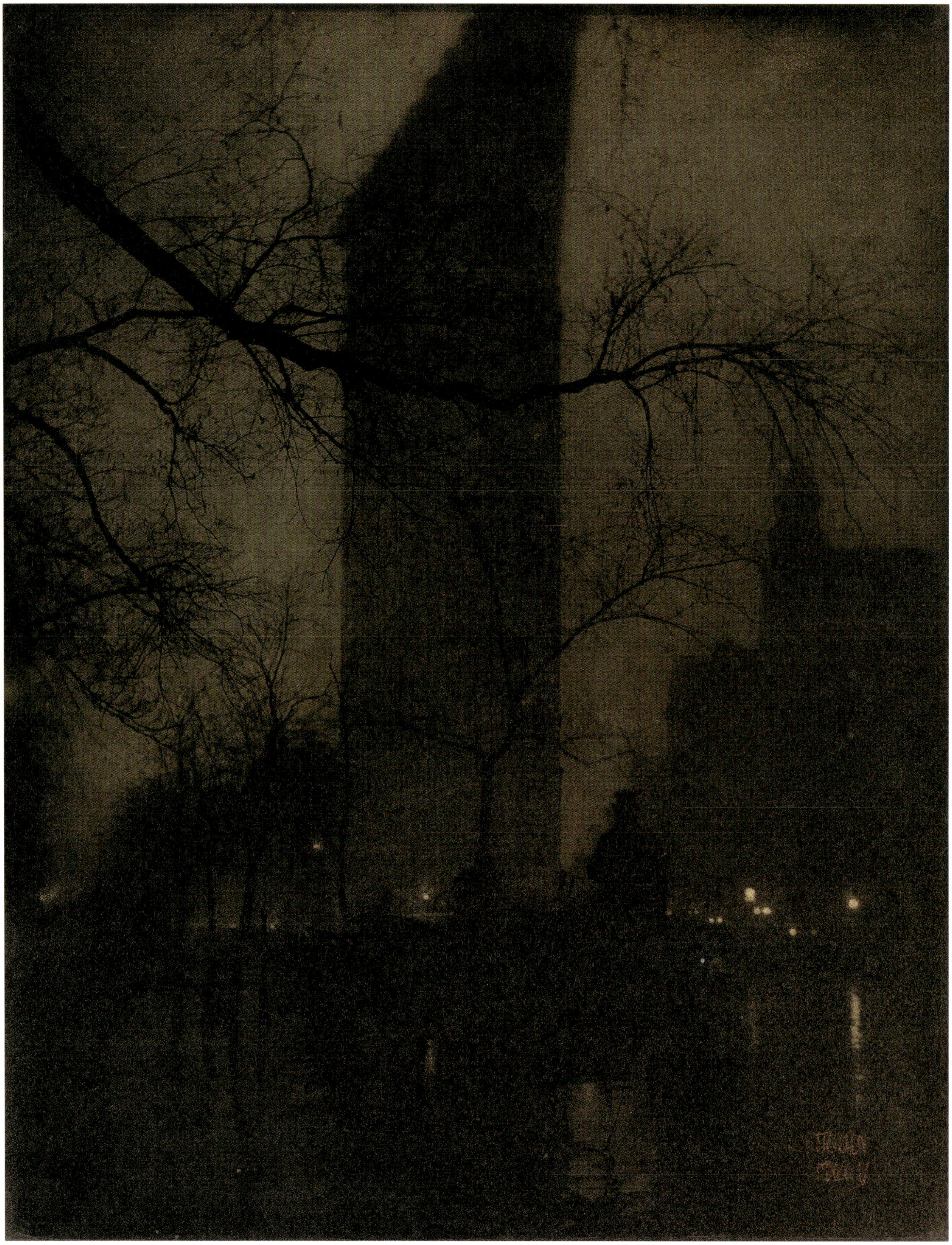

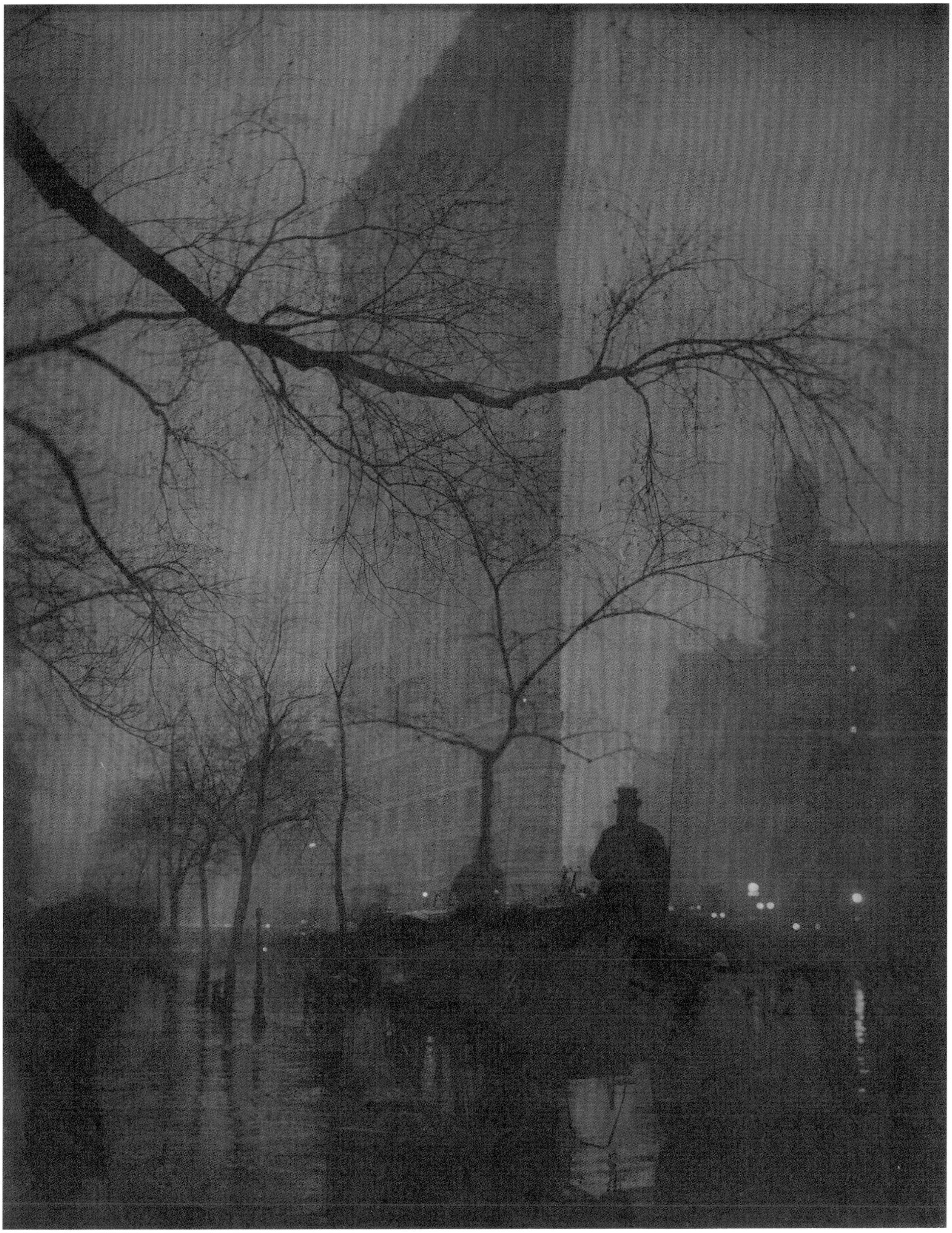

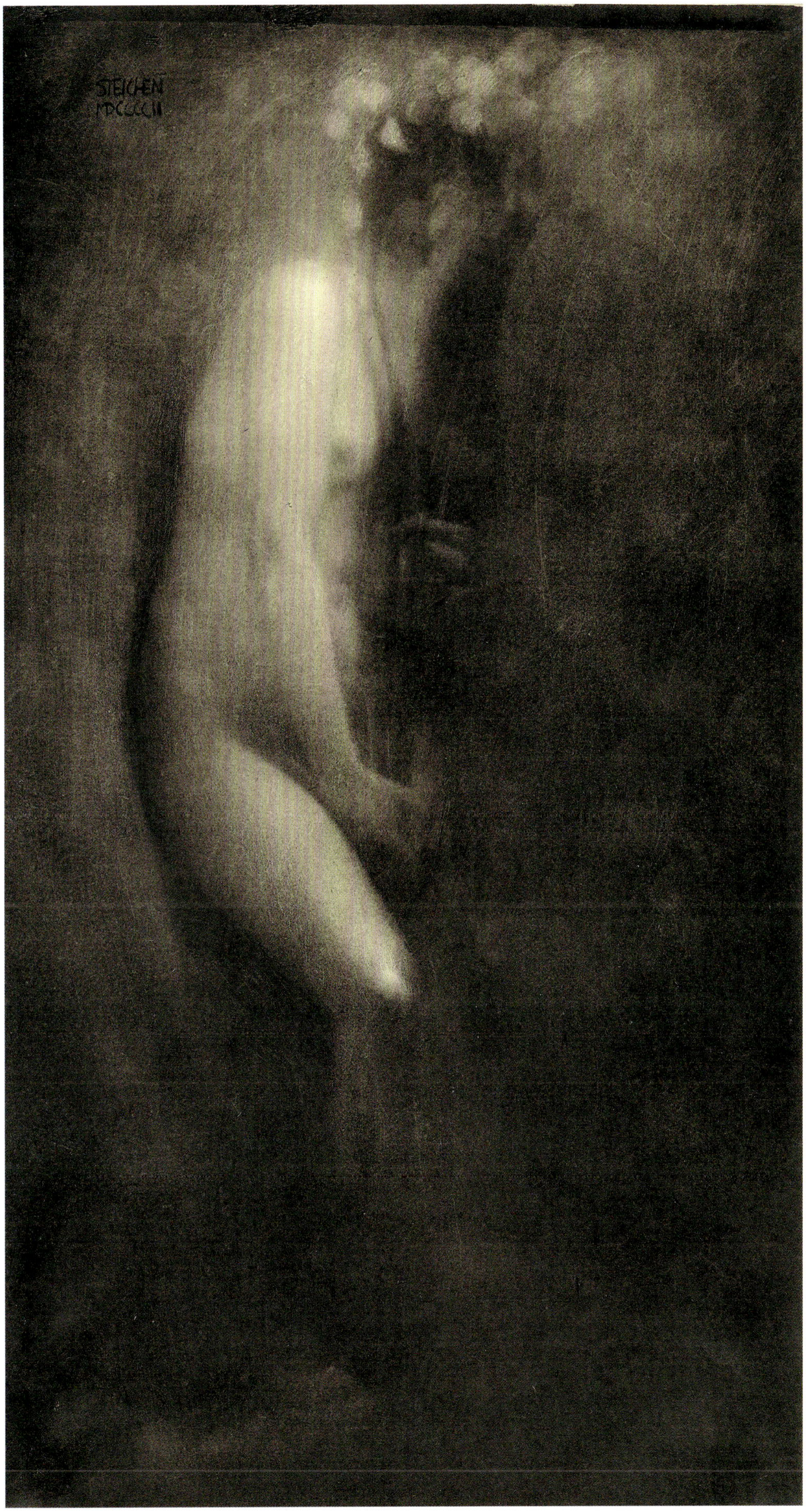

64. *Figure with Iris*
1902

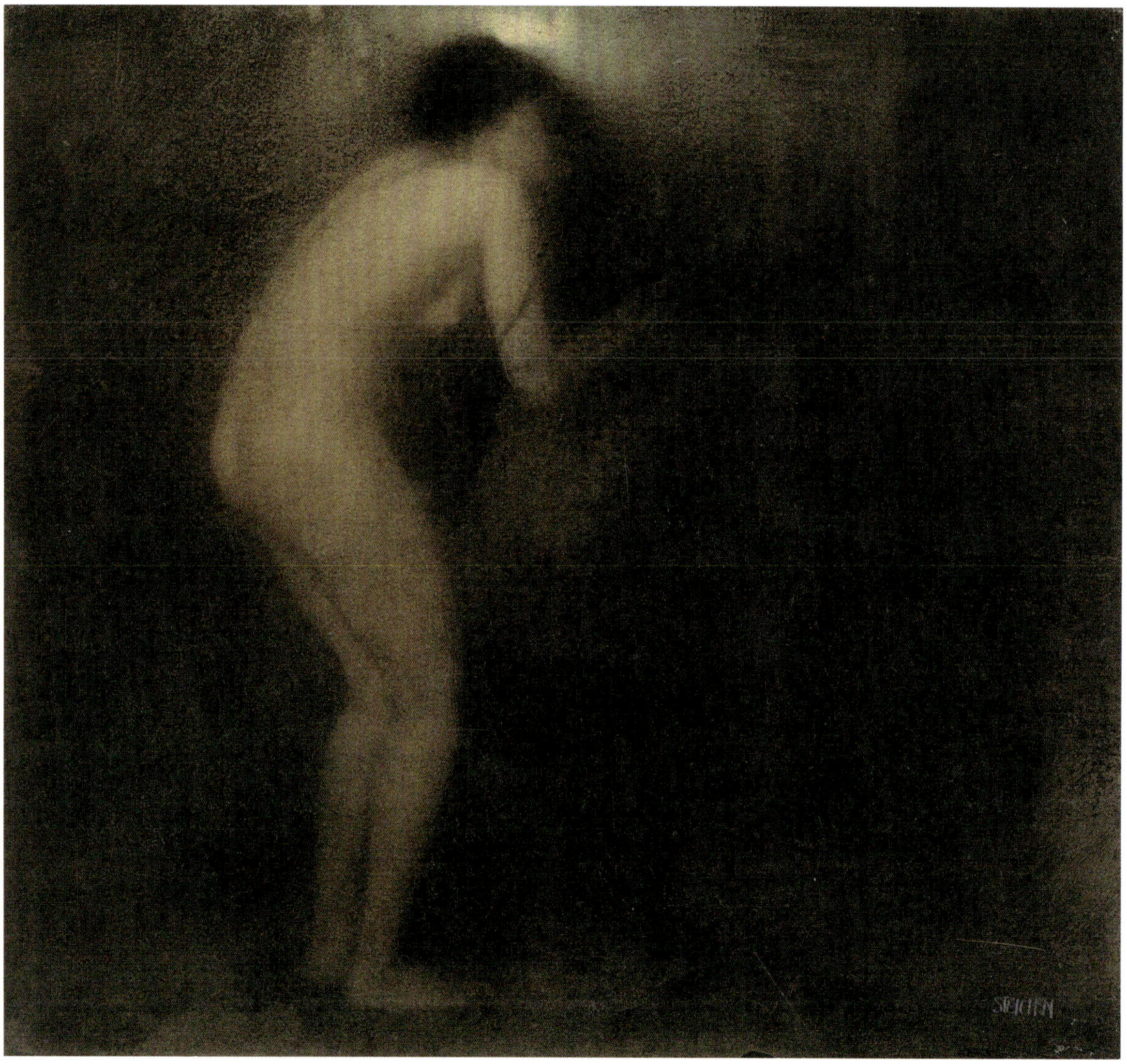

65. *La Cigale*
1901, printed 1904–5

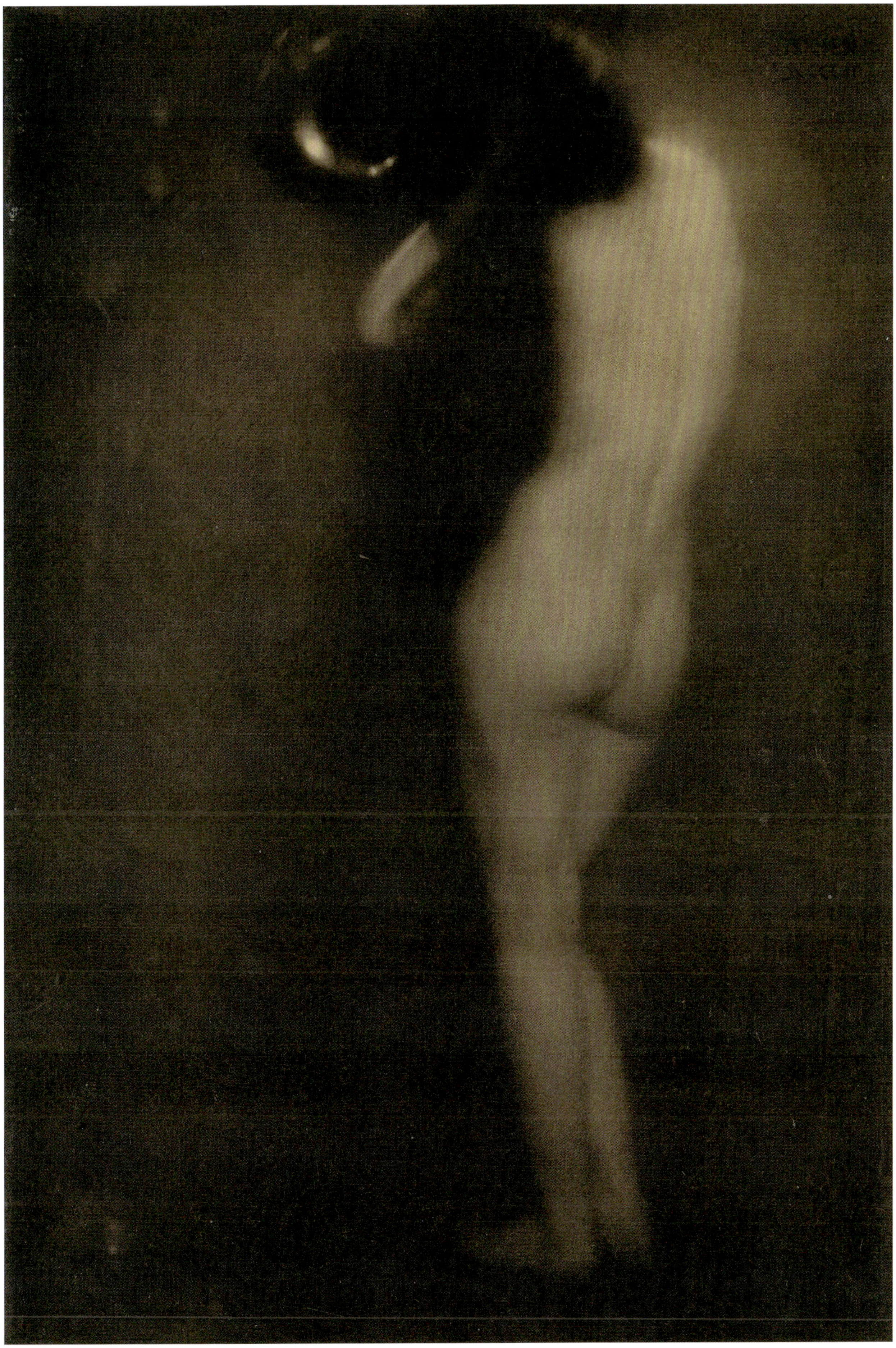

66. ***The Little Round Mirror***
1901, printed 1905

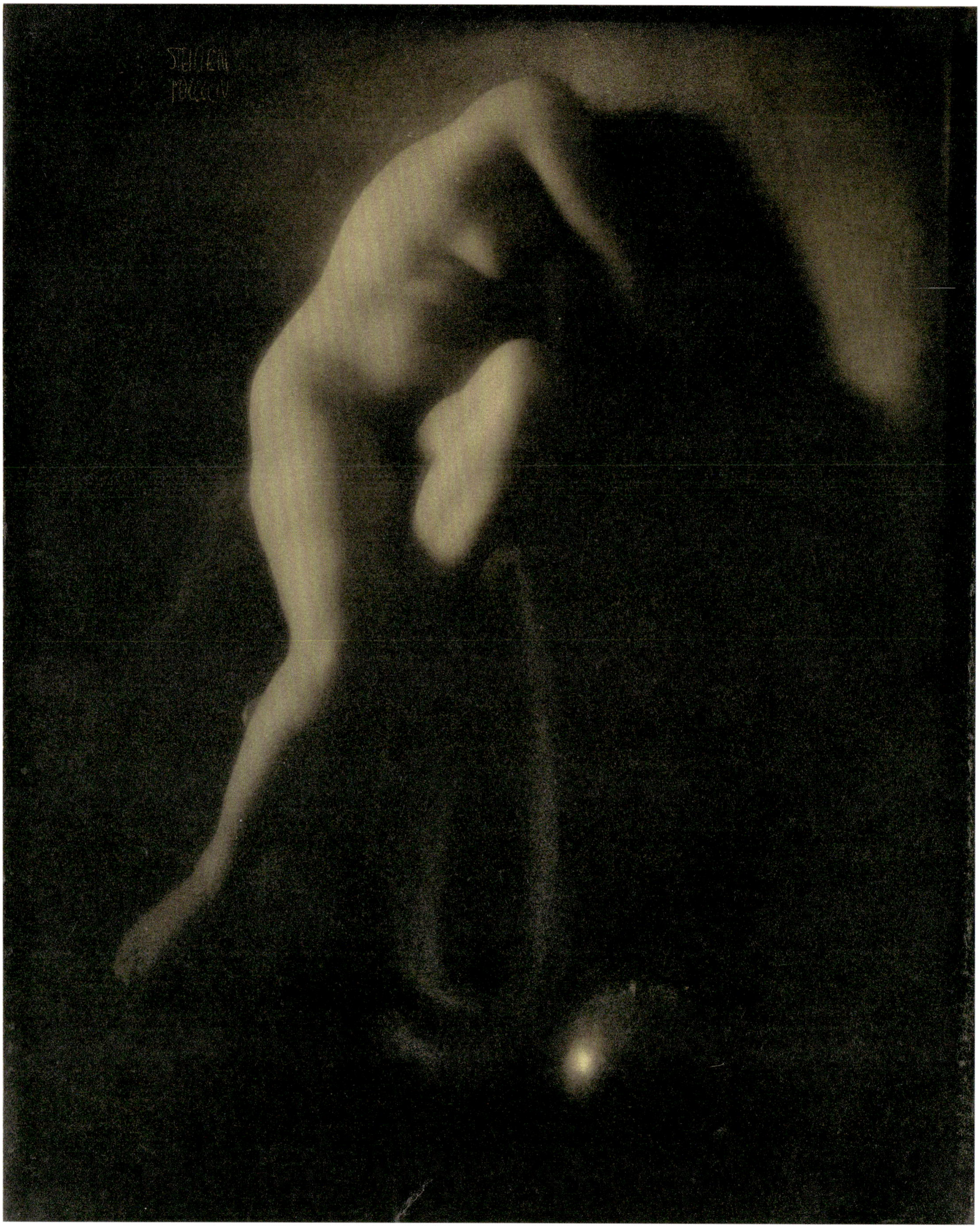

67. *In Memoriam*
1901, printed 1904

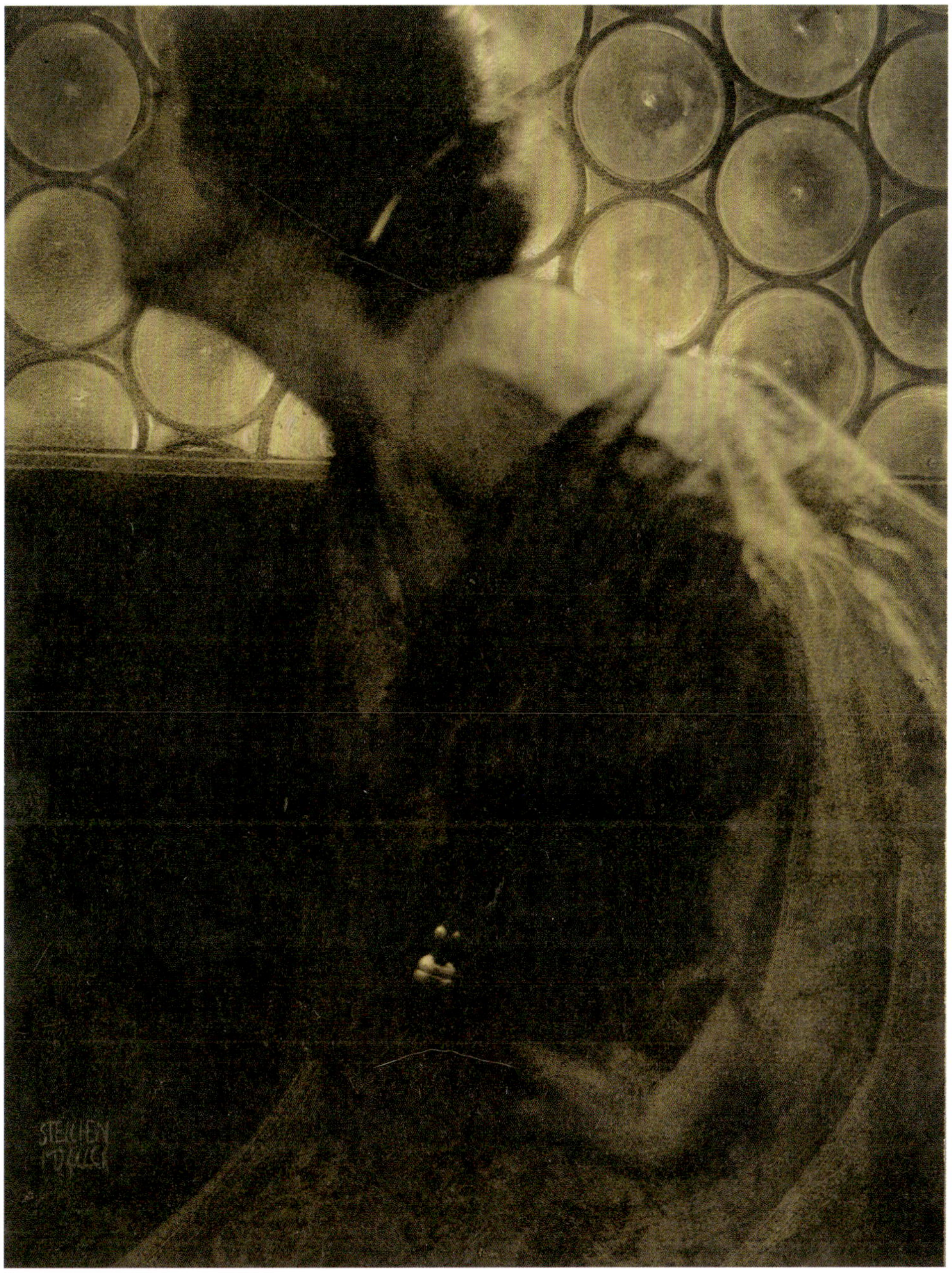

68. *The Black Vase*
1901, printed 1902

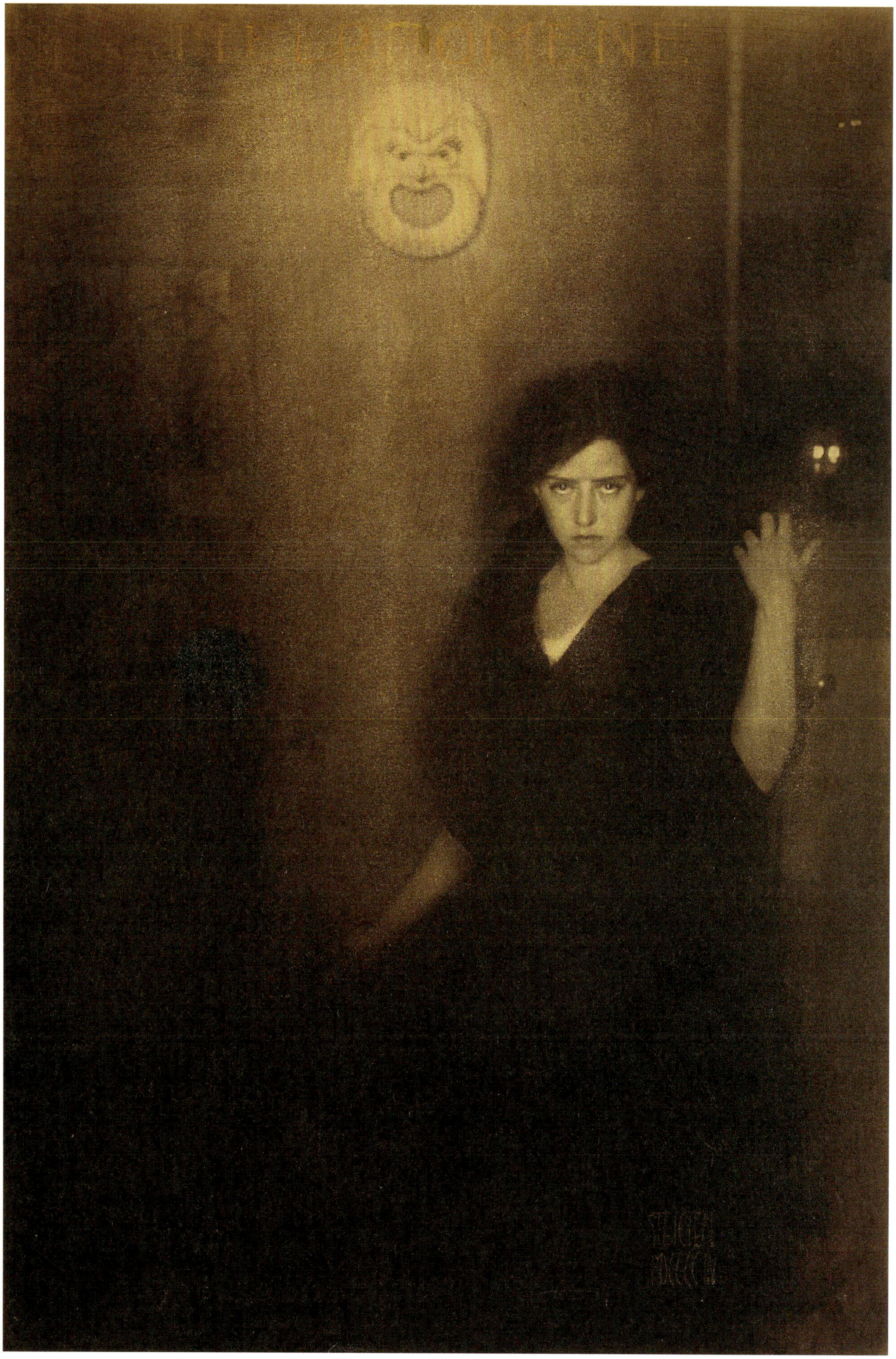

69. ***Melpomene—Landon Rives***
1904–5

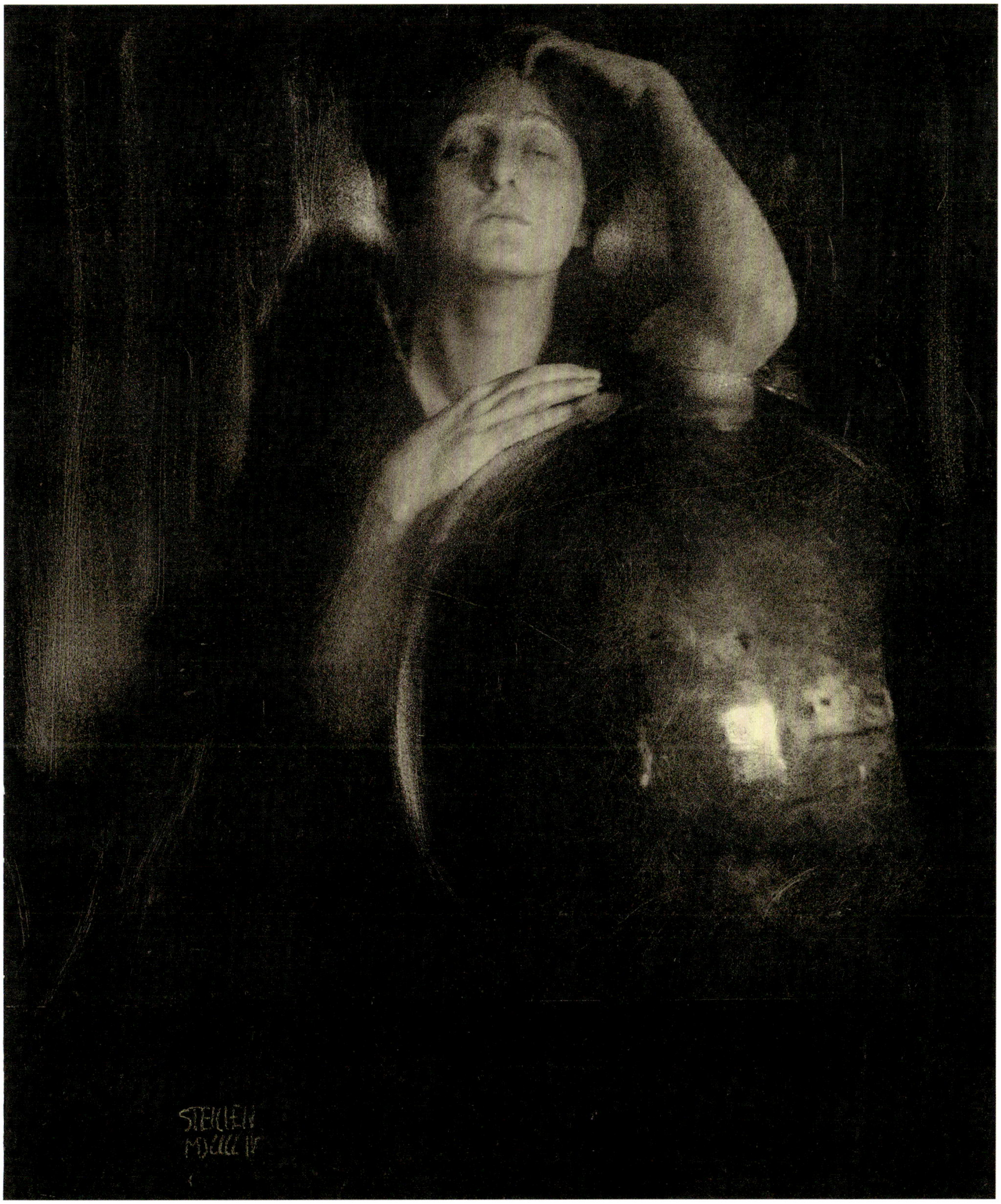

70. ***The Brass Bowl***
1904

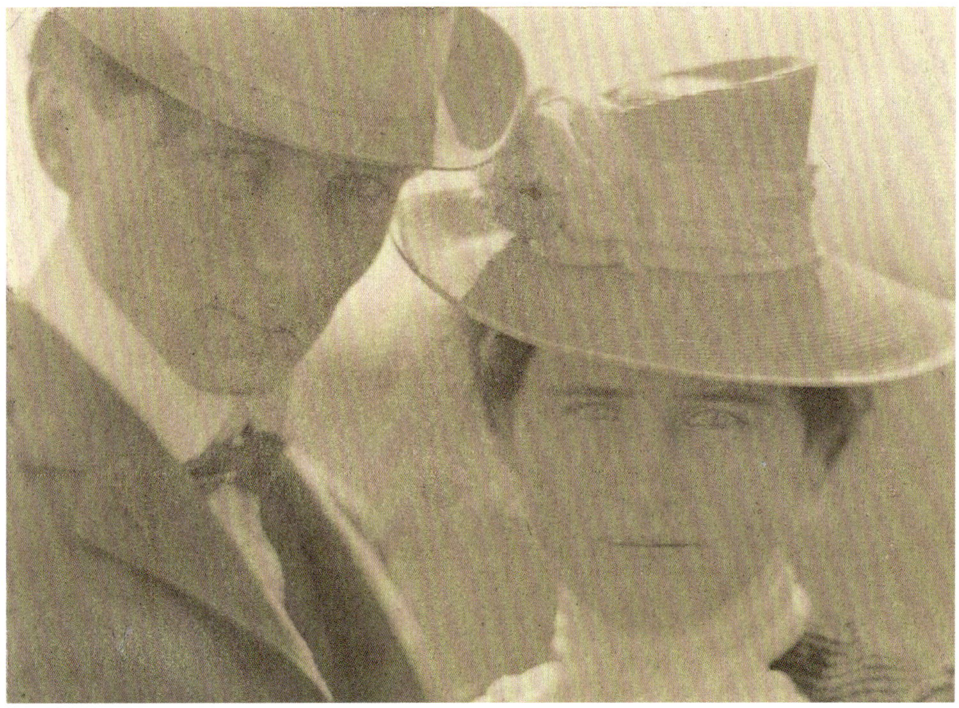

71. ***Self-Portrait with Little Sister***
1900

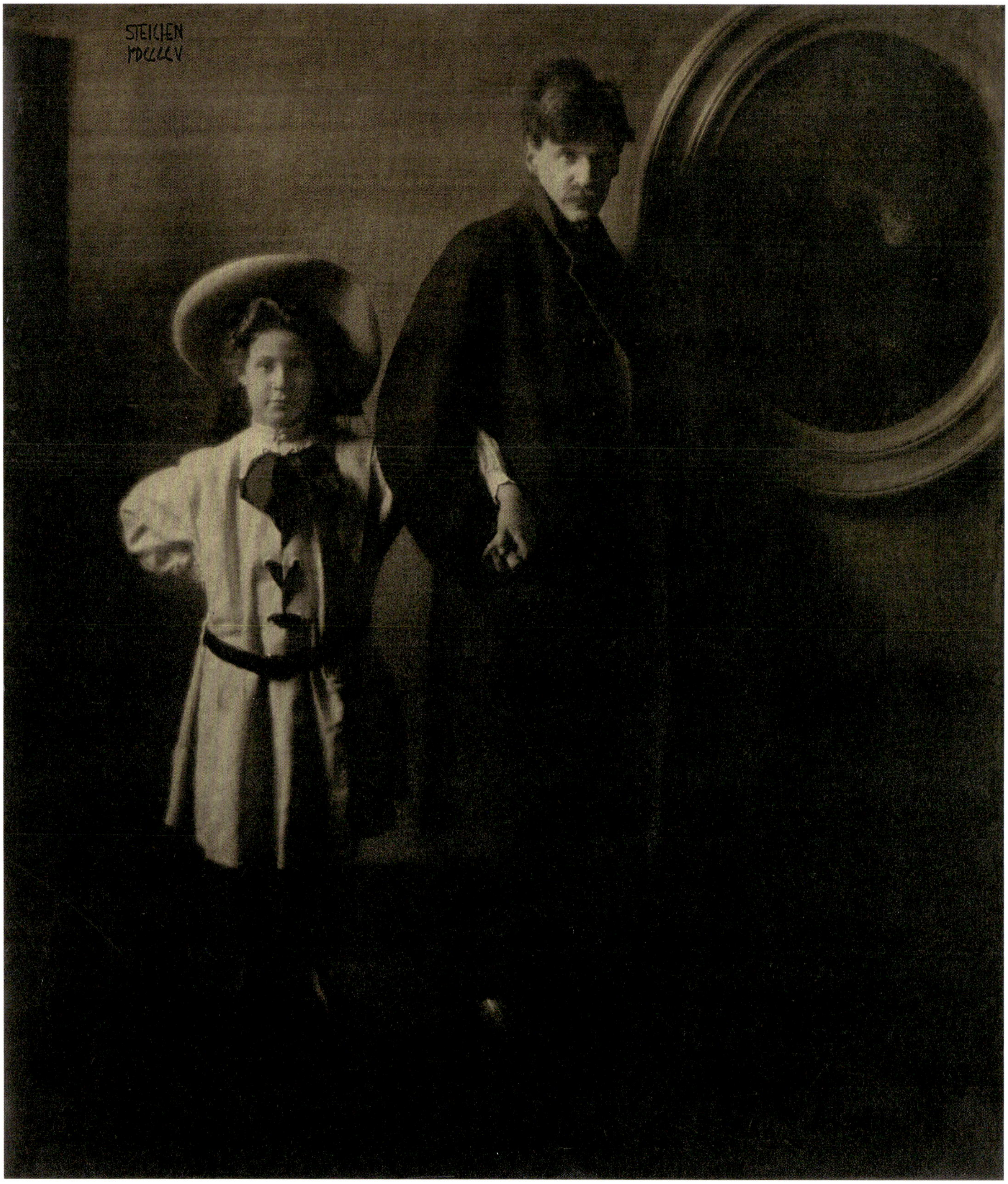

72. ***Alfred Stieglitz and His Daughter Katherine***
1904, printed 1905

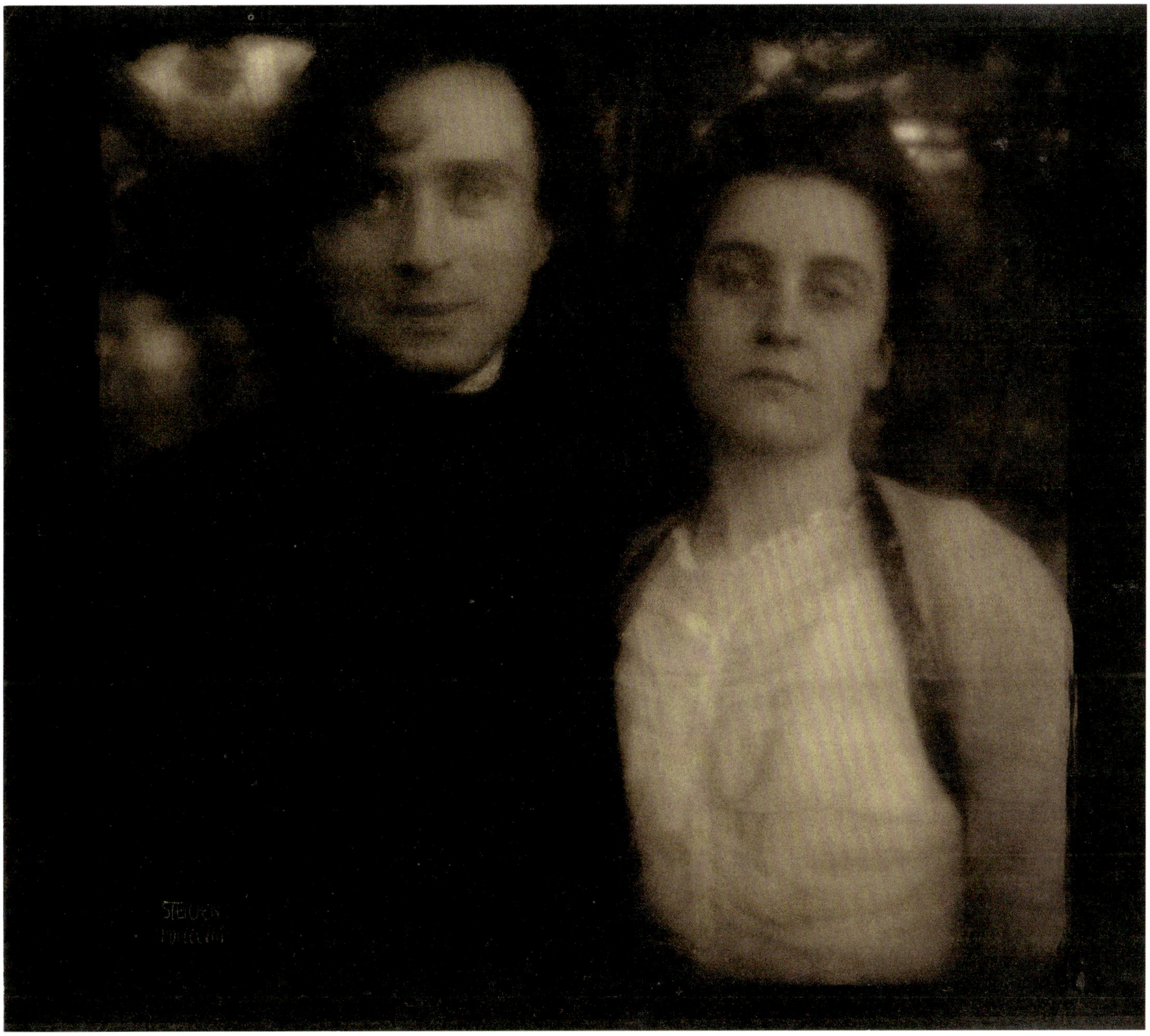

73. *Portraits—Evening*
1903, printed 1908

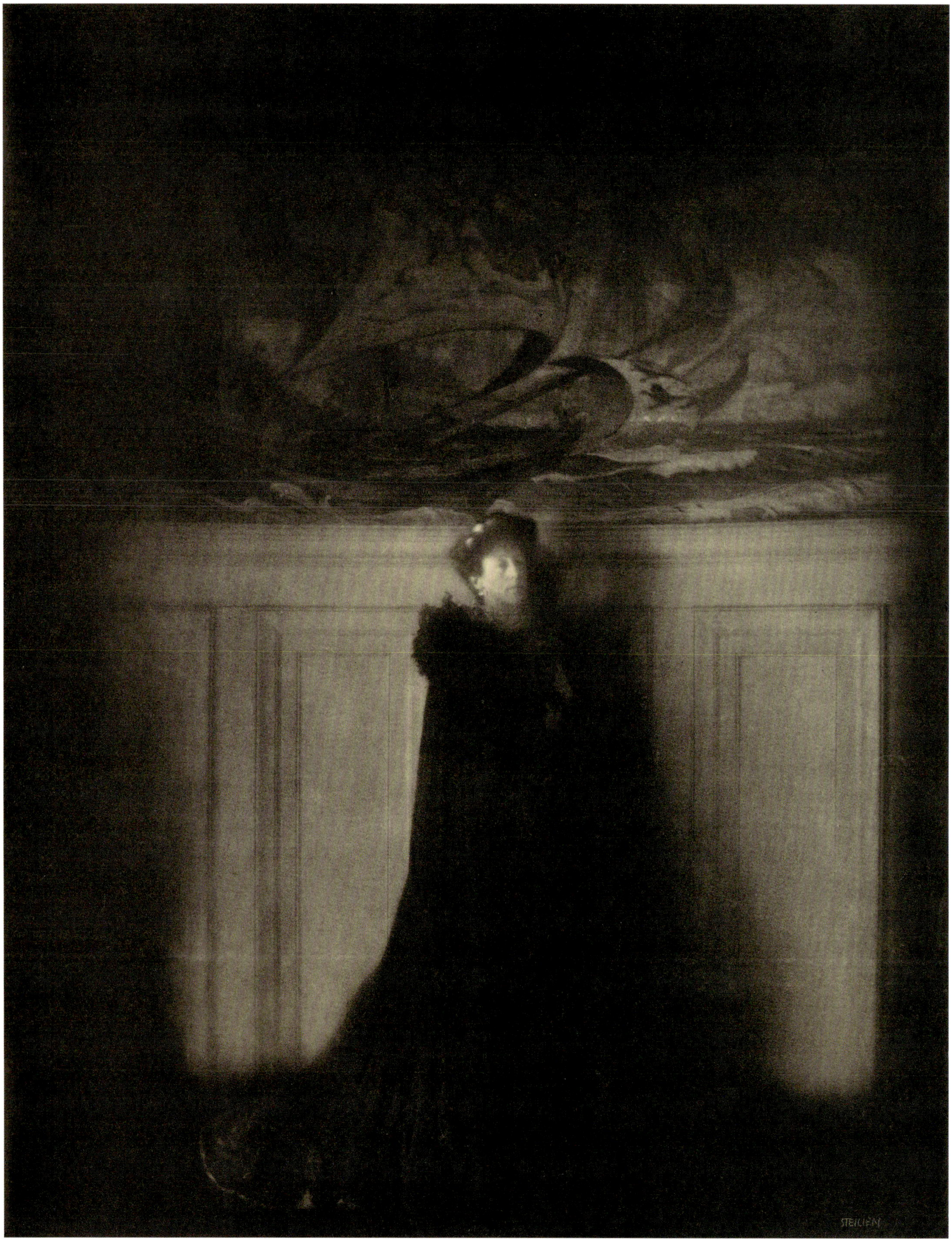

74. *Lady Ian Hamilton*
1907, printed 1909

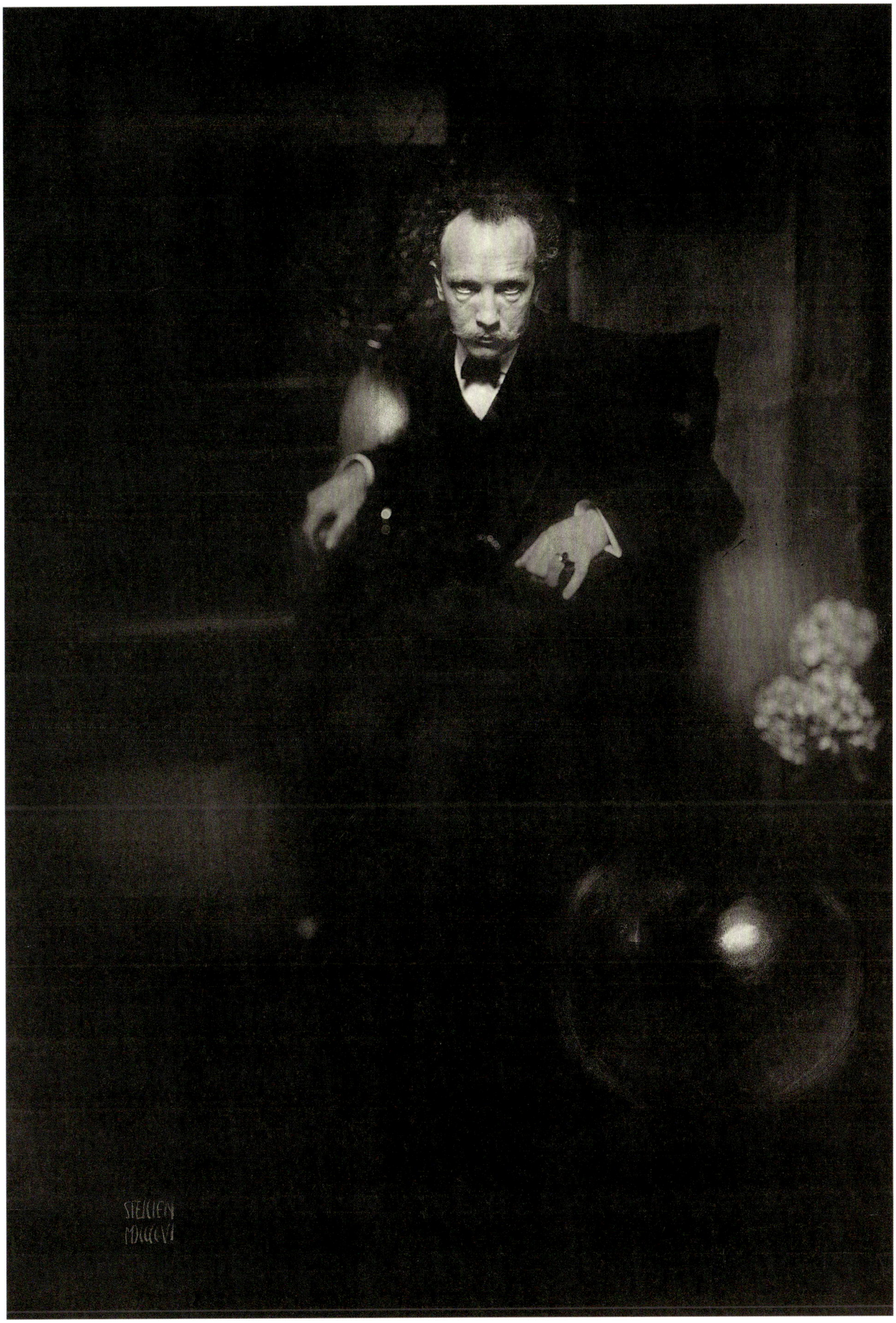

75. *Richard Strauss*
1904, printed 1906

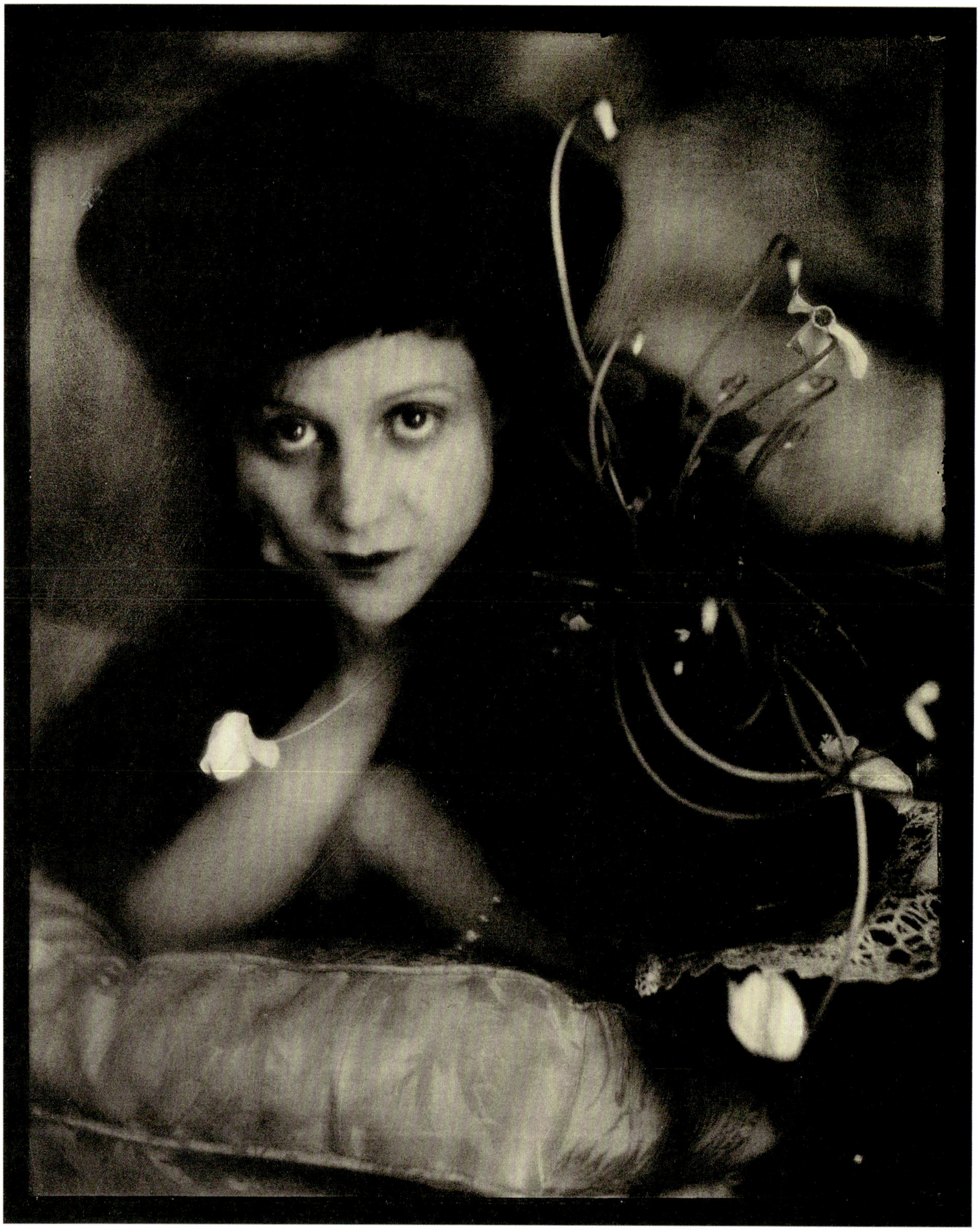

76. *Cyclamen—Mrs. Philip Lydig*
Ca. 1905

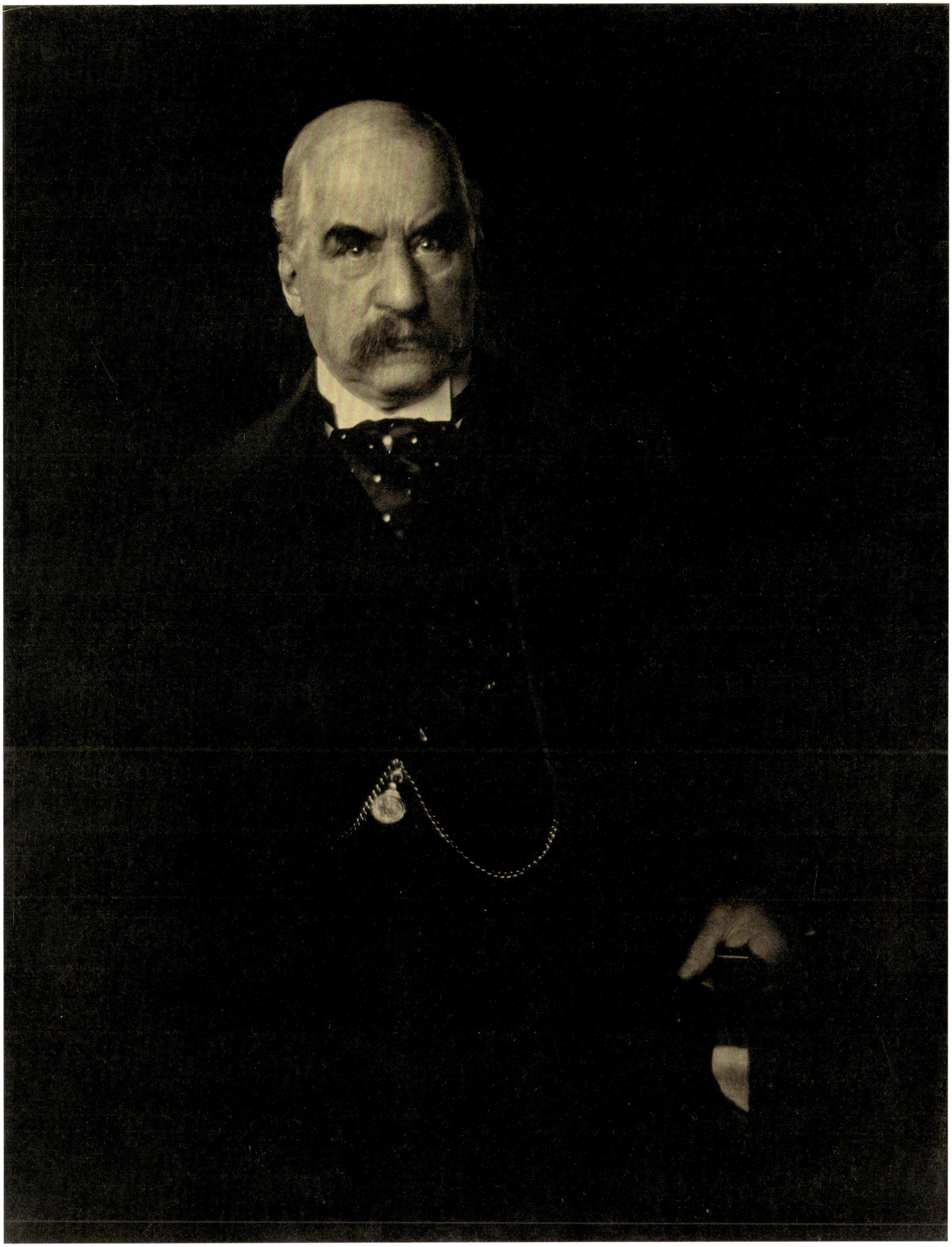

77. J. Pierpont Morgan, Esq.
1903, printed 1909–10

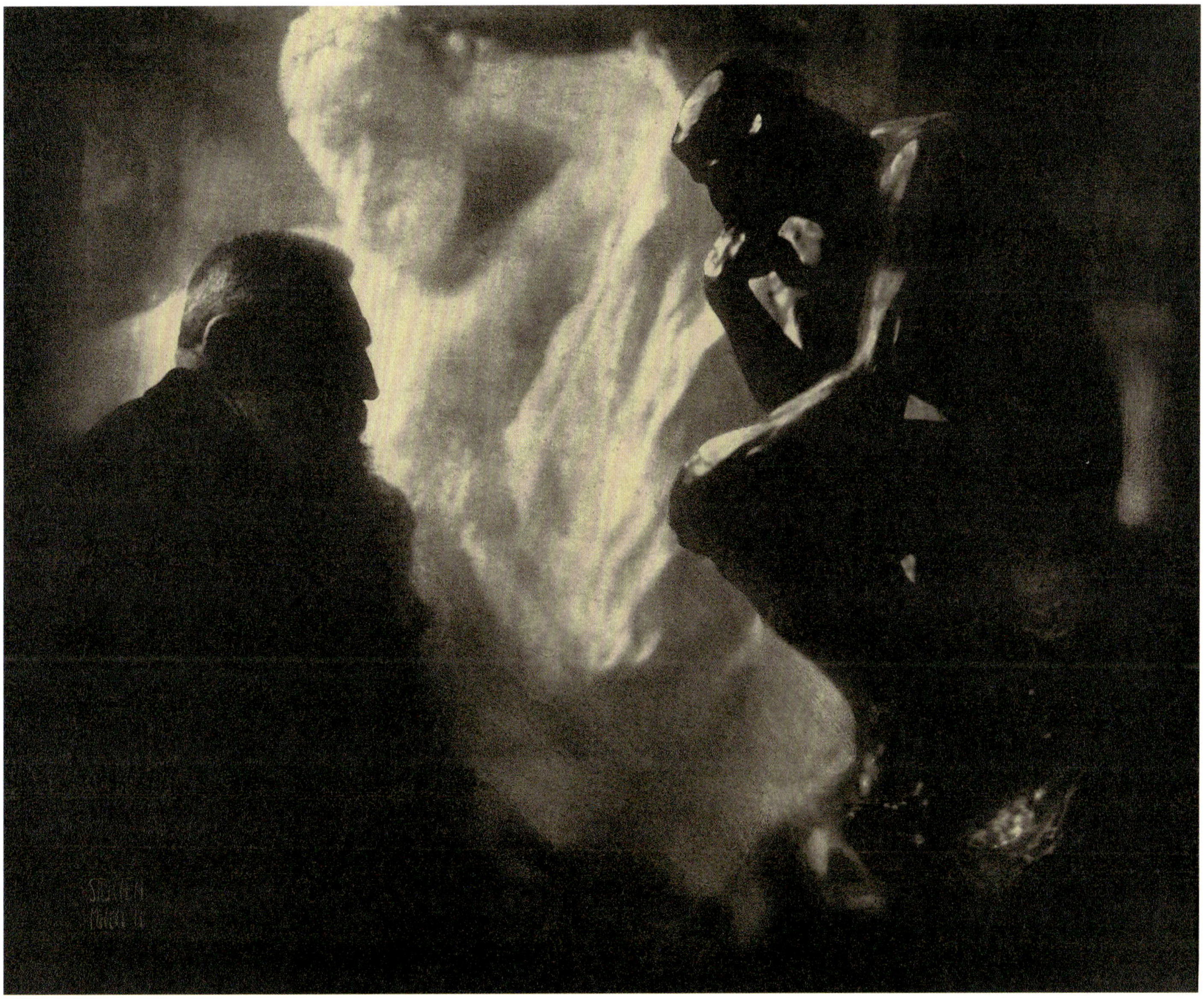

78. Rodin—The Thinker
1902

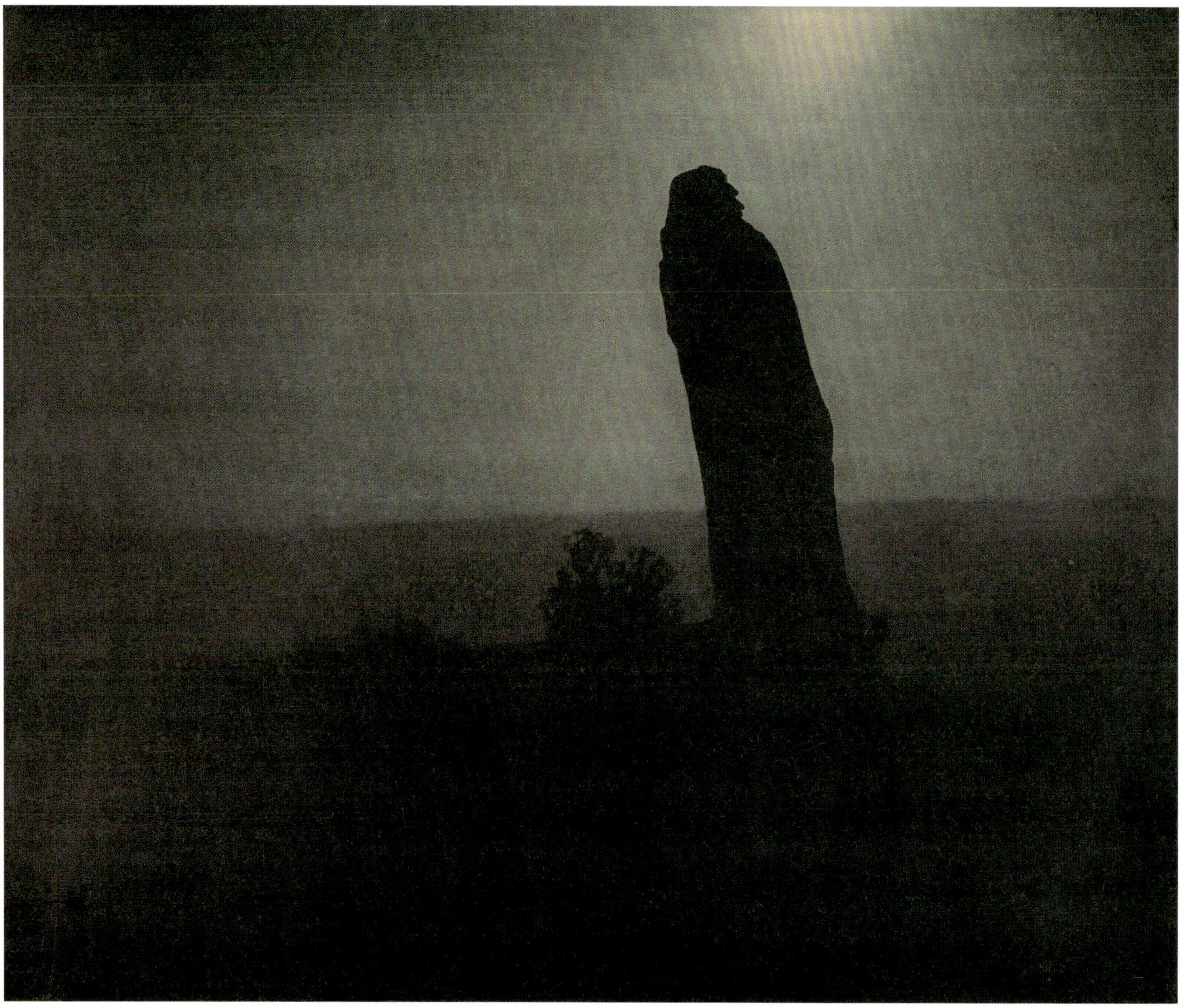

79. ***Balzac, The Silhouette—4 A.M.***
1908

80. ***Balzac, The Open Sky—11:00 P.M.***
1908, printed 1909

81. ***Balzac, Towards the Light, Midnight***
1908

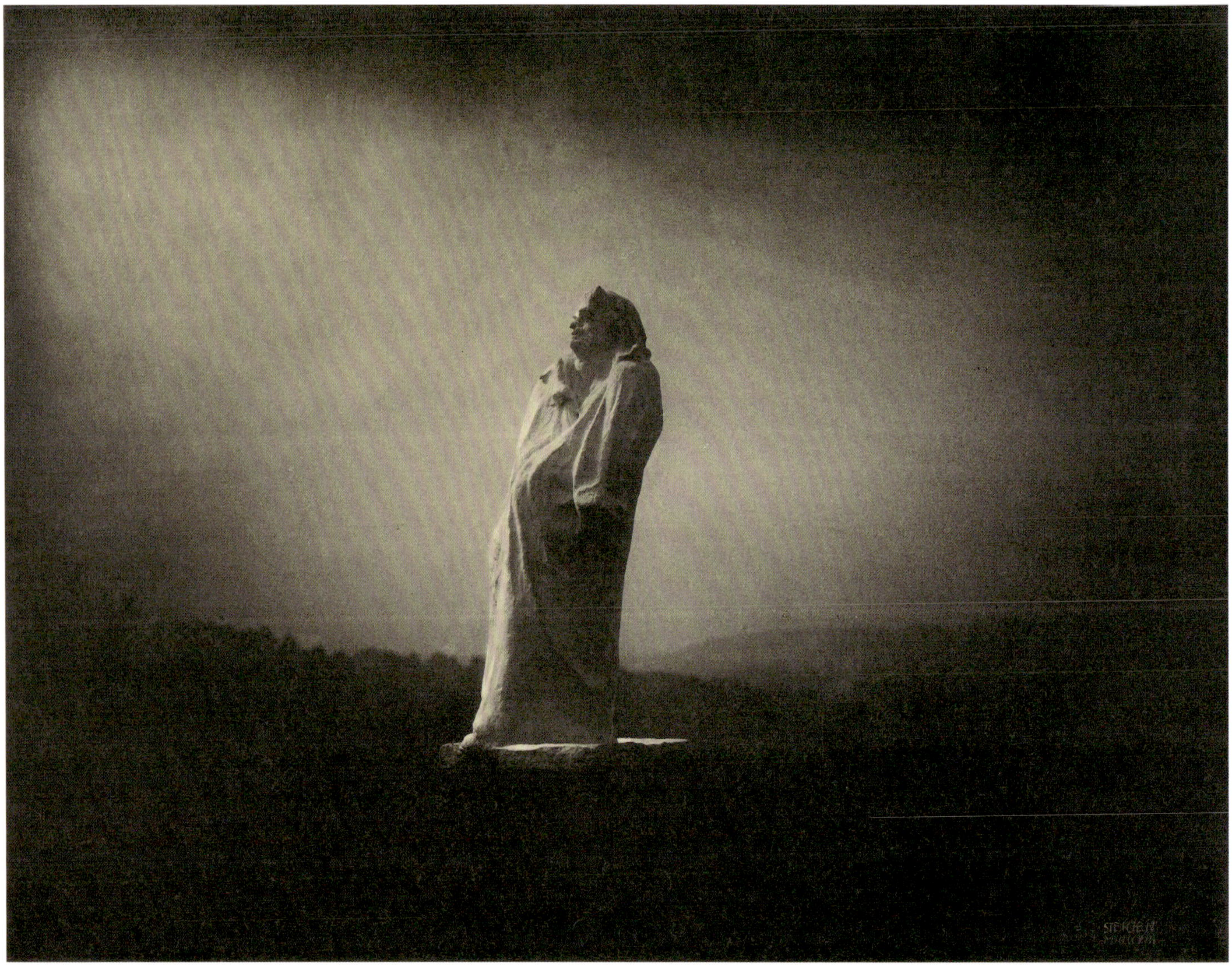

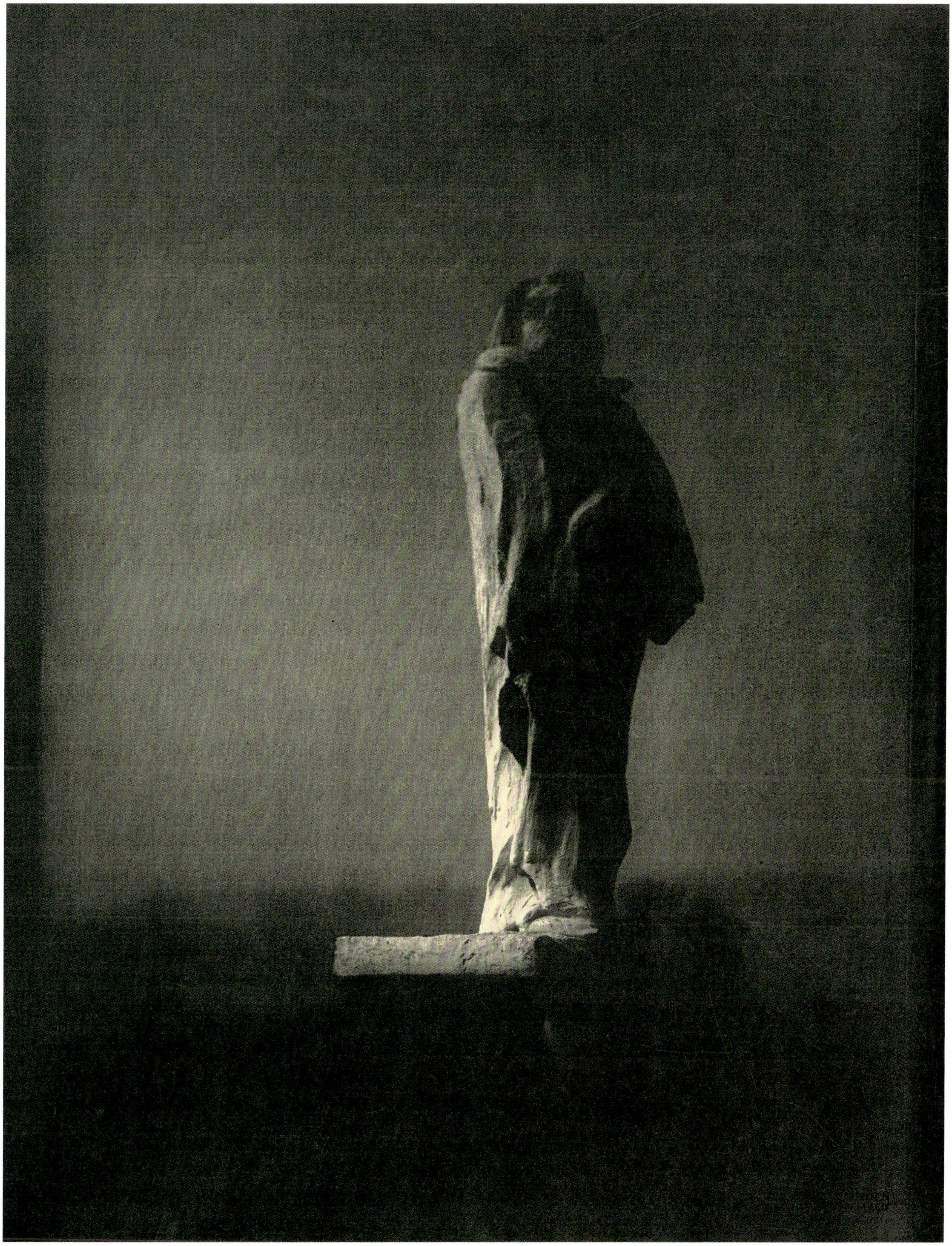

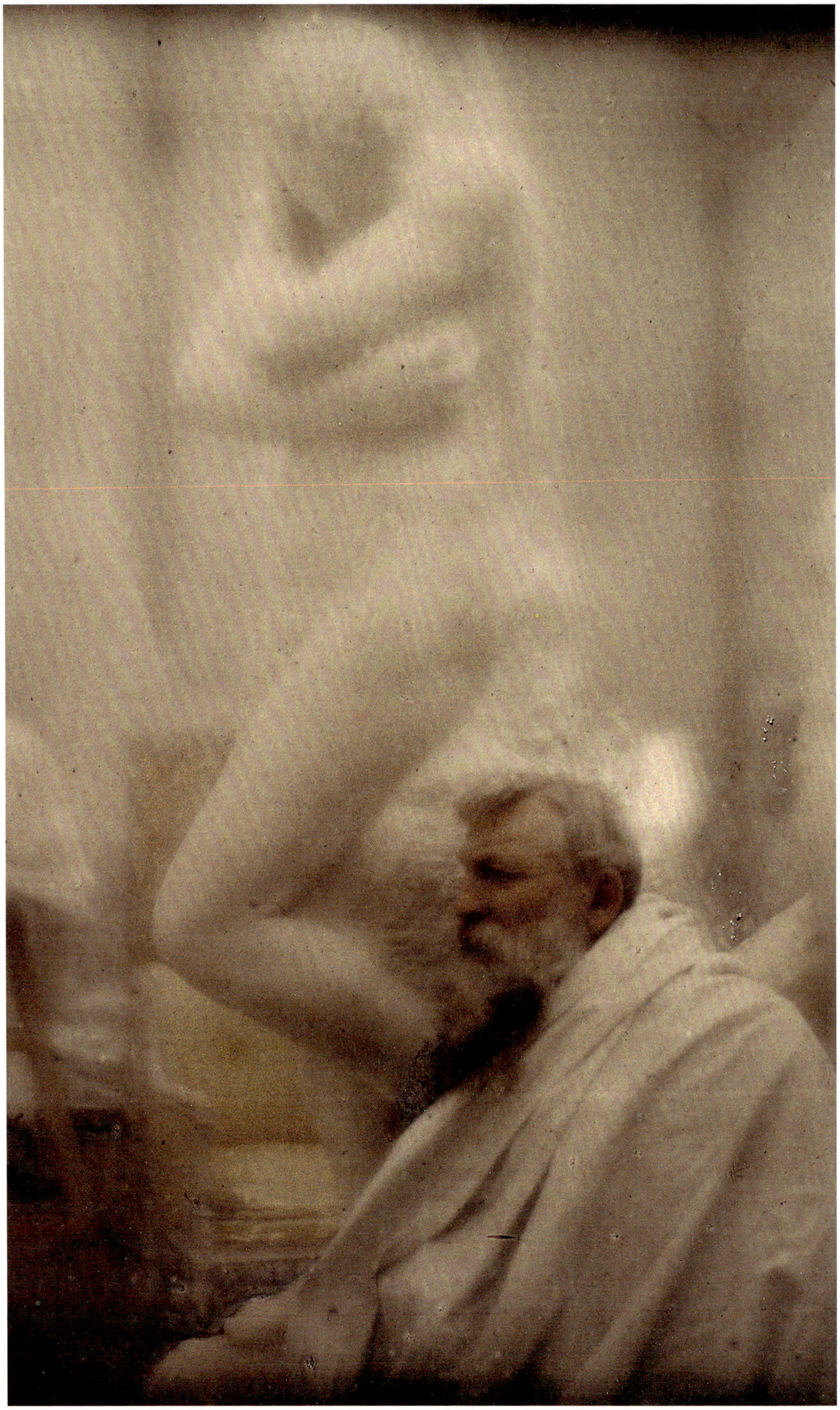

82. ***Rodin—The Eve***
1907

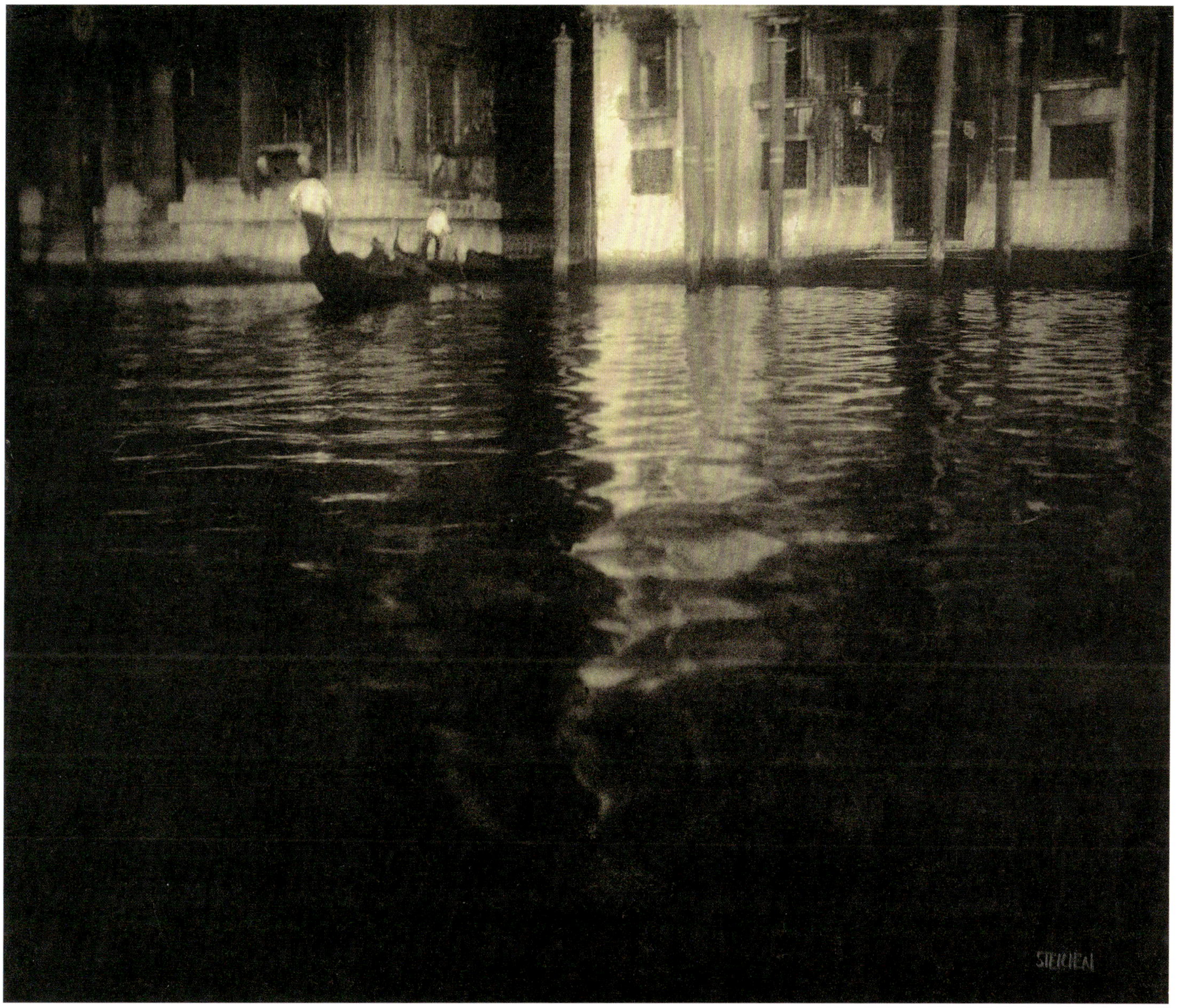

83. ***Late Afternoon—Venice***
1907

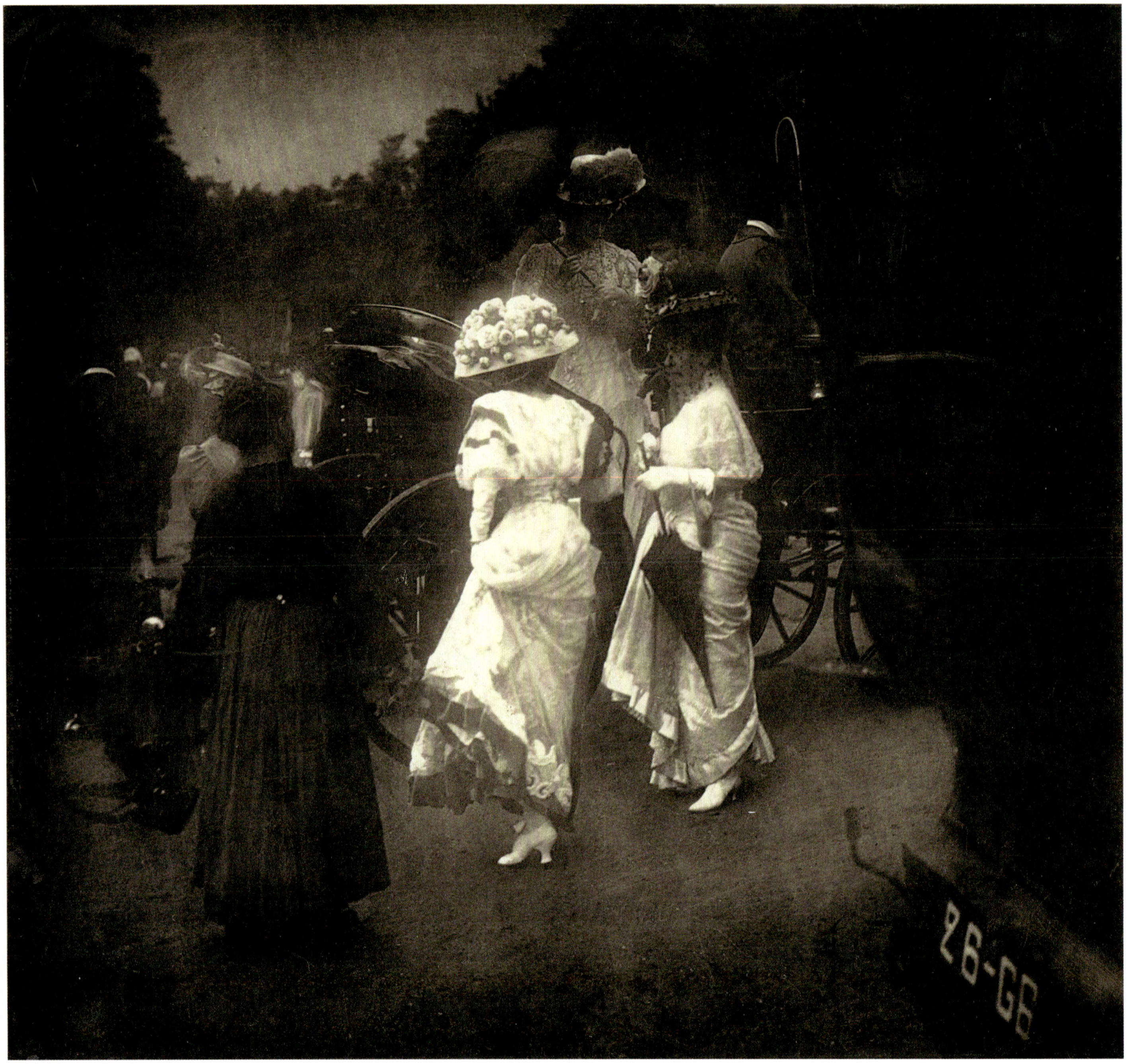

84. ***After the Grand Prix—Paris***
1907, printed 1911

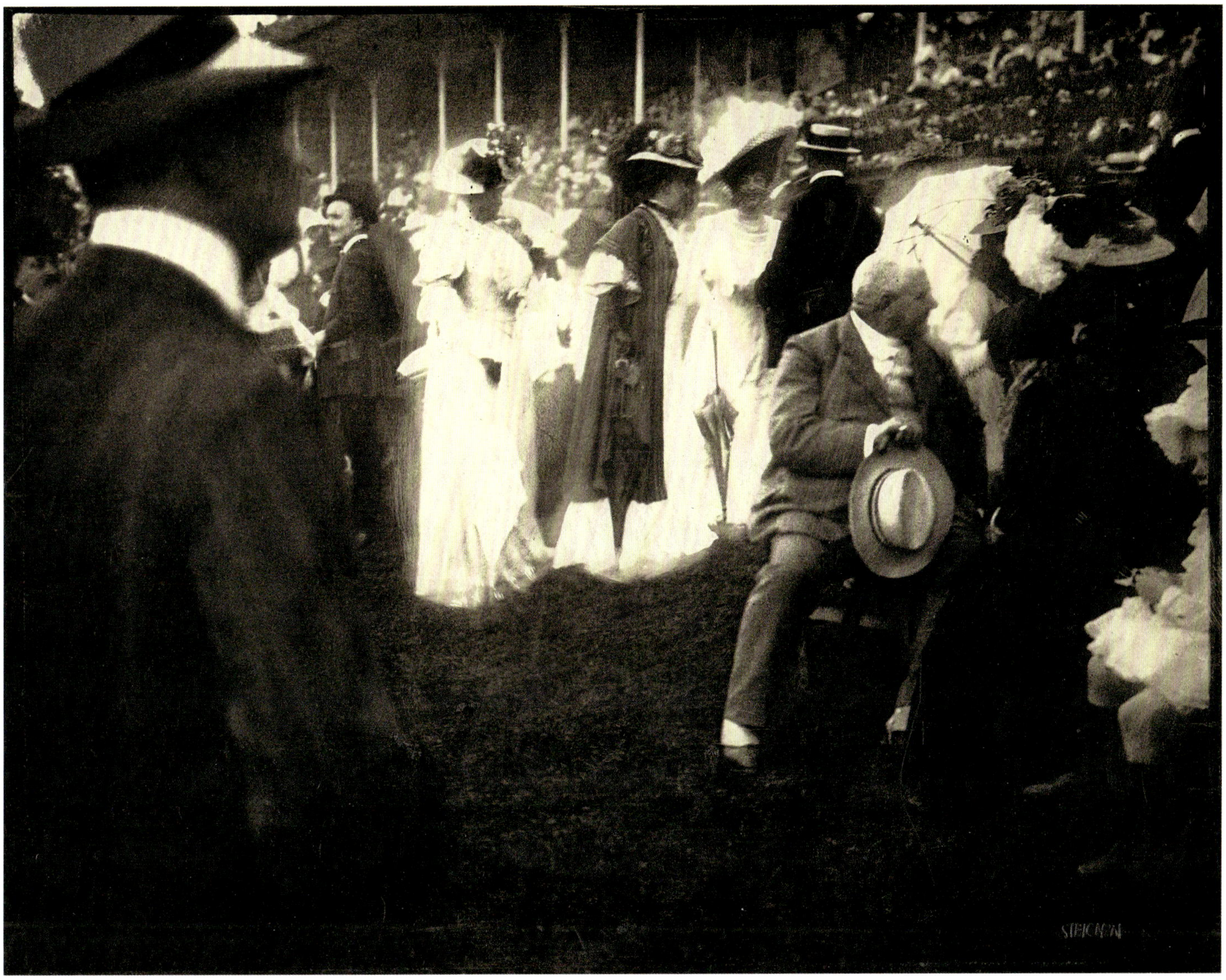

85. *Steeplechase Day, Paris—The Grandstand*
1907, printed 1911

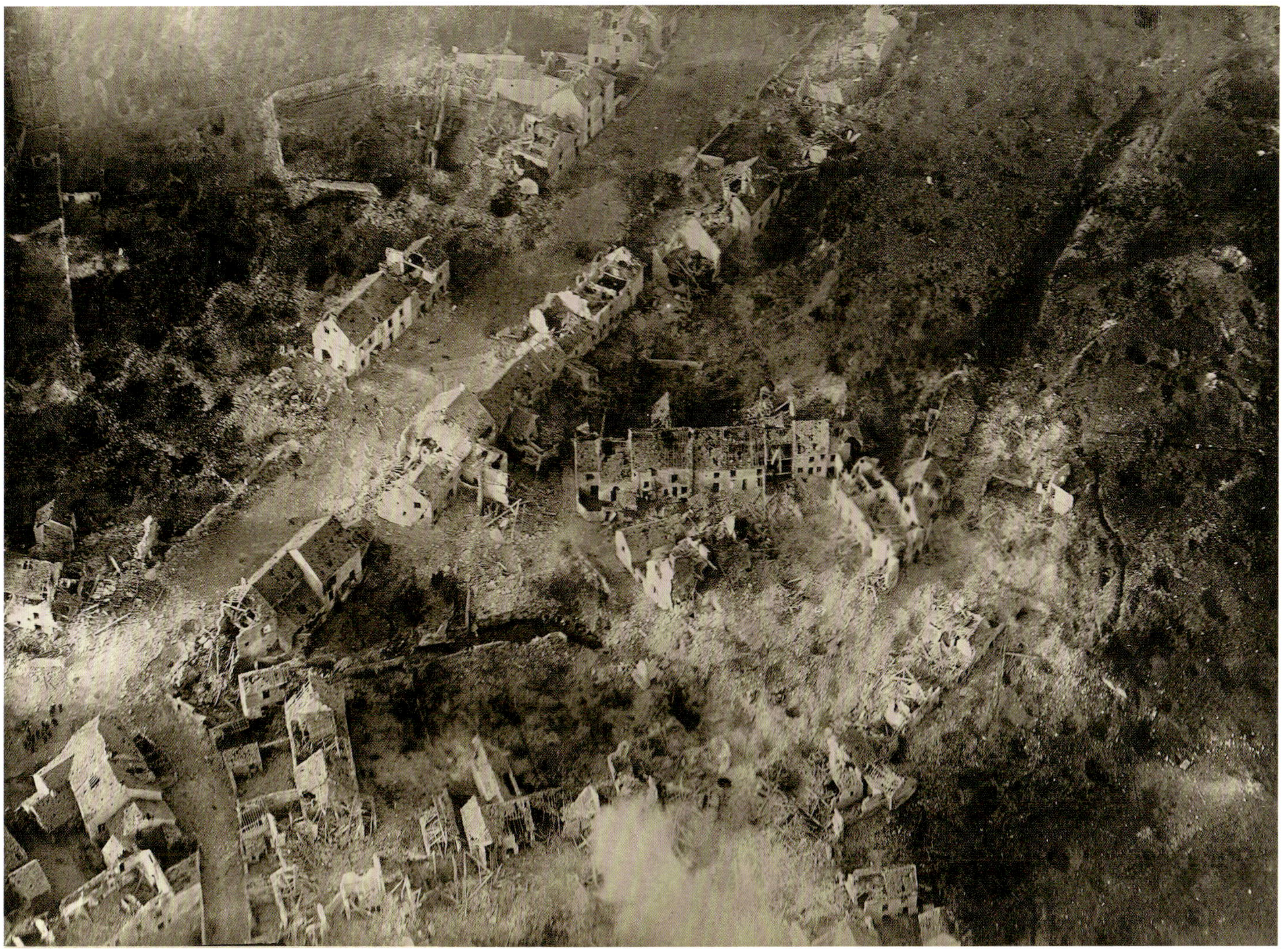

86. ***Vaux #2, After Attack***
1918

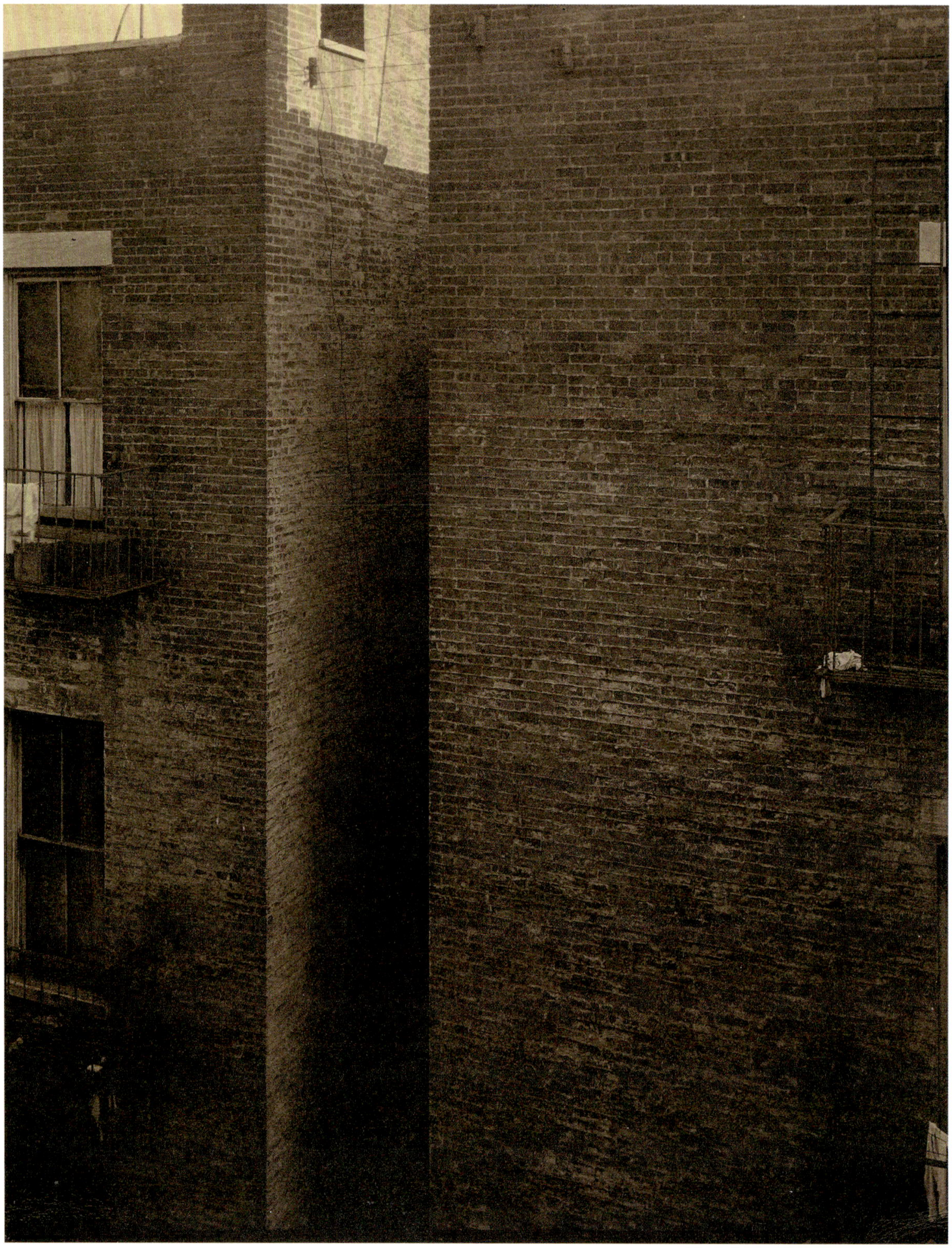

87. ***Between the Walls, New York***
Ca. 1922

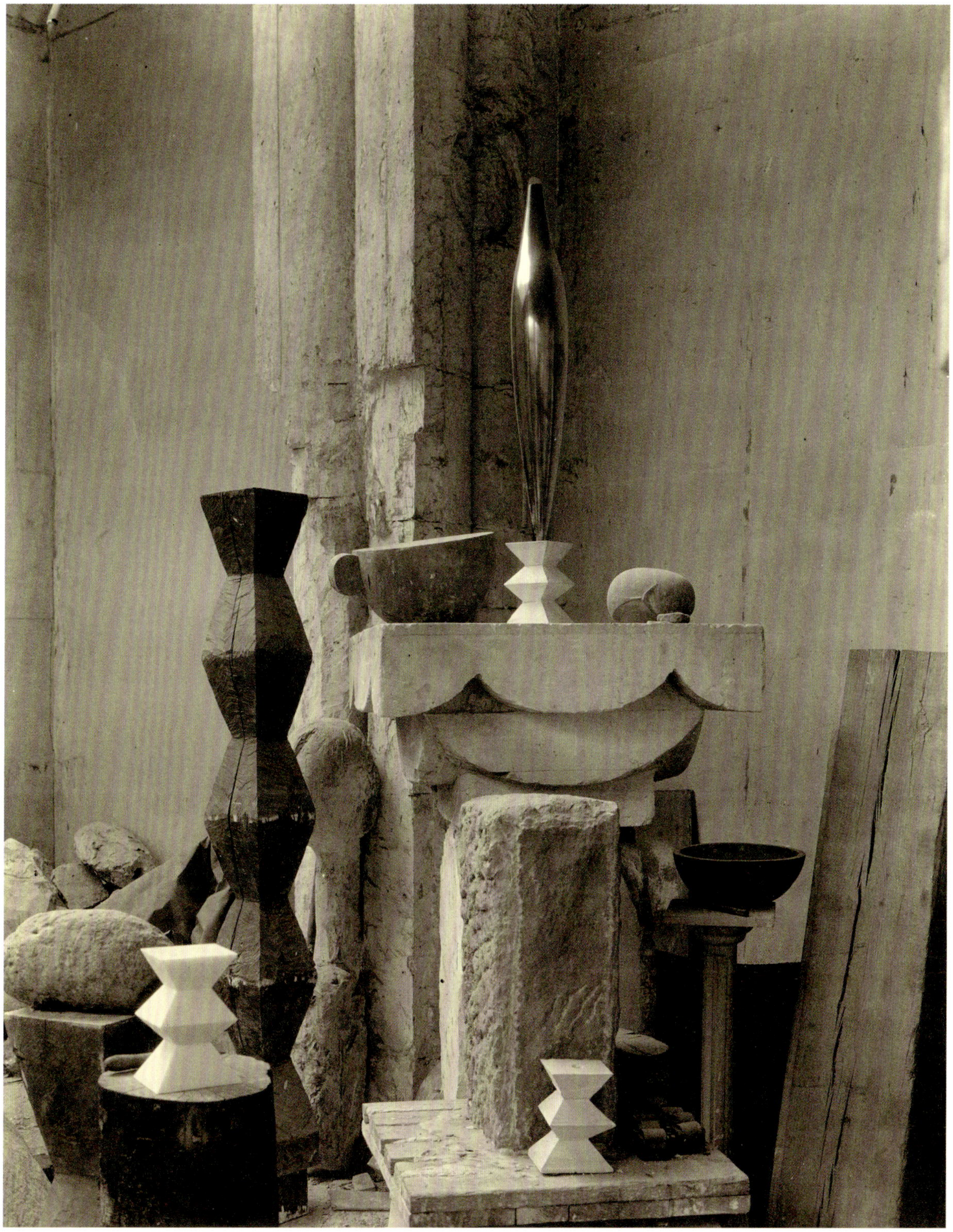

88. *[Brancusi's Studio]*
Ca. 1920

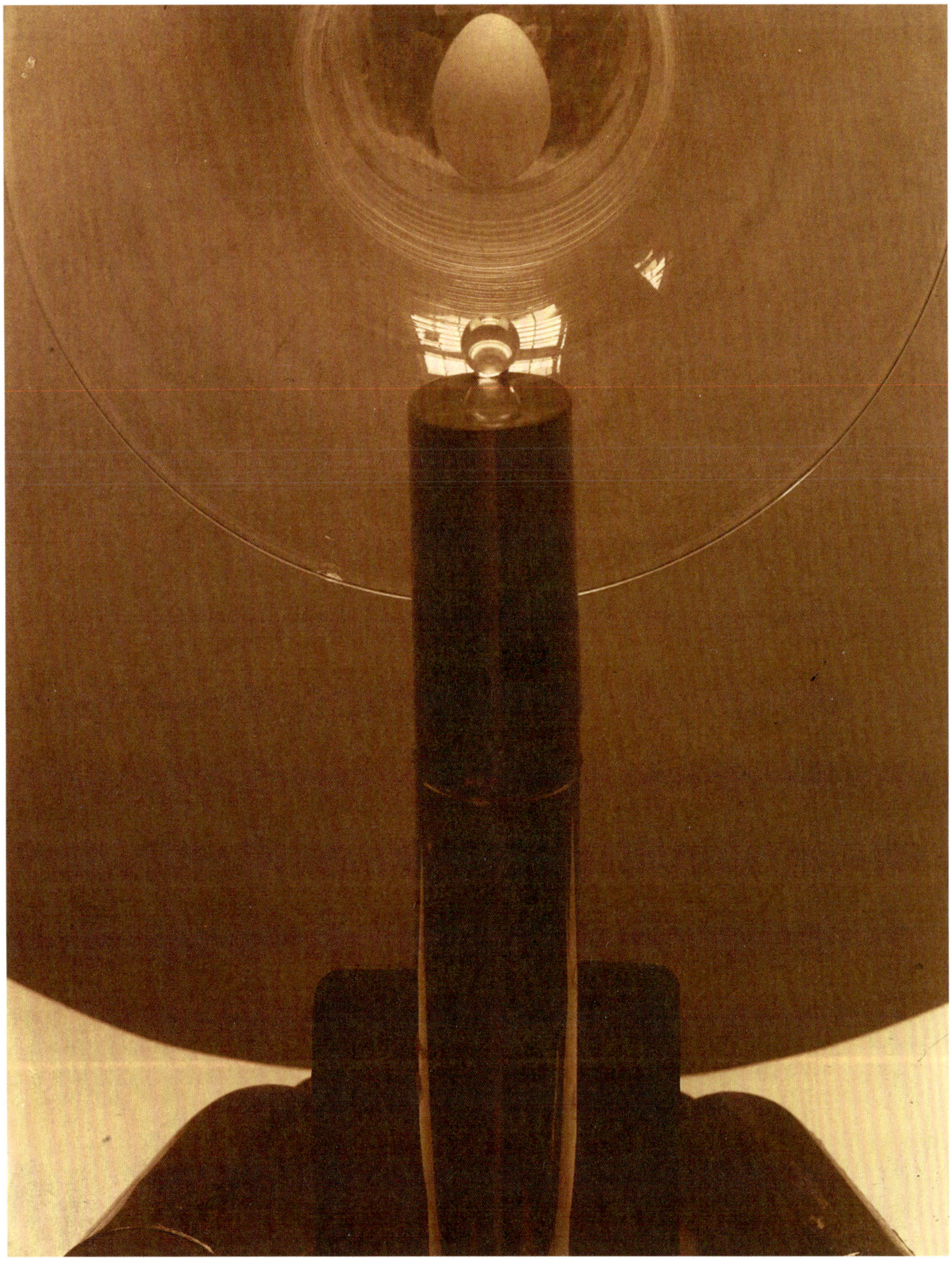

89. ***Triumph of the Egg***
1921

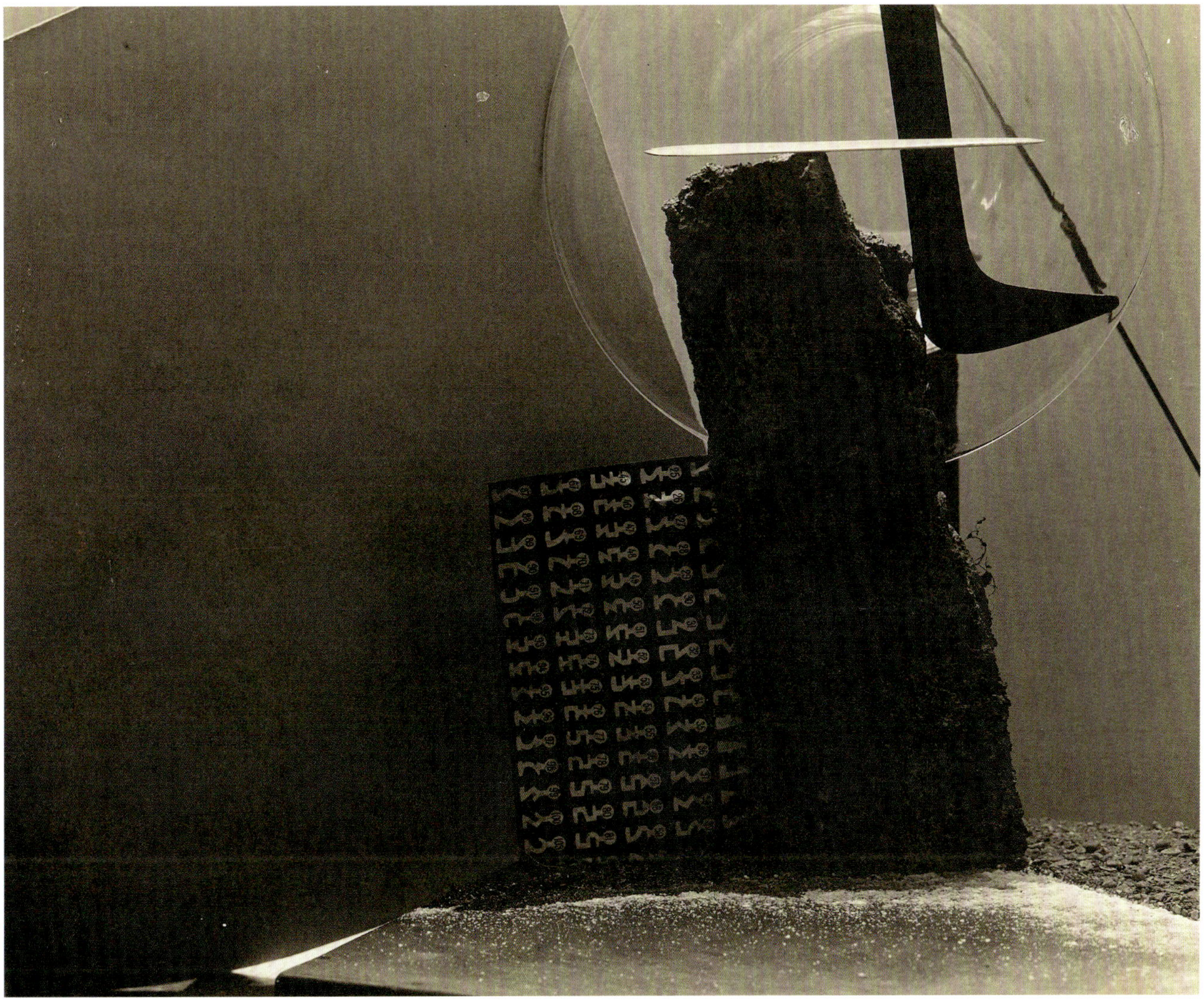

90. ***Time-Space Continuum***
Ca. 1920

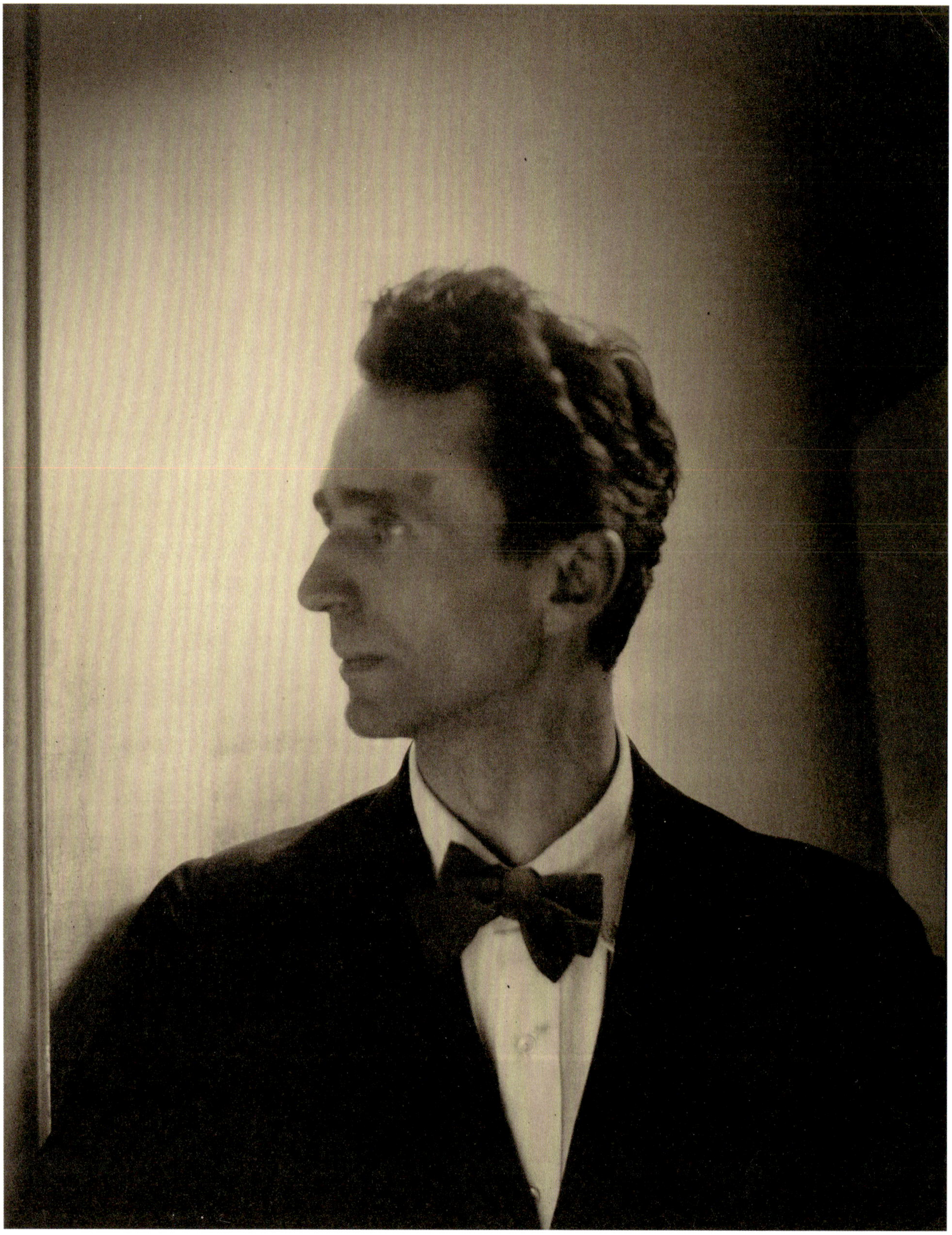

91. ***Self-Portrait***
1916

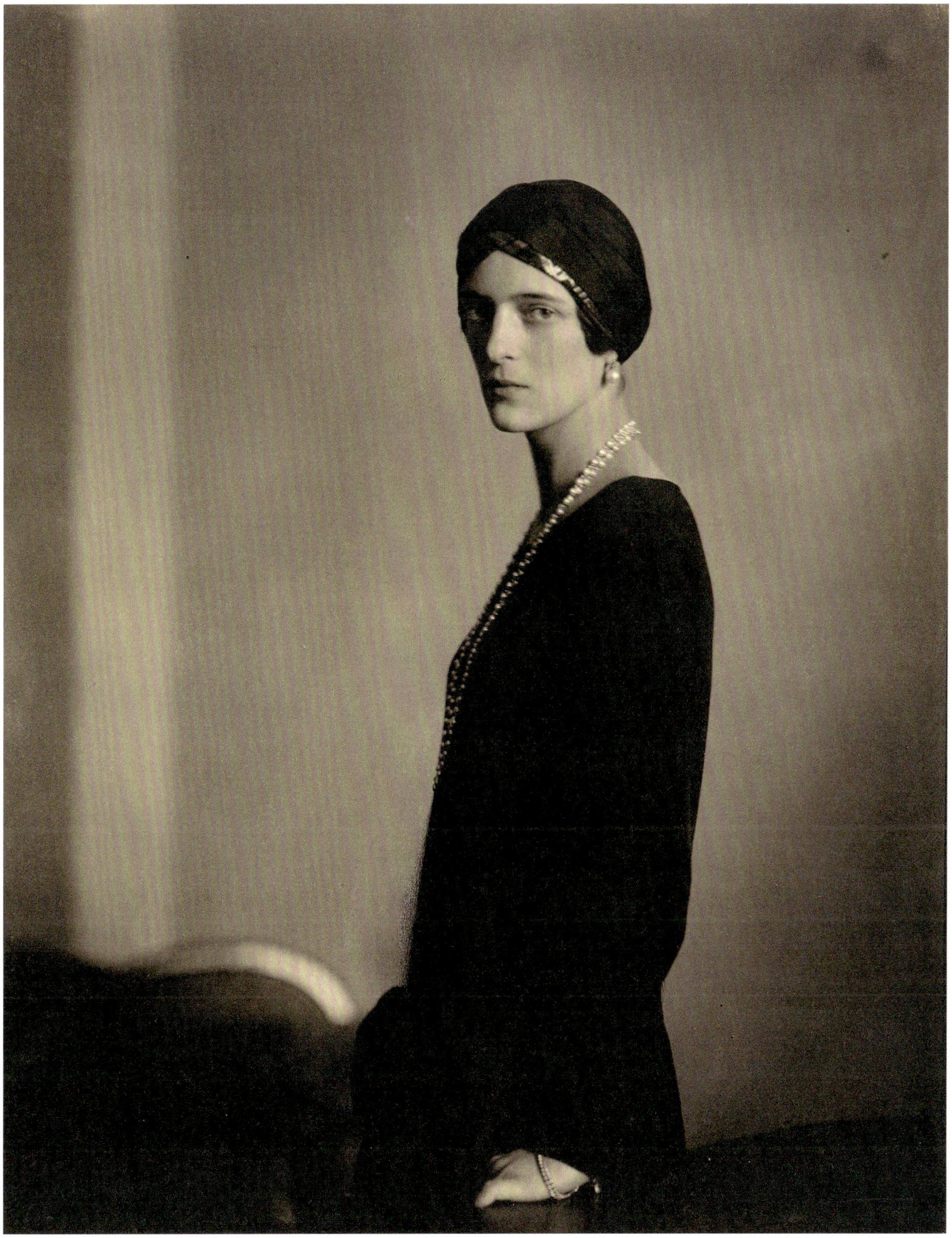

92. ***Princess Yusupov***
1924

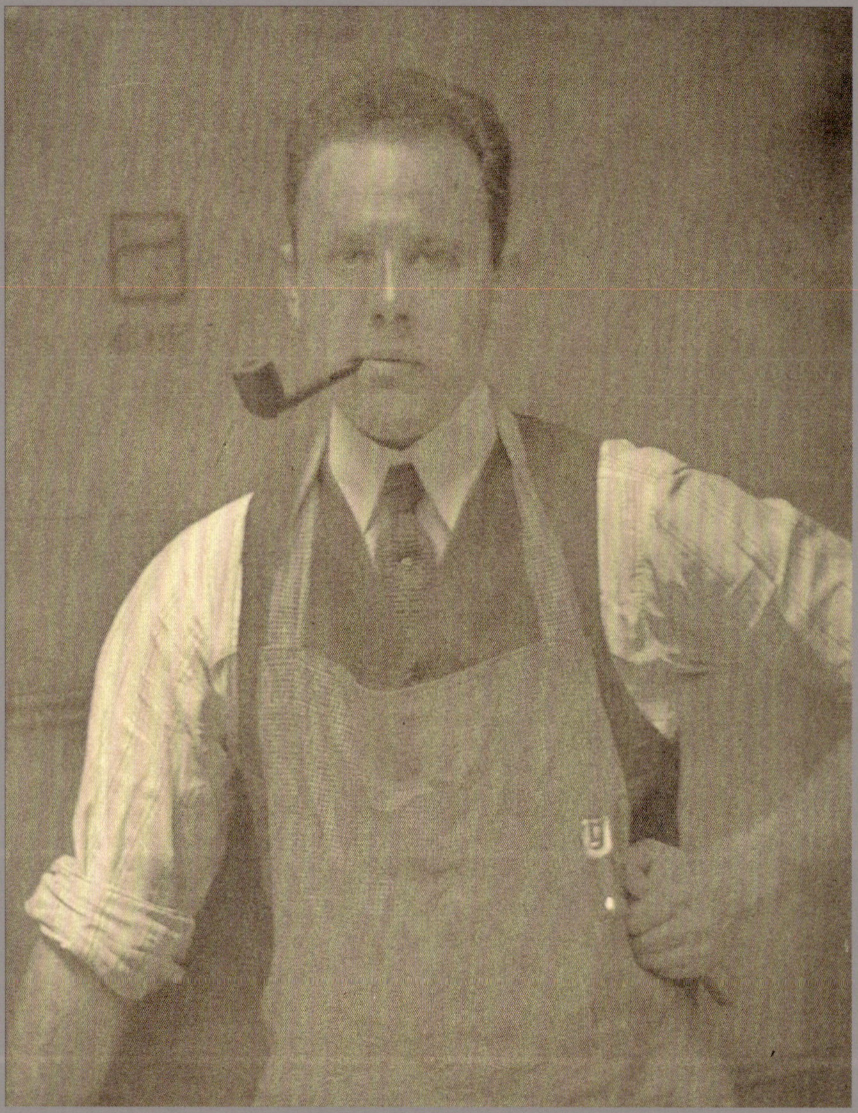

Alfred Stieglitz
Paul Strand
1917
Silver-platinum print
9 11/16 x 7 9/16 in. (24.6 x 19.3 cm)
Center for Creative Photography,
The University of Arizona, Tucson

PAUL STRAND

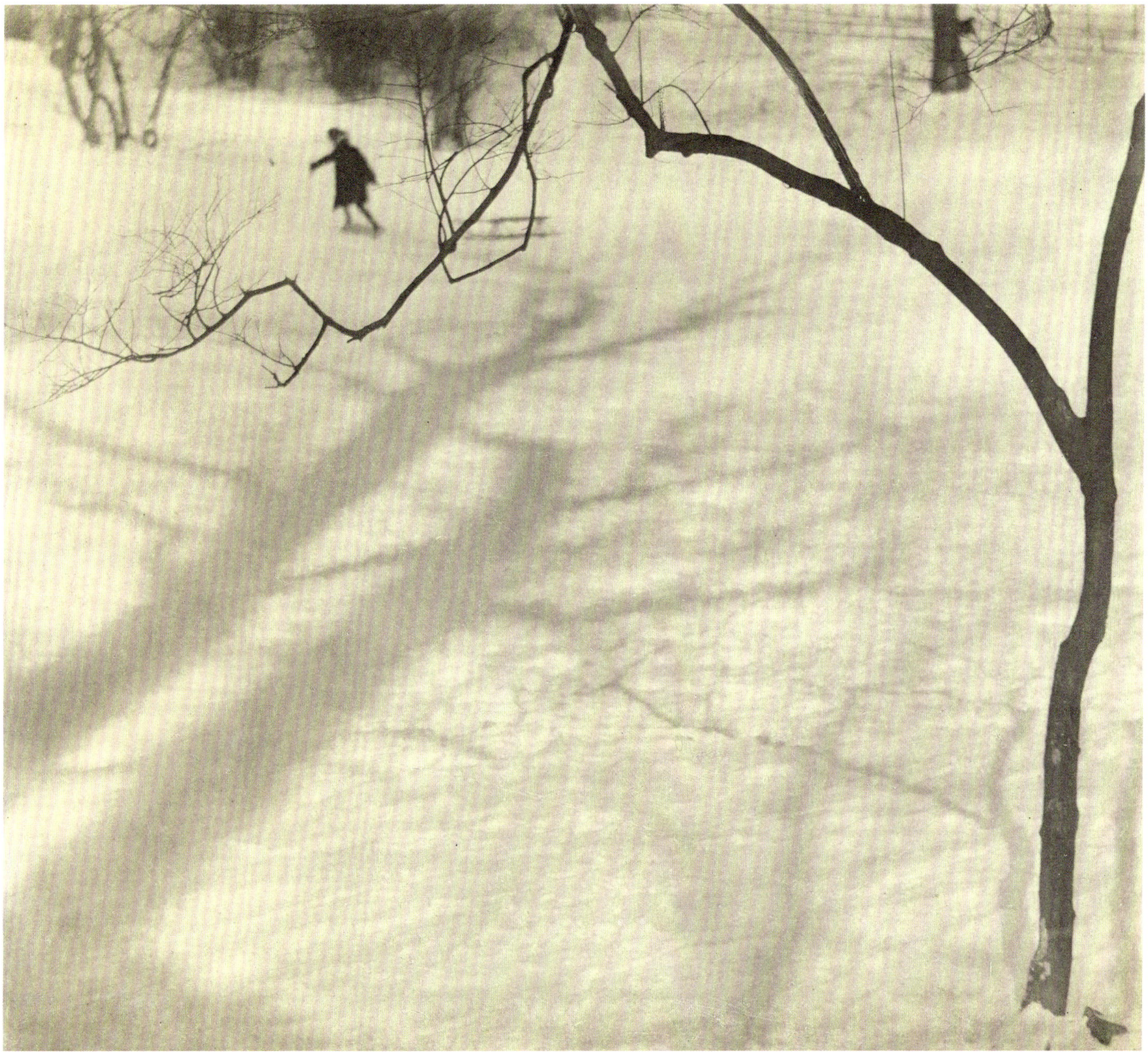

93. ***Winter, Central Park, New York***
1913–14

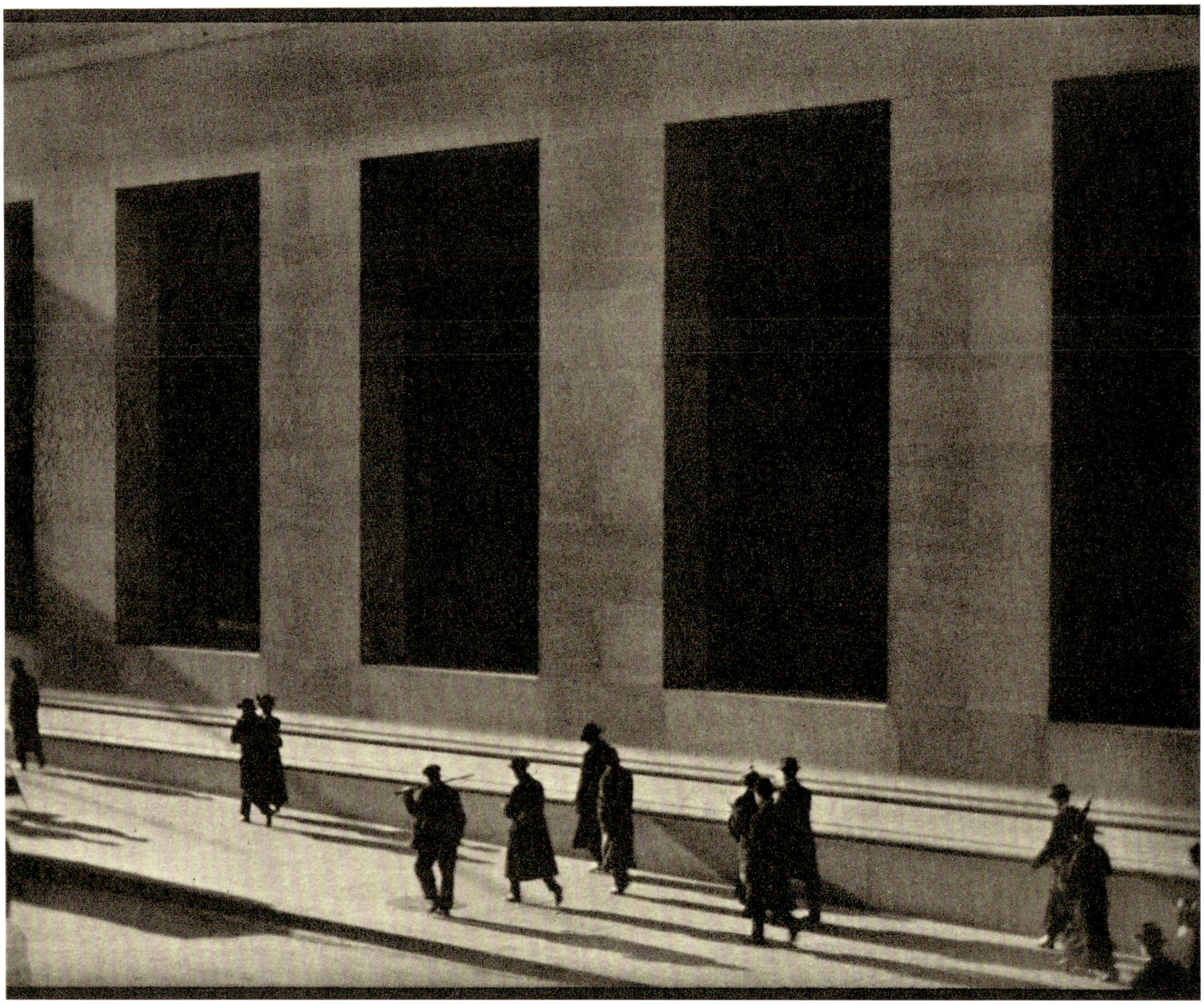

94. ***Wall Street***
1916

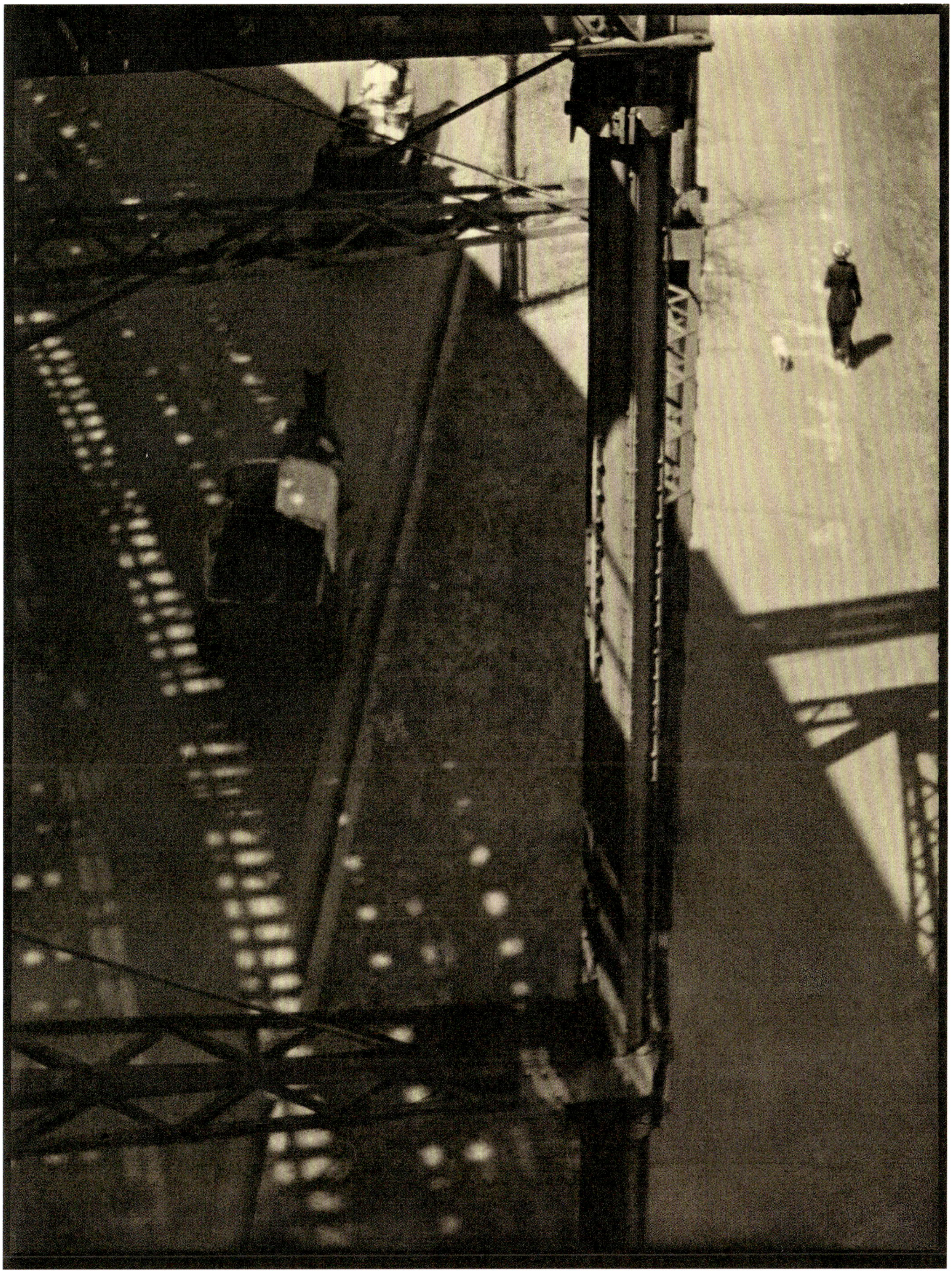

95. *From the El*
1915

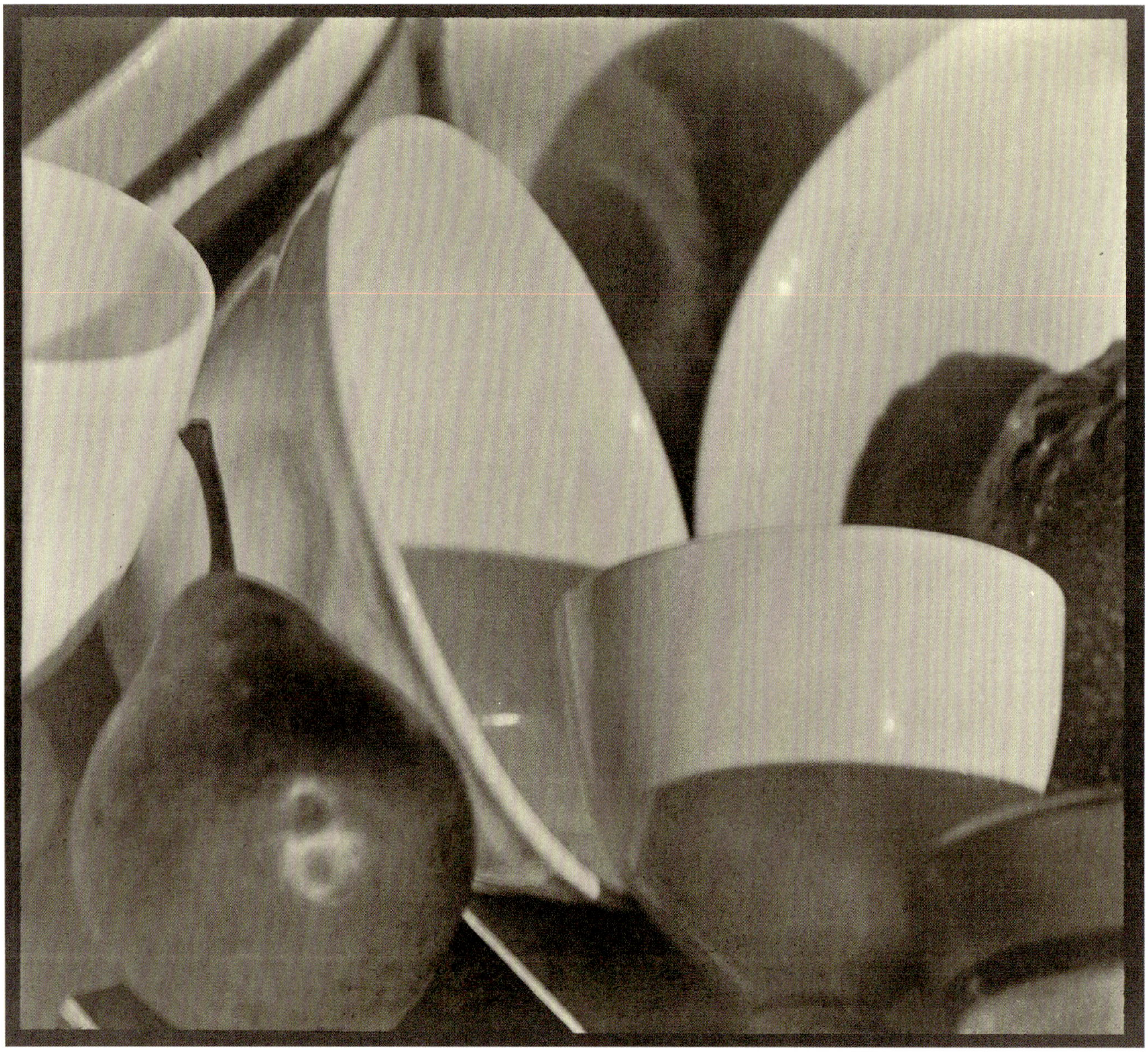

96. ***Pears and Bowls***
1916

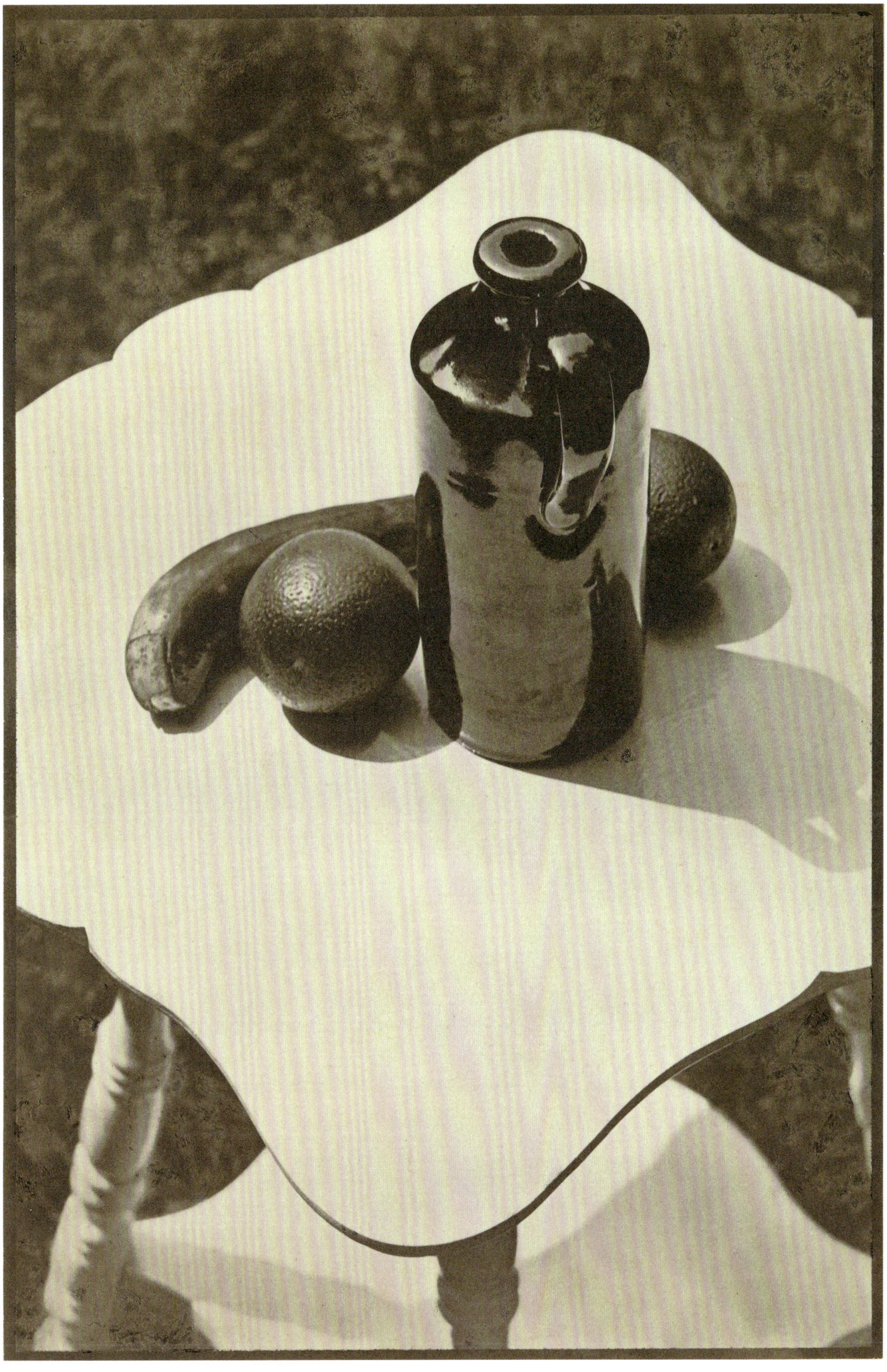

97. *Jug and Fruit*
1916

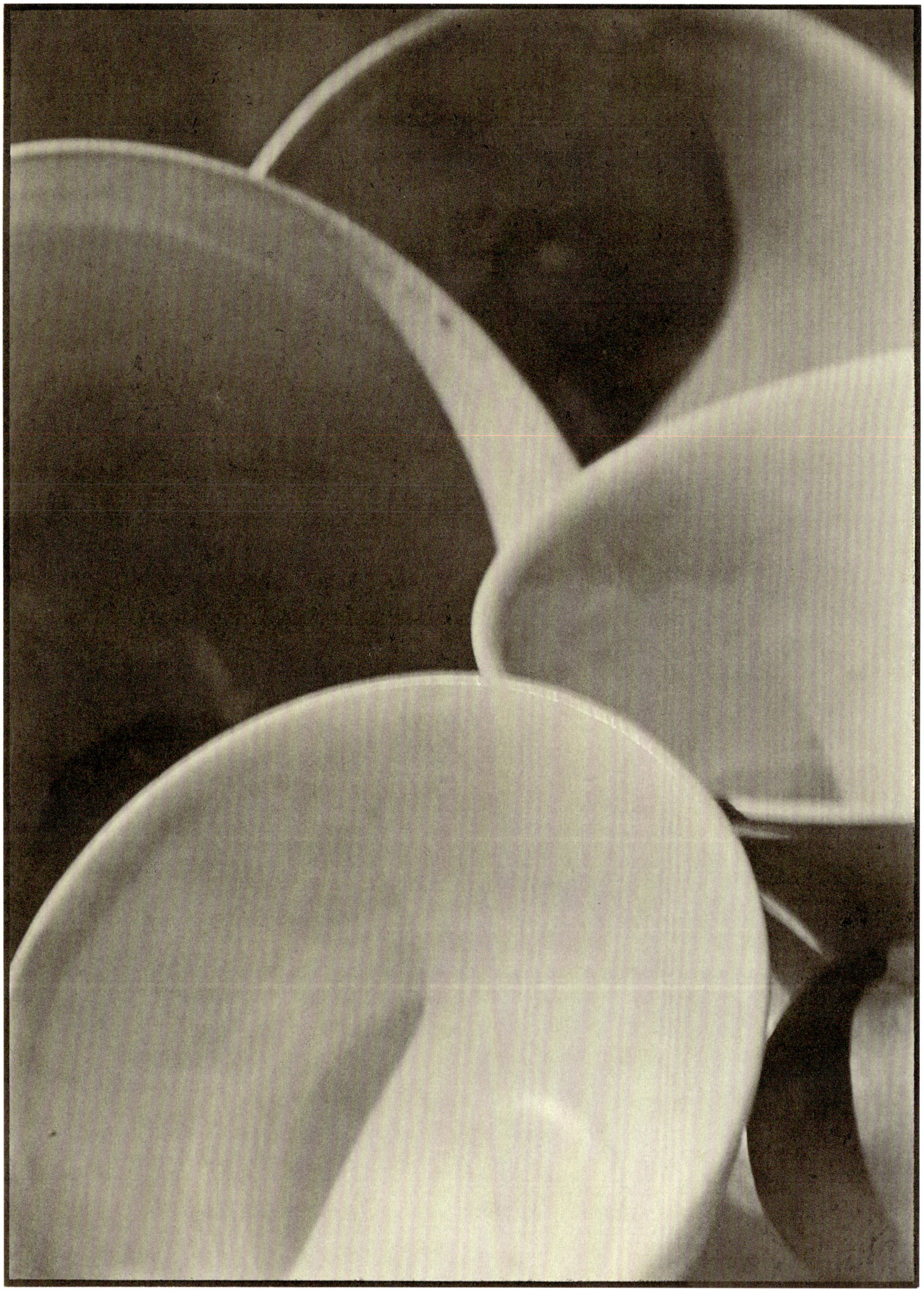

98. ***Bowls***
1916

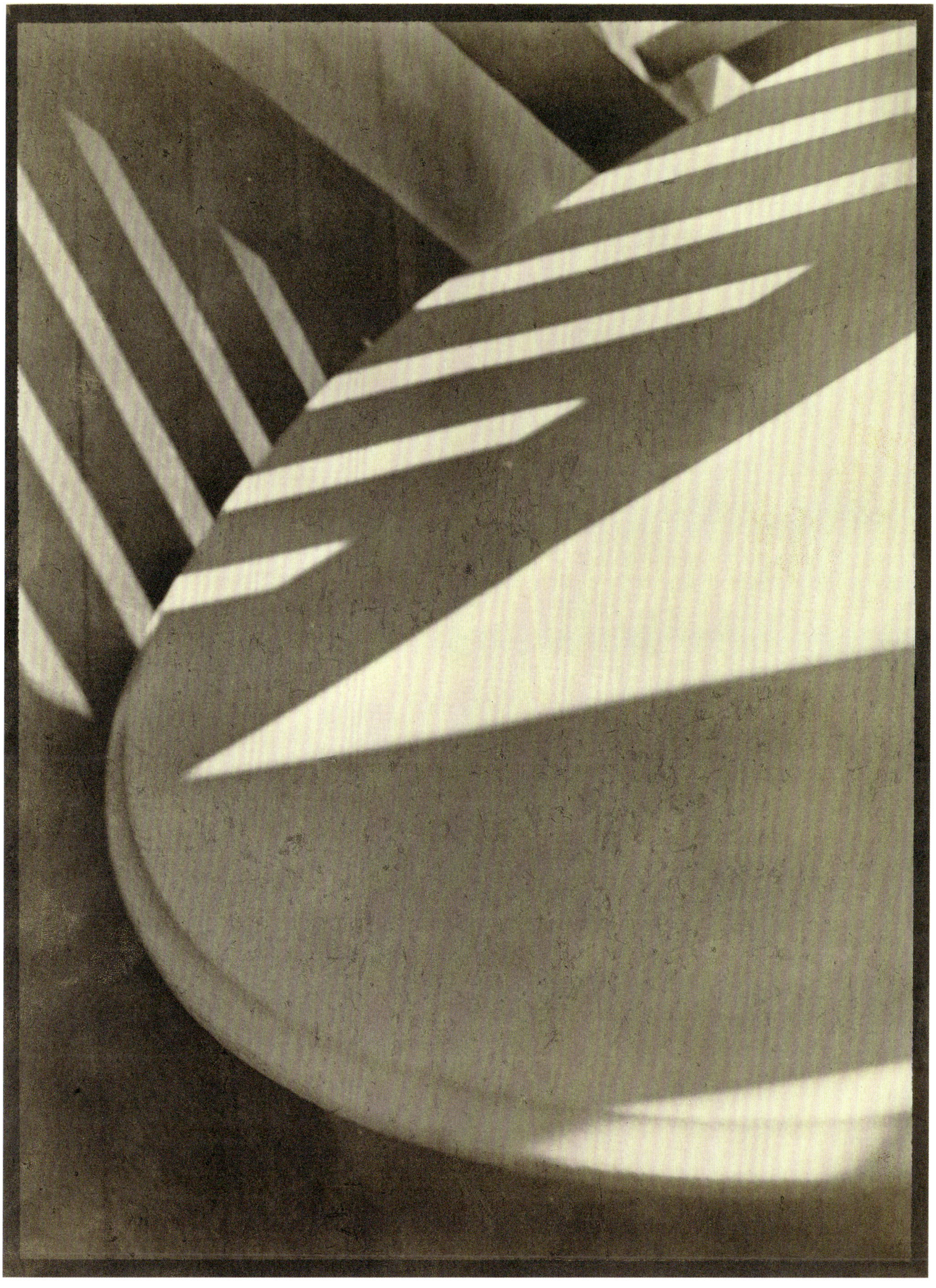

99. ***Abstraction, Twin Lakes, Connecticut***
1916

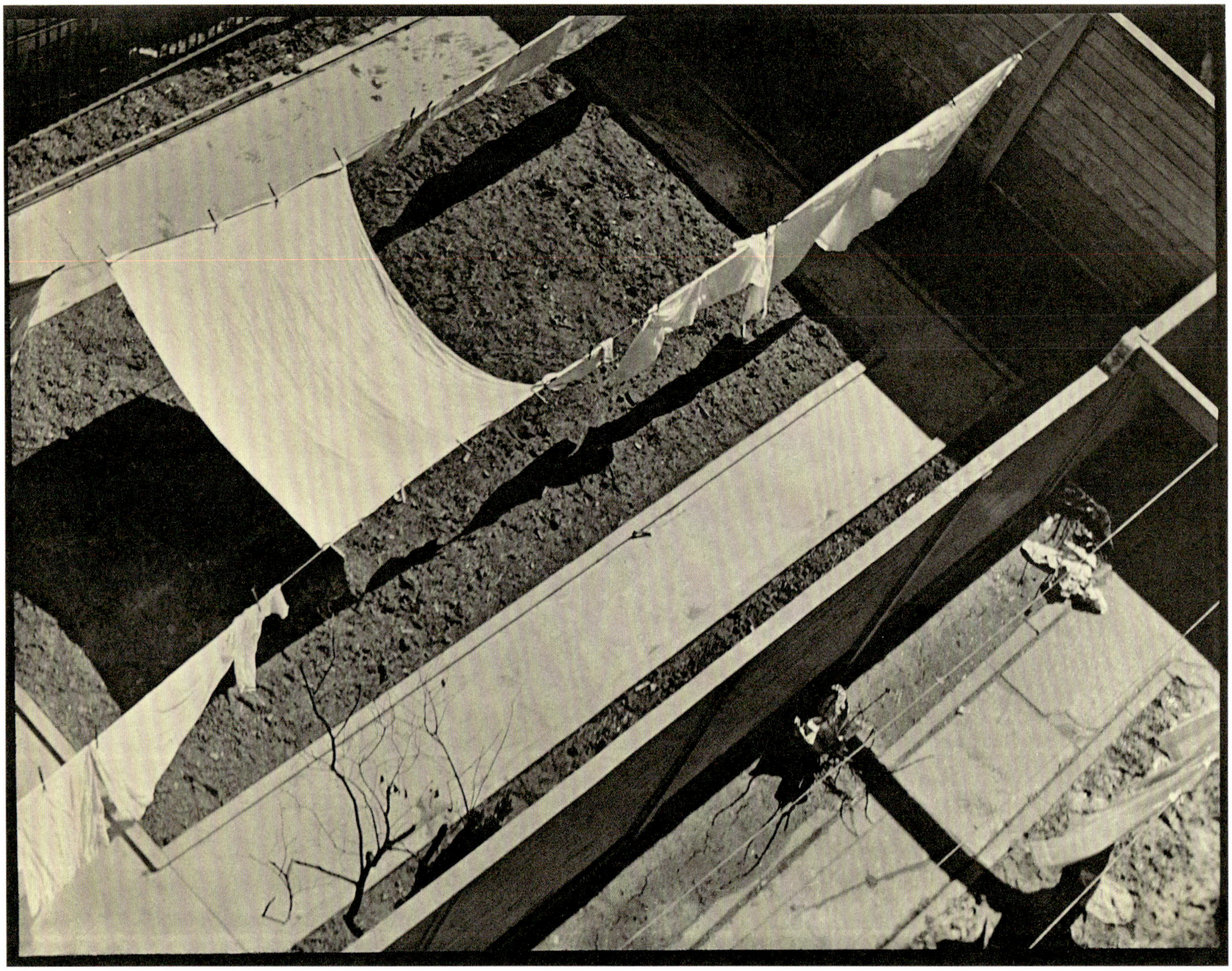

100. ***Geometric Backyards, New York***
1917

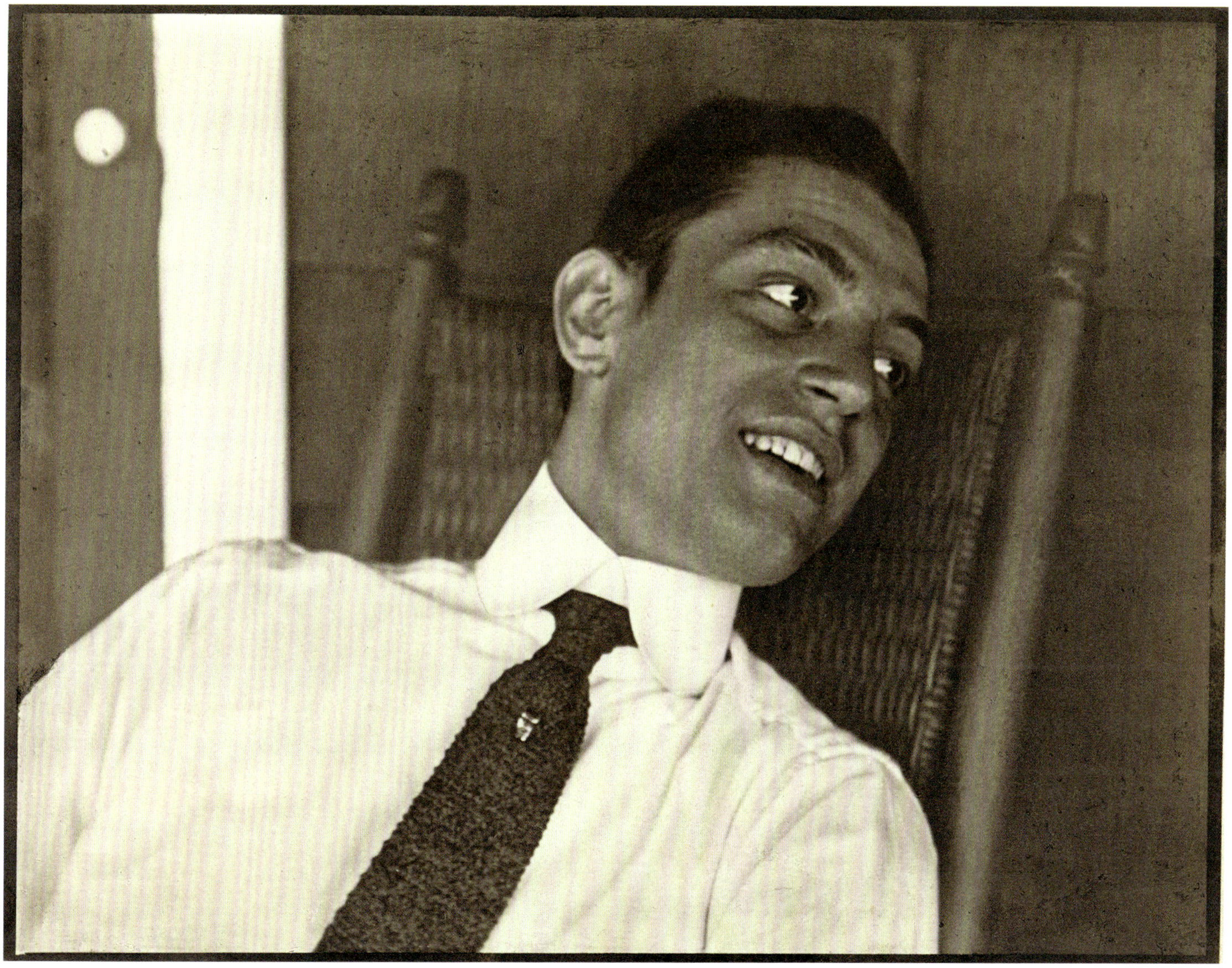

101. ***Harold Greengard, Twin Lakes, Connecticut***
1916

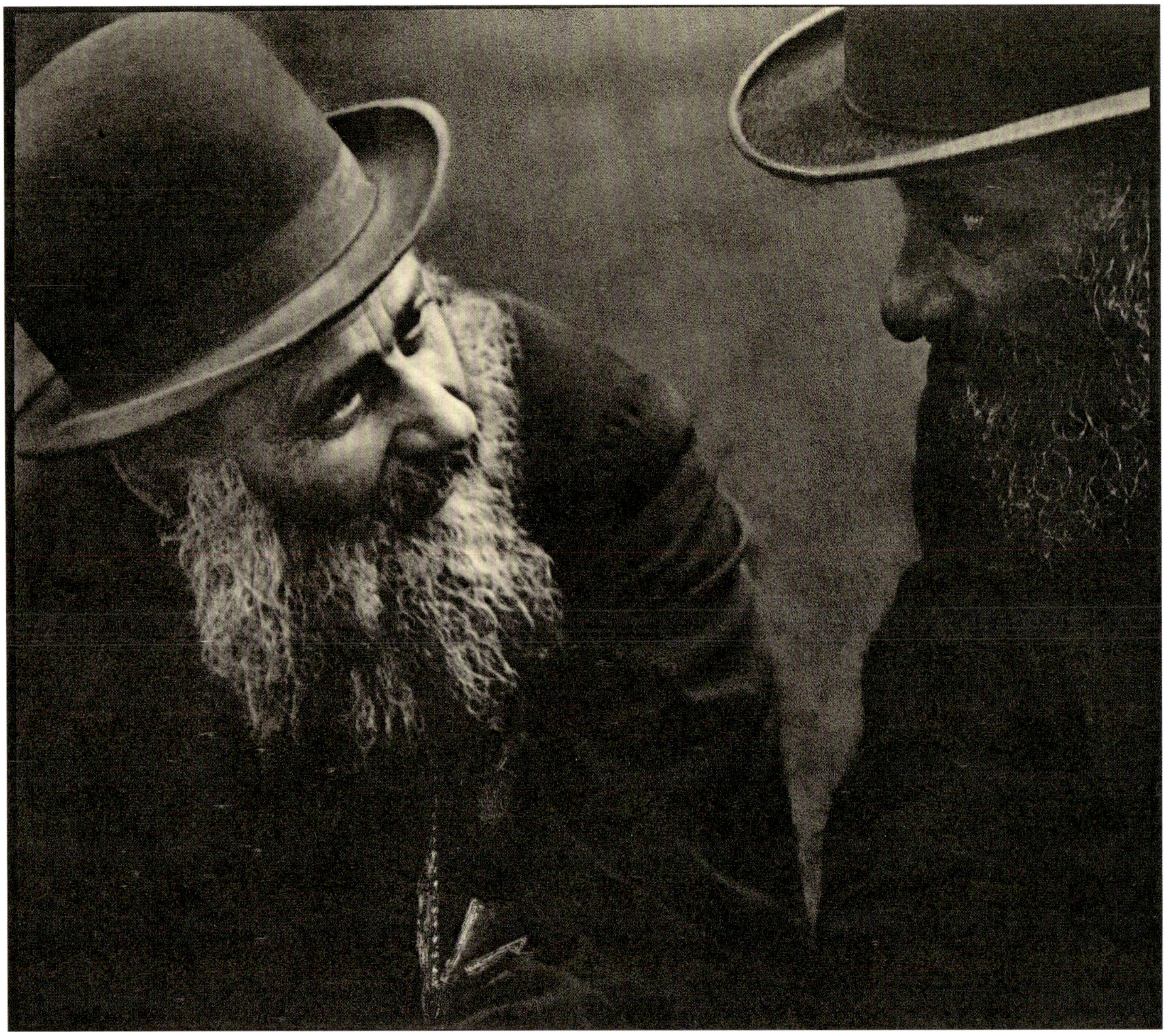

102. ***Conversation***
1916

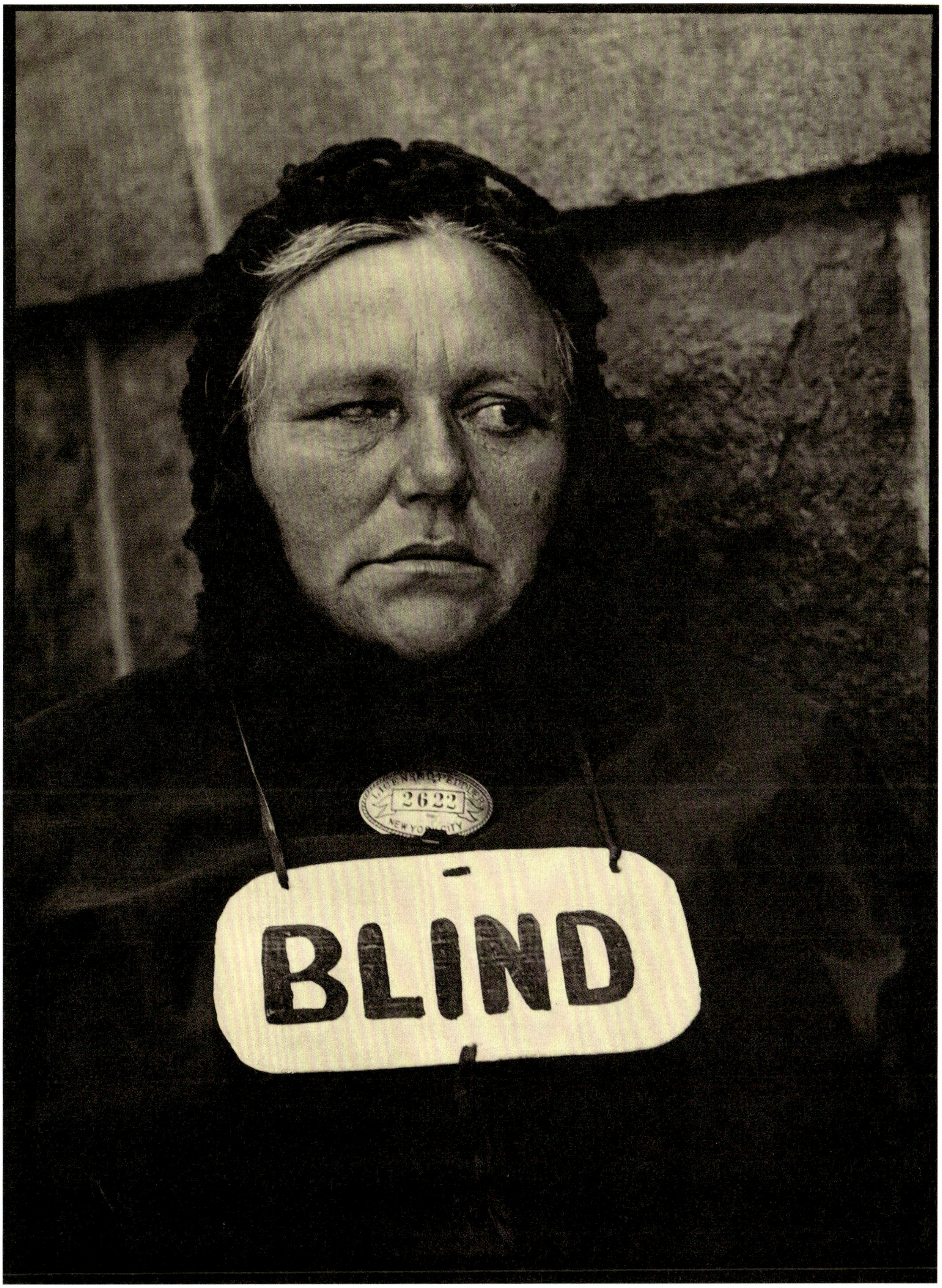

103. ***Blind***
1916

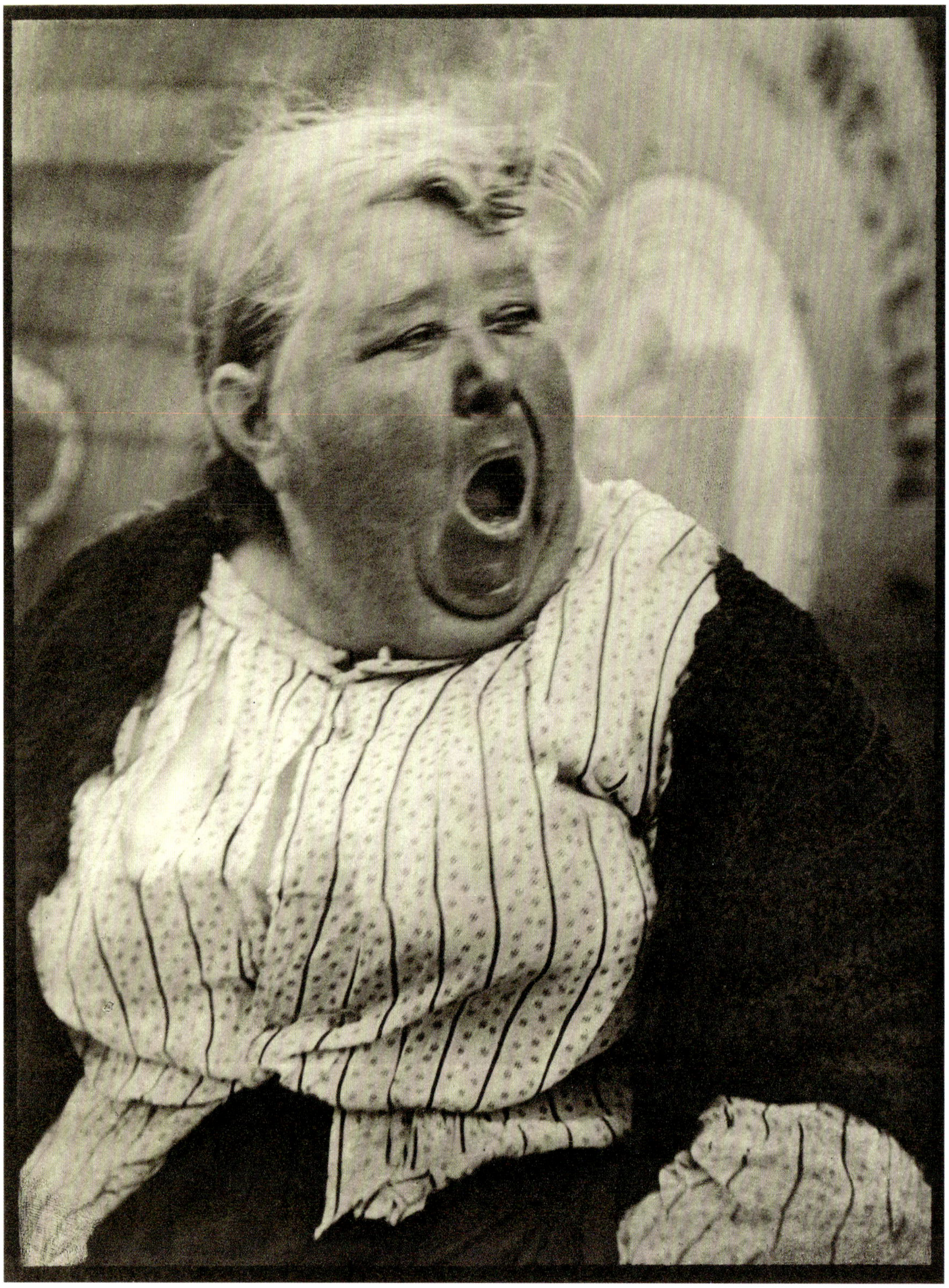

104. *[Irish Washerwoman]*
1916

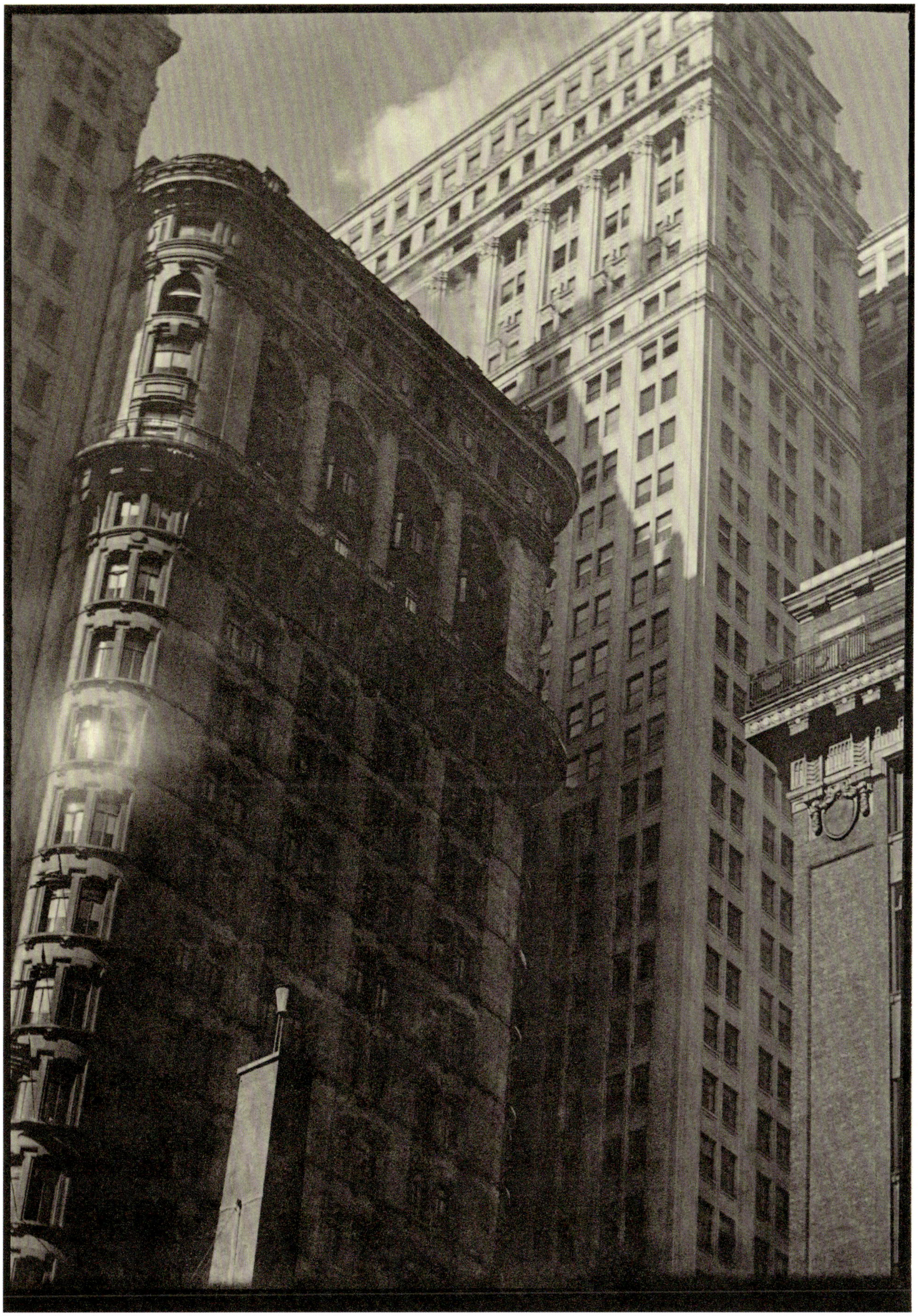

105. *[Office Buildings from Below, New York]*
1917

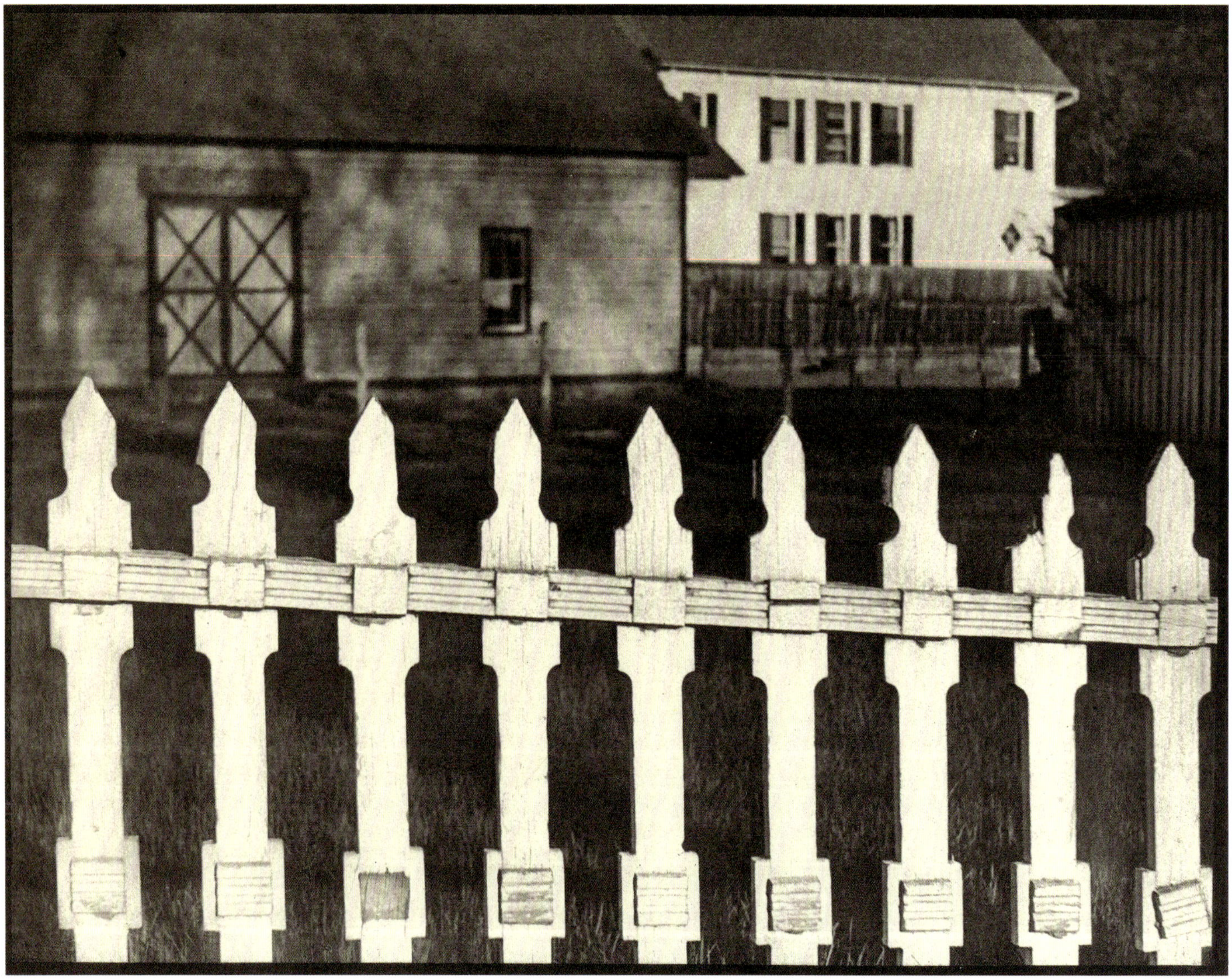

106. ***The White Fence***
1916

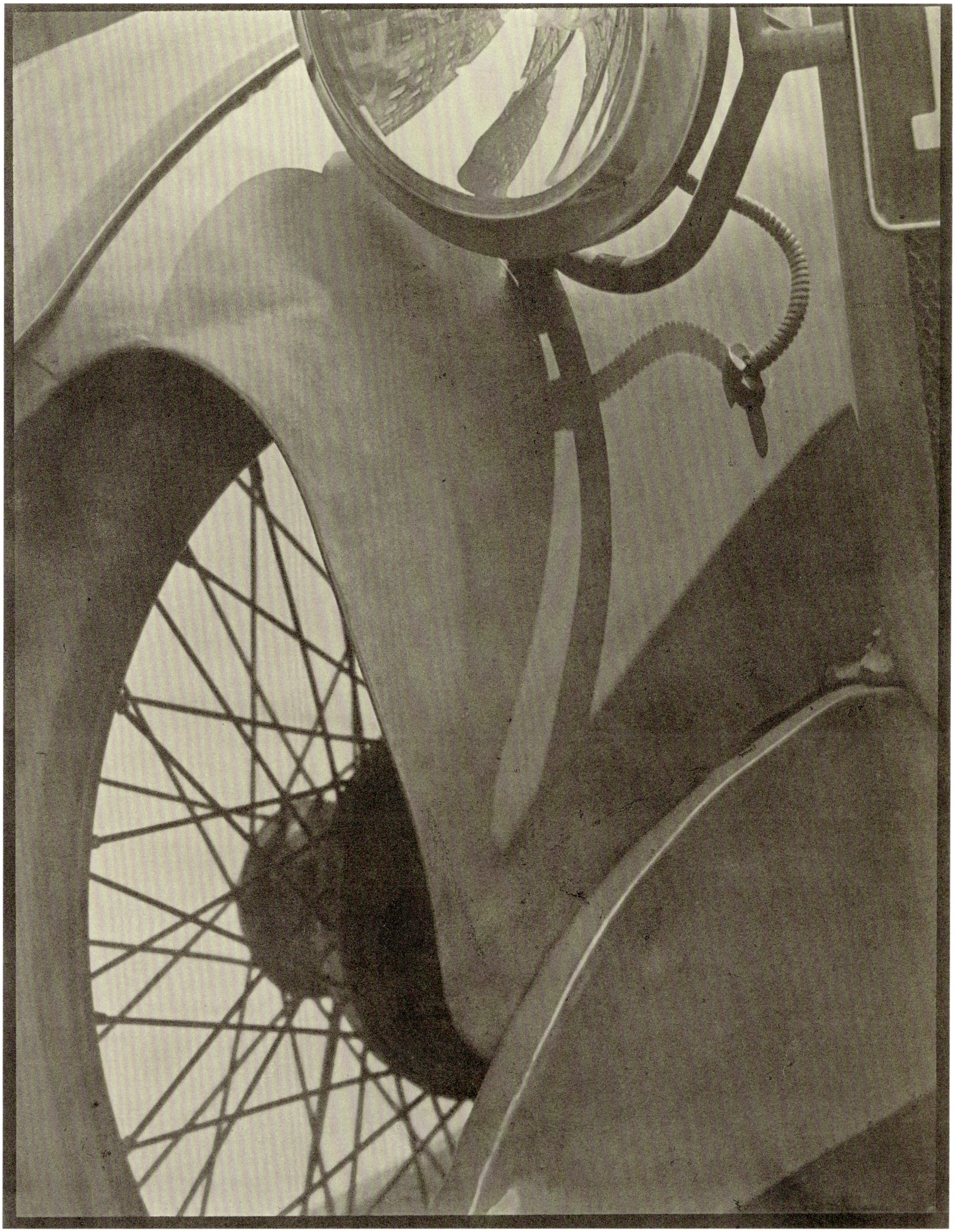

107. ***Wire Wheel***
1917

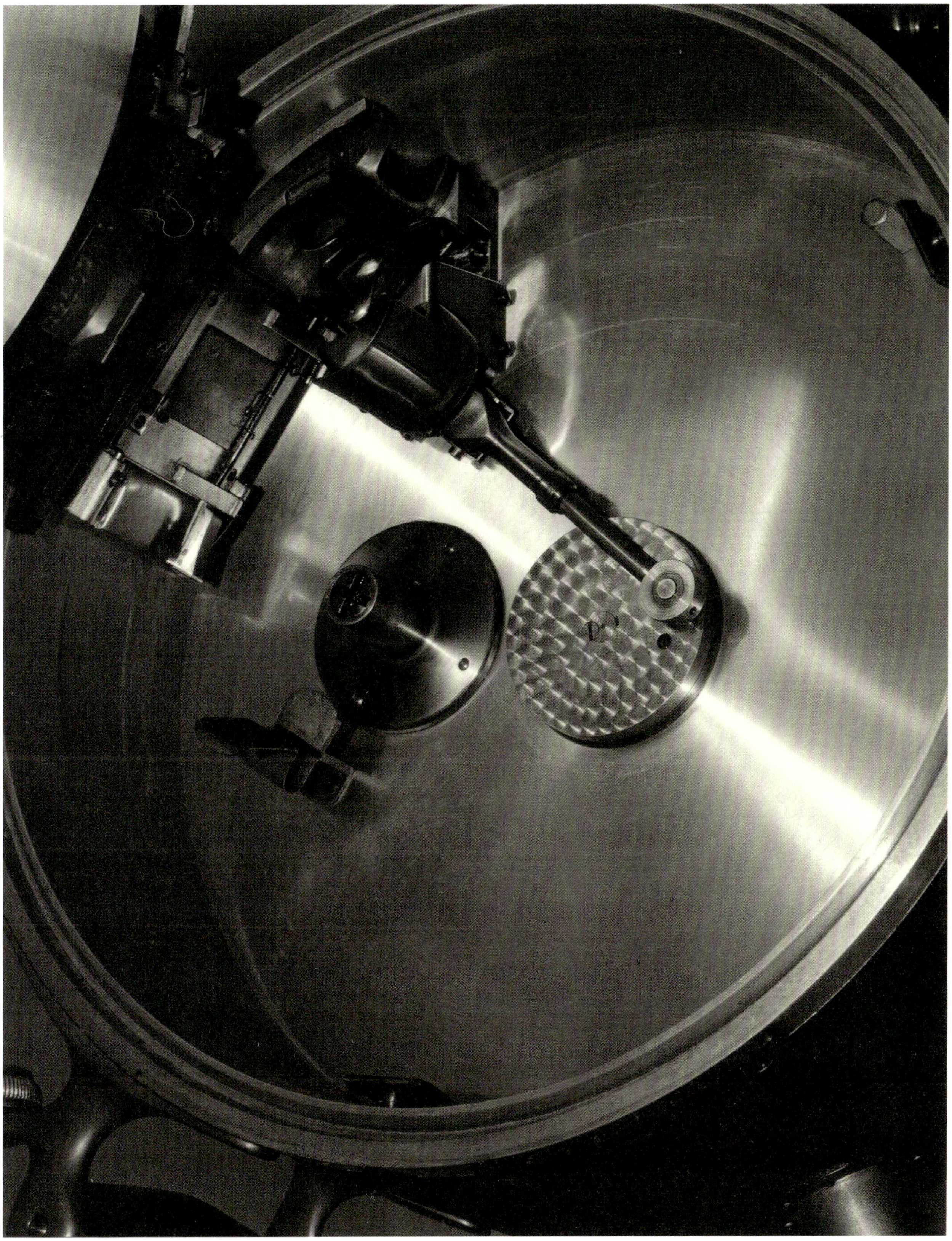

108. *Akeley Motion Picture Camera*
1922

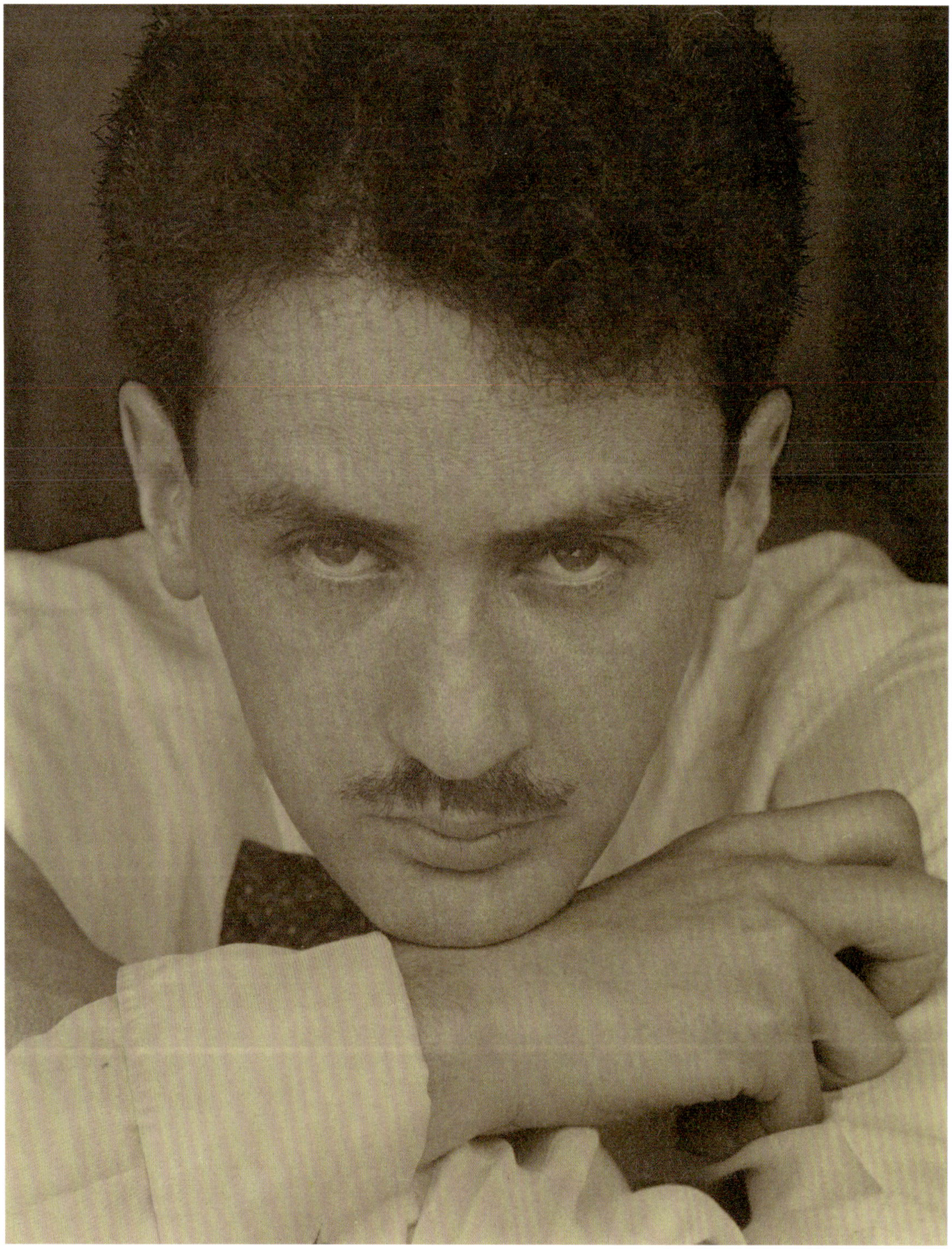

109. *Henry Churchill*
1922

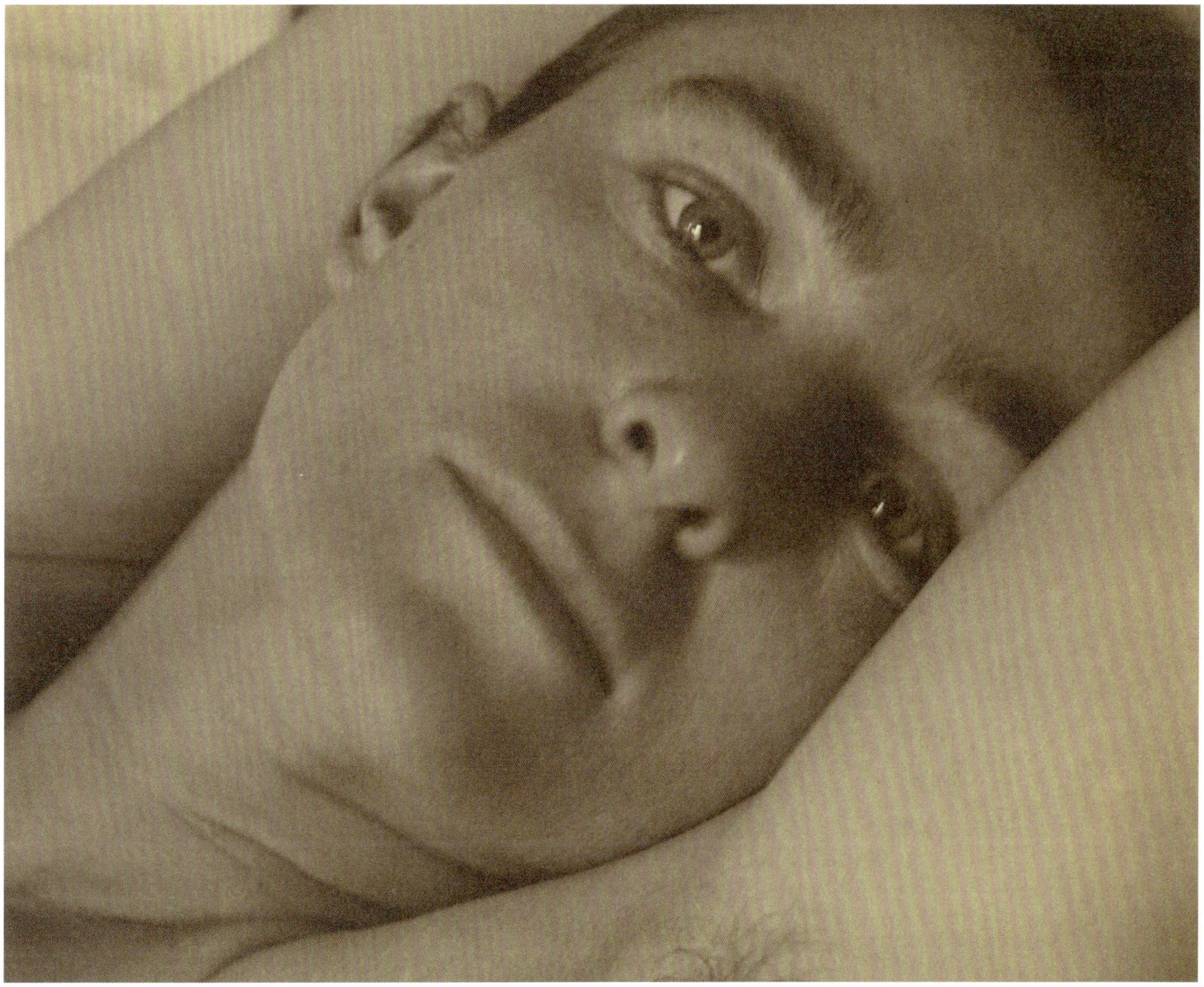

110. ***Rebecca, New York***
Ca. 1923

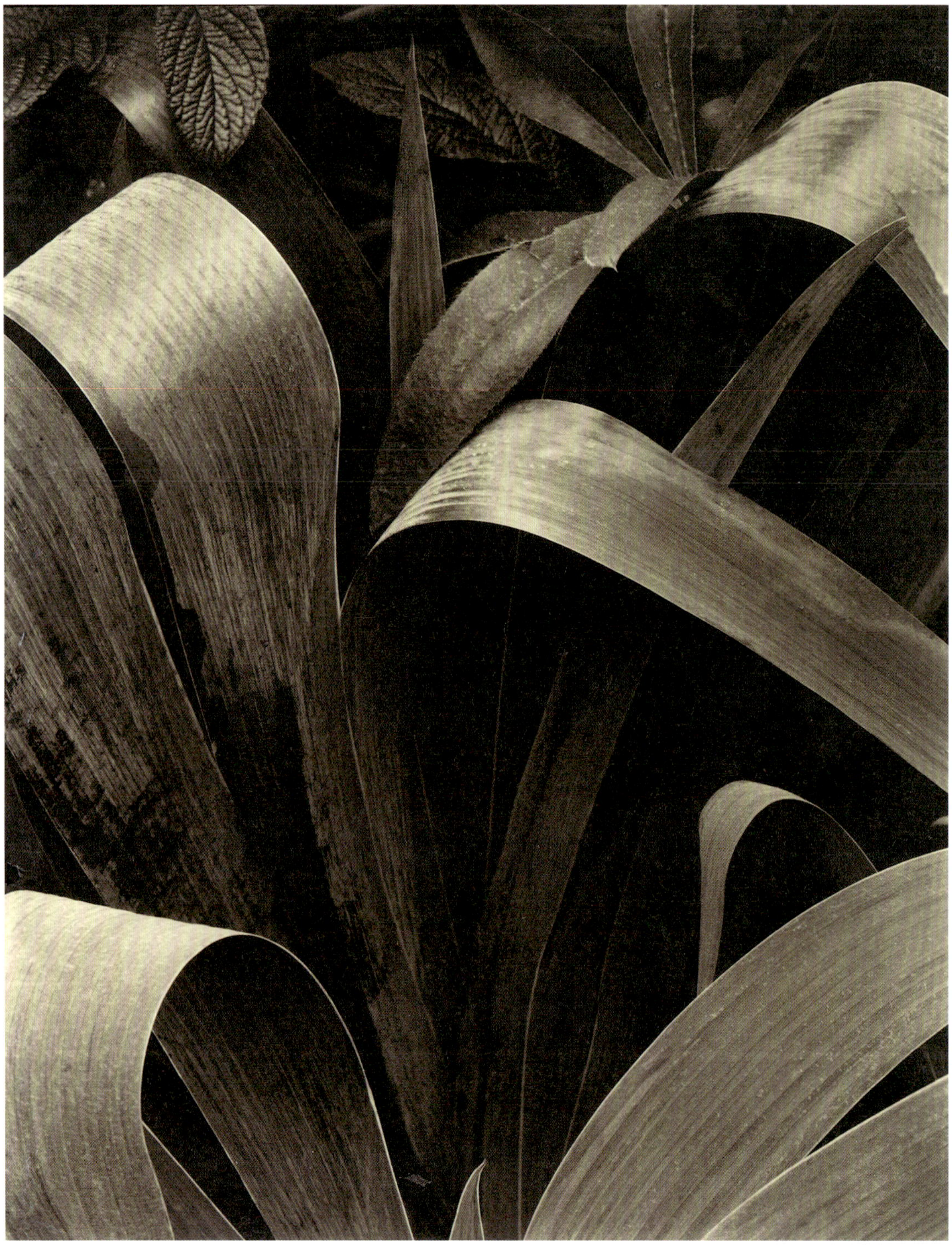

111. *Garden Iris—Georgetown, Maine*
1928

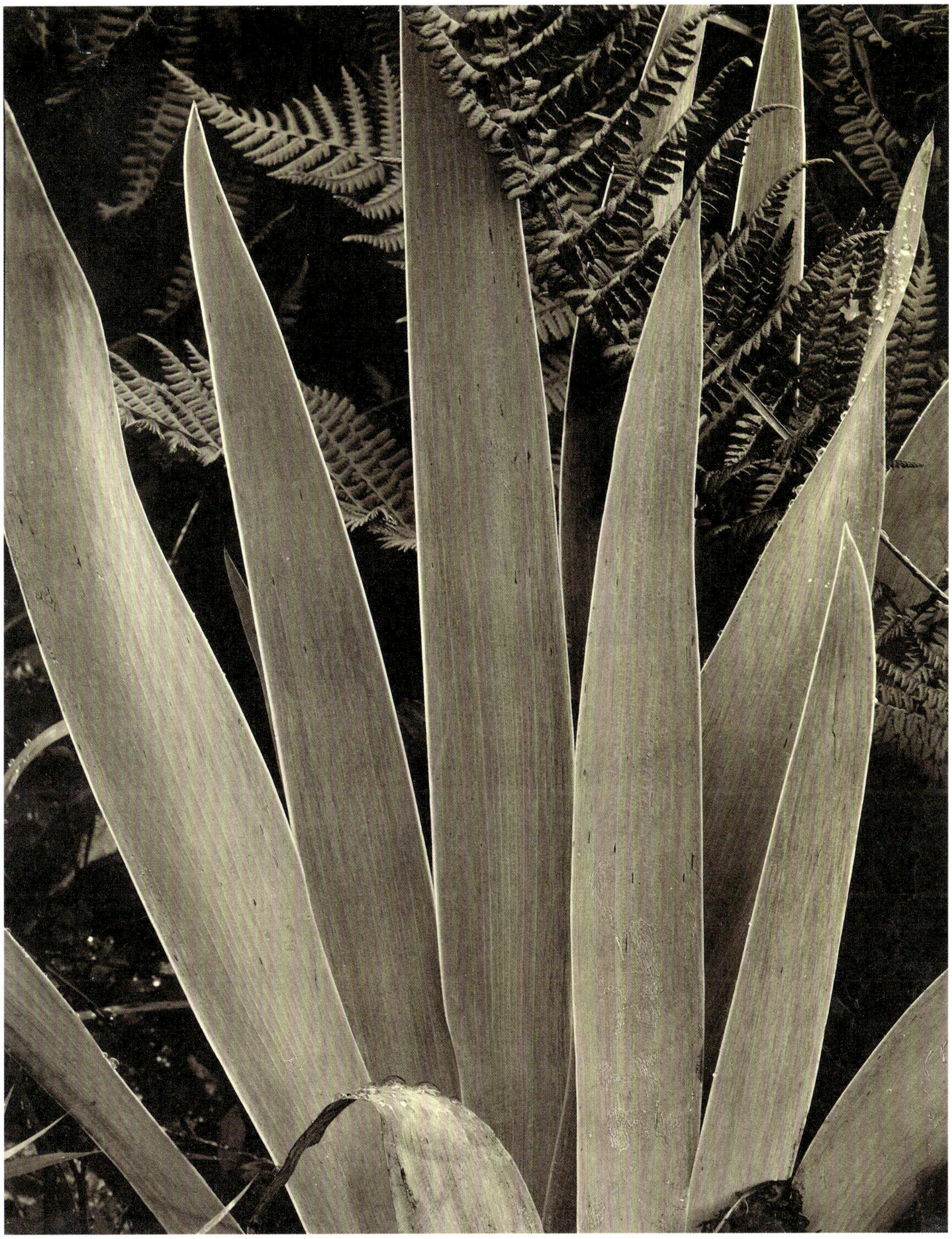

112. ***Wild Iris, Maine***
1927–28

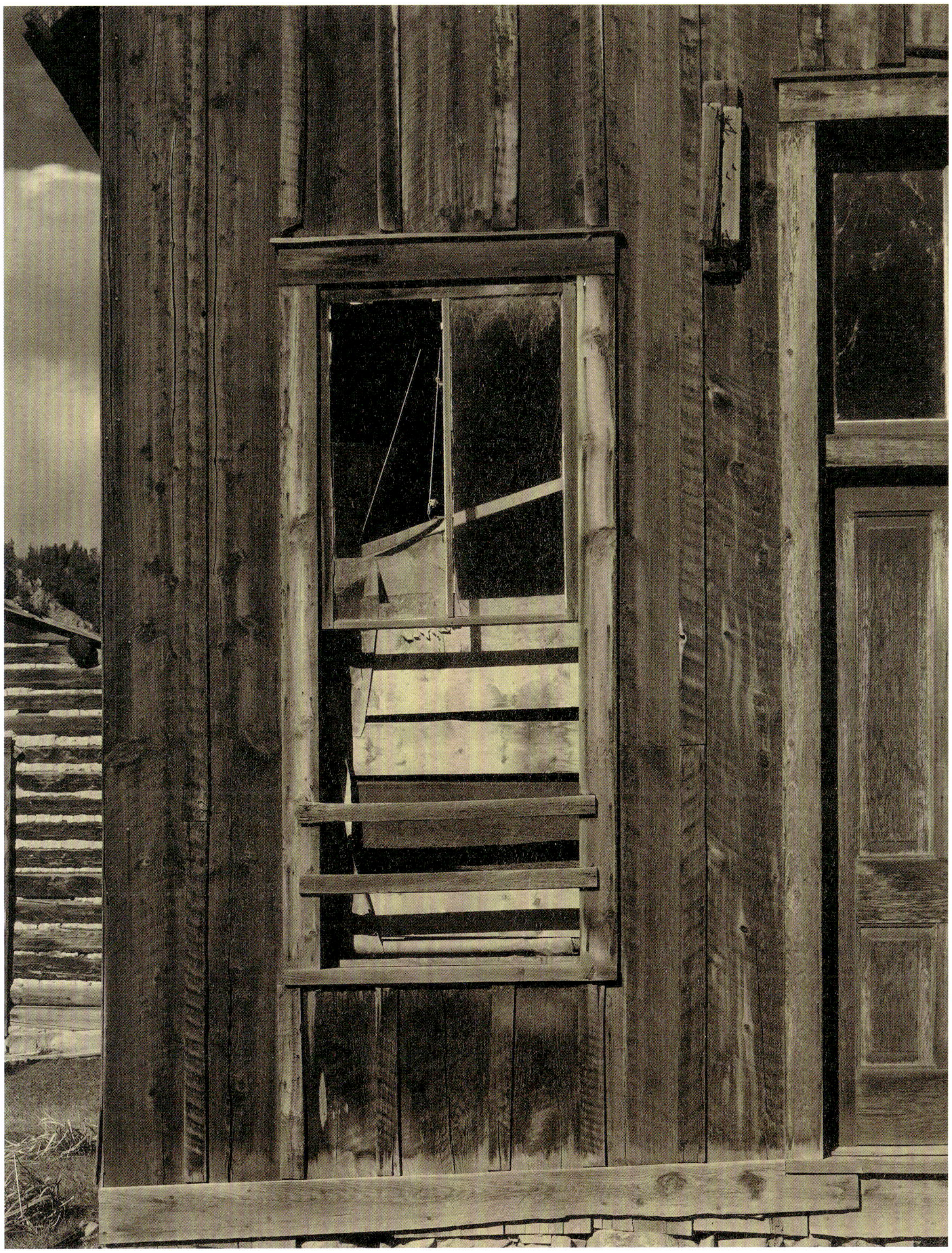

113. ***Ghost Town***
1930

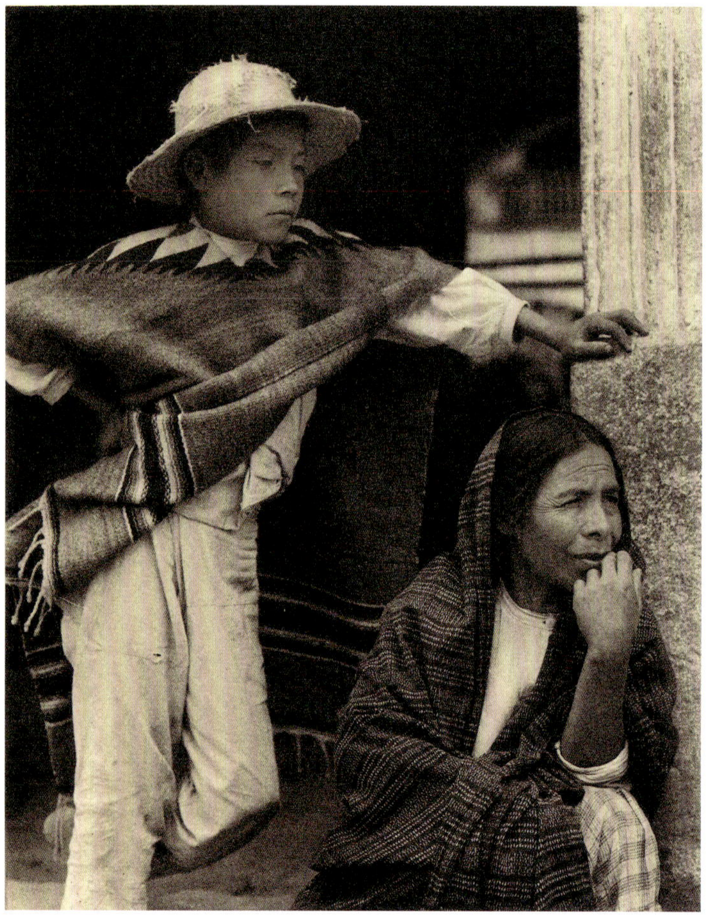

114. ***Woman and Boy, Tenancingo***
1933, printed 1940

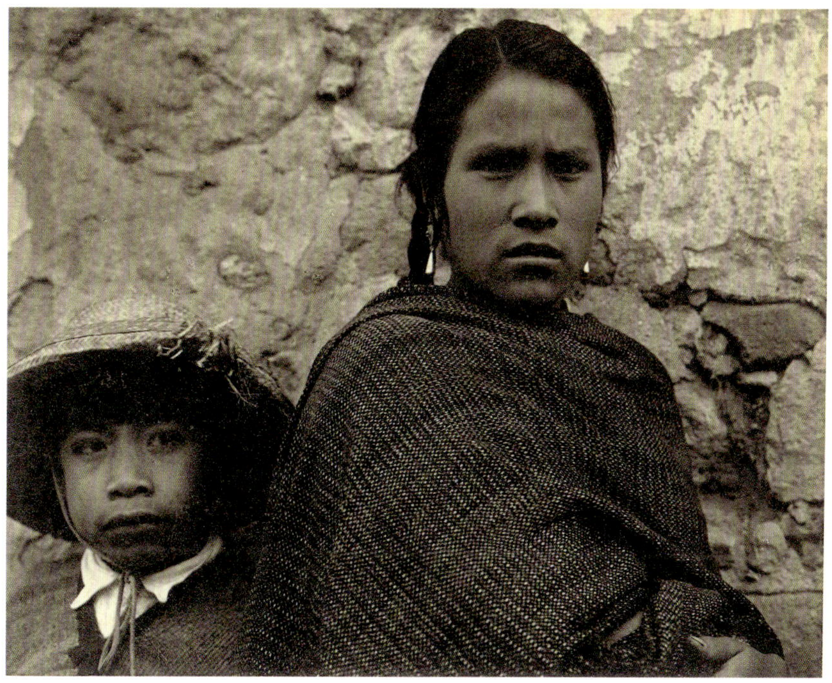

115. ***Ocoyococ***
1933

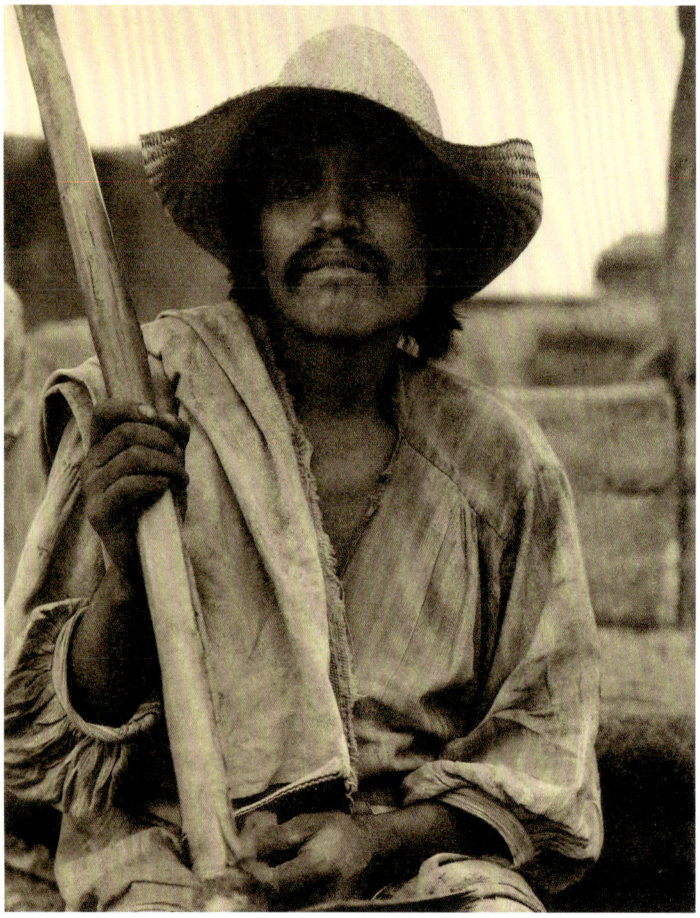

116. ***Man with a Hoe, Los Remedios***
1933, printed 1940

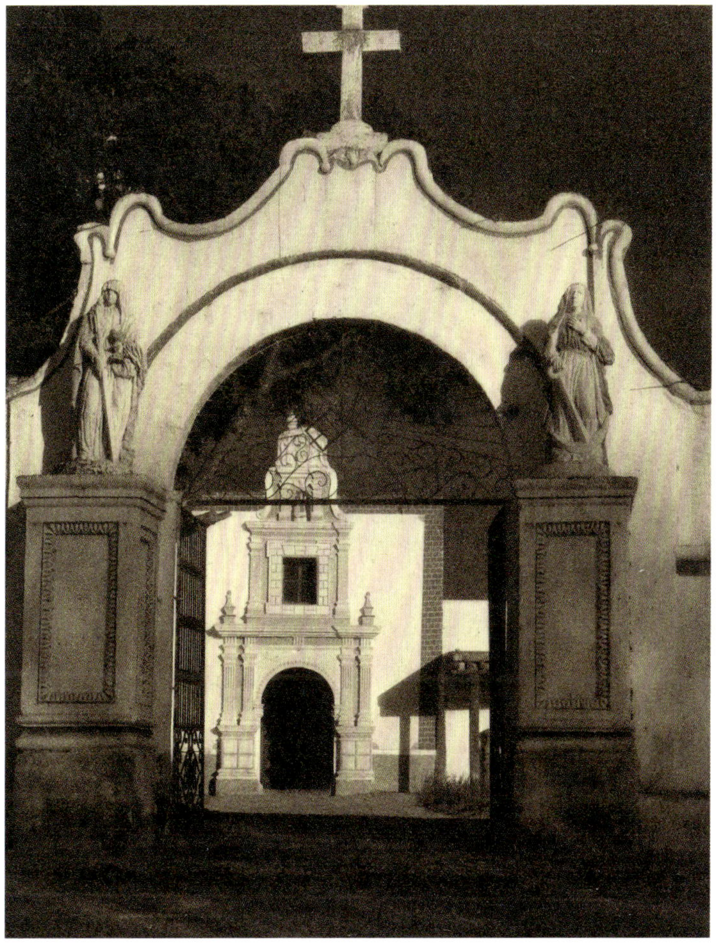

117. ***Coapiaxtla, Church***
1933, printed 1940

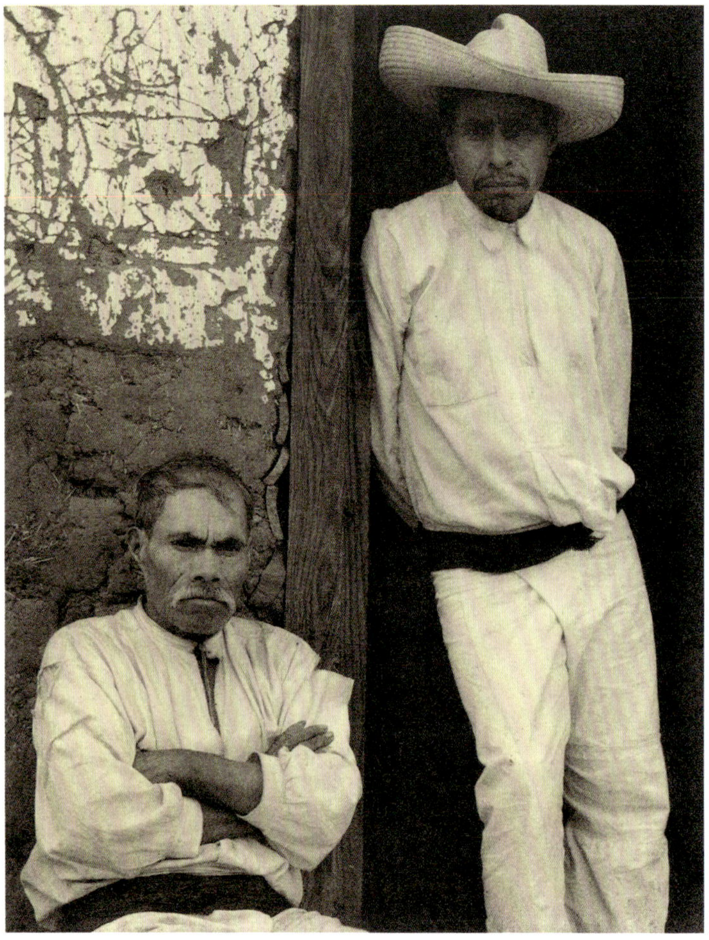

118. ***Men of Santa Anna, Michoacan***
1933, printed 1940

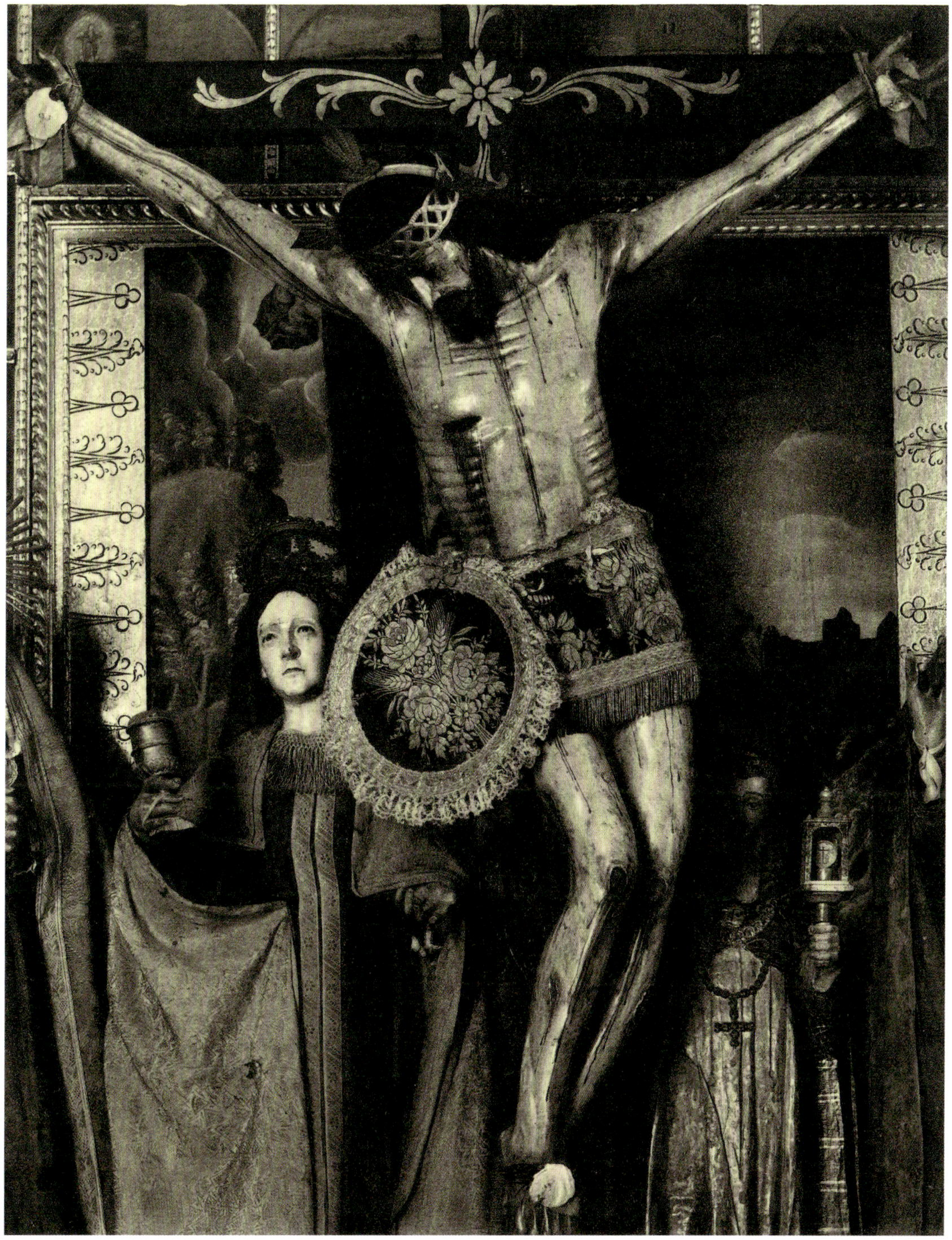

119. ***Cristo, Oaxaca***
1933, printed 1940

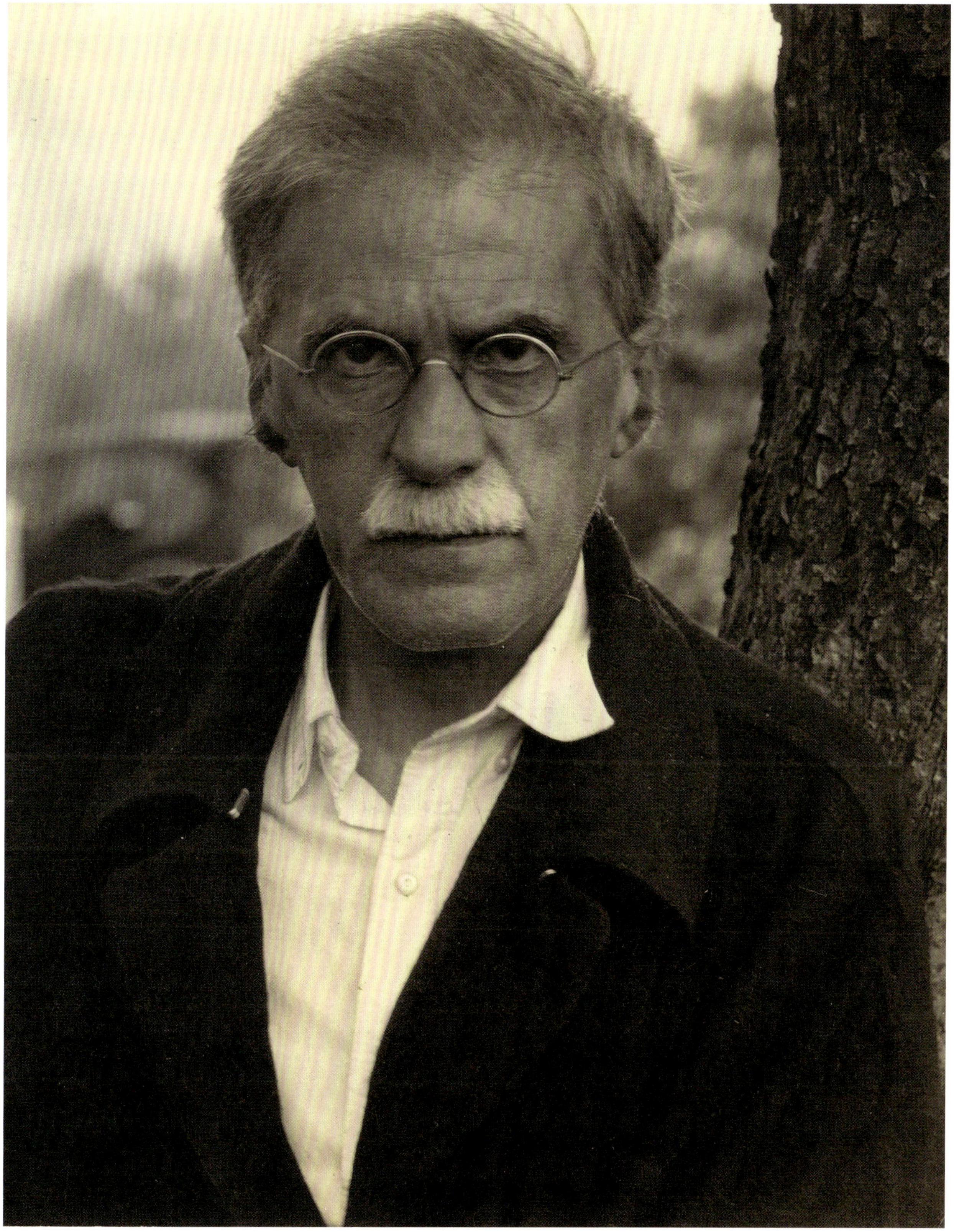

120. ***Alfred Stieglitz***
1939

LIST OF PLATES

All works are in the collection of The Metropolitan Museum of Art, New York. Titles in brackets are descriptive; all other titles were given by the photographer. Dimensions refer to the size of the printed image.

FRONTISPIECE

Edward Steichen
Alfred Stieglitz
1907
Autochrome
9 x 6 3/16 in. (22.9 x 15.7 cm)
Alfred Stieglitz Collection, 1955
55.635.10

ALFRED STIEGLITZ (1864–1946)

1. *Spring Showers, the Coach*
1899–1900
Platinum print
3 3/8 x 1 13/16 in. (8.6 x 4.6 cm)
Gilman Collection, Gift of The Howard Gilman Foundation, 2005
2005.100.178

2. *Winter, Fifth Avenue*
1893, printed 1897
Photogravure from *Picturesque Bits of New York and Other Studies* (New York: R. H. Russell, 1897)
11 3/16 x 8 3/4 in. (28.4 x 22.1 cm)
Alfred Stieglitz Collection, 1922

3. *The Street—Fifth Avenue*
1900–1901, printed 1903–4
Photogravure
12 1/16 x 9 3/16 in. (30.6 x 23.3 cm)
Alfred Stieglitz Collection, 1949
49.55.8

4. *The Terminal*
1893, printed 1920s–1930s
Gelatin silver print
3 1/2 x 4 1/2 in. (8.9 x 11.5 cm)
Alfred Stieglitz Collection, 1949
49.55.6

5. *The Terminal*
1893, printed 1913 or earlier
Photogravure
10 1/16 x 13 3/16 in. (25.5 x 33.5 cm)
Alfred Stieglitz Collection, 1949
49.55.18

6. *The Hand of Man*
1902, printed 1910
Photogravure
9 1/2 x 12 9/16 in. (24.2 x 31.9 cm)
Alfred Stieglitz Collection, 1949
49.55.9

7. *The Steerage*
1907, printed 1913 or earlier
Photogravure
12 11/16 x 10 3/16 in. (32.2 x 25.8 cm)
Alfred Stieglitz Collection, 1933
33.43.419

8. *Old and New New York*
1910, printed 1913 or earlier
Photogravure
13 1/16 x 10 1/16 in. (33.2 x 25.5 cm)
Alfred Stieglitz Collection, 1949
49.55.17

9. *The City of Ambition*
1910, printed 1913 or earlier
Photogravure
13 5/16 x 10 1/4 in. (33.8 x 26 cm)
Alfred Stieglitz Collection, 1949
49.55.15

10. *[Two Men Playing Chess]*
1907
Autochrome
3 1/2 x 4 3/4 in. (9 x 12 cm)
Gilman Collection, Purchase, Mr. and Mrs. Henry R. Kravis Gift, 2005
2005.100.476

11. *Mrs. Selma Schubart*
1907
Autochrome
7 1/16 x 5 1/16 in. (18 x 12.8 cm)
Alfred Stieglitz Collection, 1955
55.635.14

12. *Hodge Kirnon*
1917
Palladium print
9 11/16 x 7 13/16 in. (24.6 x 19.9 cm)
Alfred Stieglitz Collection, 1949
49.55.38

13. *Marsden Hartley*
1916
Gelatin silver print
$9\frac{3}{4}$ x $7\frac{13}{16}$ in. (24.8 x 19.8 cm)
Gilman Collection, Purchase, Gift of Marsden Hartley, by exchange, and Gift of Grace M. Mayer, by exchange, 2005
2005.100.290

14. *John Marin*
1921–22
Palladium print
$9\frac{1}{2}$ x $7\frac{5}{8}$ in. (24.2 x 19.3 cm)
Alfred Stieglitz Collection, 1949
49.55.39

15. *Dorothy True*
1919
Gelatin silver print
$9\frac{9}{16}$ x $7\frac{5}{8}$ in. (24.3 x 19.3 cm)
Gift of Paul Rosenfeld, 1928
28.126

16. *Margaret Treadwell*
1921
Platinum-palladium print
10 x 8 in. (25.4 x 20.3 cm)
Gift of John Pritzker, 2007
2007.469

17. *Dancing Trees*
1921–22
Palladium print
$9\frac{1}{2}$ x $7\frac{5}{8}$ in. (24.2 x 19.3 cm)
Gift of David A. Schulte, 1928
28.127.7

18. *Shadows in Lake*
1916
Gelatin silver print
$4\frac{1}{2}$ x $3\frac{9}{16}$ in. (11.5 x 9.1 cm)
Alfred Stieglitz Collection, 1949
49.55.21

19. *Katherine*
1921
Gelatin silver print
$4\frac{1}{8}$ x $3\frac{1}{4}$ in. (10.4 x 8.2 cm)
Alfred Stieglitz Collection, 1949
49.55.23

20. *Rebecca Salsbury Strand*
1922
Gelatin silver print
$3\frac{11}{16}$ x $4\frac{1}{2}$ in. (9.3 x 11.5 cm)
Alfred Stieglitz Collection, 1949
49.55.22

21. *House and Grape Leaves*
1934
Gelatin silver print
$9\frac{1}{2}$ x $7\frac{5}{8}$ in. (24.2 x 19.3 cm)
Alfred Stieglitz Collection, 1949
49.55.41

22. *Gable and Apples*
1922
Gelatin silver print
$4\frac{1}{2}$ x $3\frac{9}{16}$ in. (11.4 x 9 cm)
Ford Motor Company Collection, Gift of Ford Motor Company and John C. Waddell, 1987
1987.1100.103

23. *Georgia O'Keeffe—Hands*
1917
Platinum print
$8\frac{7}{8}$ x $6\frac{5}{8}$ in. (22.6 x 16.8 cm)
Gift of Georgia O'Keeffe, through the generosity of The Georgia O'Keeffe Foundation and Jennifer and Joseph Duke, 1997
1997.61.2

24. *Georgia O'Keeffe—Hand*
1918
Platinum print
$4\frac{5}{8}$ x $3\frac{9}{16}$ in. (11.8 x 9.1 cm)
Gift of Georgia O'Keeffe, through the generosity of The Georgia O'Keeffe Foundation and Jennifer and Joseph Duke, 1997
1997.61.26

25. *Georgia O'Keeffe*
1918
Platinum print
$4\frac{5}{8}$ x $3\frac{9}{16}$ in. (11.7 x 9 cm)
Gift of Georgia O'Keeffe, through the generosity of The Georgia O'Keeffe Foundation and Jennifer and Joseph Duke, 1997
1997.61.25

26. *Georgia O'Keeffe—Feet*
1918
Palladium print
$9\frac{1}{2}$ x $7\frac{11}{16}$ in. (24.1 x 19.5 cm)
Gift of Georgia O'Keeffe, through the generosity of The Georgia O'Keeffe Foundation and Jennifer and Joseph Duke, 1997
1997.61.55

27. *Georgia O'Keeffe*
1918
Platinum-palladium print
$9\frac{5}{8}$ x $7\frac{11}{16}$ in. (24.5 x 19.6 cm)
Gift of David A. Schulte, 1928
28.127.1

28. *Georgia O'Keeffe*
1918
Palladium print
$9\frac{1}{8}$ x $7\frac{9}{16}$ in. (23.2 x 19.2 cm)
Gift of Georgia O'Keeffe, through the generosity of The Georgia O'Keeffe Foundation and Jennifer and Joseph Duke, 1997
1997.61.21

29. *Georgia O'Keeffe—Torso*
1918
Gelatin silver print
$9\frac{5}{16}$ x $7\frac{3}{8}$ in. (23.6 x 18.8 cm)
Gift of Mrs. Alma Wertheim, 1928
28.130.2

30. *Georgia O'Keeffe—Hands*
1919
Palladium print
9 x $7\frac{7}{16}$ in. (22.9 x 18.9 cm)
Gift of Georgia O'Keeffe, through the generosity of The Georgia O'Keeffe Foundation and Jennifer and Joseph Duke, 1997
1997.61.18

31. *Georgia O'Keeffe*
1919
Palladium print
$9\frac{1}{4}$ x $7\frac{1}{4}$ in. (23.5 x 18.4 cm)
Gift of Mrs. Rebecca S. Strand, 1928
28.129

32. *Georgia O'Keeffe*
1918
Palladium print
9 x $7\frac{5}{16}$ in. (22.8 x 18.6 cm)
Gift of Georgia O'Keeffe, through the generosity of The Georgia O'Keeffe Foundation and Jennifer and Joseph Duke, 1997
1997.61.20

33. *Georgia O'Keeffe—Hand and Breasts*
1919
Palladium print
$7\frac{3}{16}$ x $9\frac{1}{8}$ in. (18.2 x 23.1 cm)
Gift of Mrs. Alma Wertheim, 1928
28.130.1

34. *Georgia O'Keeffe—Breasts*
1919
Palladium print
$9\frac{5}{8}$ x $7\frac{5}{8}$ in. (24.4 x 19.3 cm)
Gift of Georgia O'Keeffe, through the generosity of The Georgia O'Keeffe Foundation and Jennifer and Joseph Duke, 1997
1997.61.23

35. ***Georgia O'Keeffe—Neck***
1921
Palladium print
$9\frac{5}{16} \times 7\frac{9}{16}$ in. (23.6 x 19.2 cm)
Gift of Georgia O'Keeffe, through the generosity of The Georgia O'Keeffe Foundation and Jennifer and Joseph Duke, 1997
1997.61.19

36. ***Georgia O'Keeffe***
1919–21
Palladium print
$9\frac{5}{16} \times 7\frac{1}{2}$ in. (23.7 x 19 cm)
Gift of Georgia O'Keeffe, through the generosity of The Georgia O'Keeffe Foundation and Jennifer and Joseph Duke, 1997
1997.61.61

37. ***Georgia O'Keeffe***
1922
Palladium print
$7\frac{7}{16} \times 9\frac{7}{16}$ in. (18.9 x 24 cm)
Gift of Georgia O'Keeffe, through the generosity of The Georgia O'Keeffe Foundation and Jennifer and Joseph Duke, 1997
1997.61.66

38. ***Georgia O'Keeffe—Hands and Horse Skull***
1931
Gelatin silver print
$7\frac{9}{16} \times 9\frac{7}{16}$ in. (19.2 x 24 cm)
Gift of Georgia O'Keeffe, through the generosity of The Georgia O'Keeffe Foundation and Jennifer and Joseph Duke, 1997
1997.61.37

39. ***Georgia O'Keeffe—Hand and Wheel***
1933
Gelatin silver print
$9\frac{1}{2} \times 7\frac{11}{16}$ in. (24.1 x 19.5 cm)
Gift of Georgia O'Keeffe, through the generosity of The Georgia O'Keeffe Foundation and Jennifer and Joseph Duke, 1997
1997.61.39

40. ***Music No. 1***
1922
Platinum print
$7\frac{9}{16} \times 9\frac{1}{2}$ in. (19.2 x 24.1 cm)
Gift of David A. Schulte, 1928
28.127.6

41. ***Equivalent***
1924
Gelatin silver print
$3\frac{5}{8} \times 4\frac{5}{8}$ in. (9.2 x 11.8 cm)
Alfred Stieglitz Collection, 1928
28.128.5

42. ***Equivalent***
1925
Gelatin silver print
$4\frac{5}{8} \times 3\frac{5}{8}$ in. (11.8 x 9.2 cm)
Alfred Stieglitz Collection, 1928
28.128.7

43. ***Equivalent***
1925
Gelatin silver print
$3\frac{11}{16} \times 4\frac{11}{16}$ in. (9.3 x 11.9 cm)
Alfred Stieglitz Collection, 1928
28.128.8

44. ***Equivalent***
1925
Gelatin silver print
$4\frac{11}{16} \times 3\frac{9}{16}$ in. (11.9 x 9.1 cm)
Alfred Stieglitz Collection, 1928
28.128.9

45. ***Equivalent***
1927
Gelatin silver print
$3\frac{9}{16} \times 4\frac{5}{8}$ in. (9.1 x 11.8 cm)
Alfred Stieglitz Collection, 1928
28.128.11

46. ***Equivalent***
1935
Gelatin silver print
$9\frac{7}{16} \times 7\frac{1}{2}$ in. (24 x 19.1 cm)
Alfred Stieglitz Collection, 1949
49.55.44

47. ***Grass***
1933
Gelatin silver print
$5\frac{7}{8} \times 7\frac{5}{16}$ in. (14.9 x 18.6 cm)
Gilman Collection, Purchase, Ann Tenenbaum and Thomas H. Lee Gift, 2005
2005.100.479

48. ***Spiritual America***
1923
Gelatin silver print
$4\frac{9}{16} \times 3\frac{5}{8}$ in. (11.6 x 9.2 cm)
Alfred Stieglitz Collection, 1949
49.55.24

49. ***From the Back Window, 291***
1915
Platinum print
$9\frac{7}{8} \times 7\frac{15}{16}$ in. (25.1 x 20.2 cm)
Alfred Stieglitz Collection, 1949
49.55.35

50. ***From My Window at An American Place, Southwest***
1932
Gelatin silver print
$7\frac{9}{16} \times 9\frac{1}{2}$ in. (19.2 x 24.1 cm)
Alfred Stieglitz Collection, 1949
49.55.48

51. ***From My Window at An American Place, North***
1931
Gelatin silver print
$9\frac{1}{4} \times 7\frac{5}{16}$ in. (23.5 x 18.6 cm)
Alfred Stieglitz Collection, 1949
49.55.47

52. ***From My Window at the Shelton, West***
1931
Gelatin silver print
$9\frac{1}{2} \times 7\frac{1}{2}$ in. (24.2 x 19.1 cm)
Alfred Stieglitz Collection, 1949
49.55.45

53. ***Looking Northwest from the Shelton, New York***
1932
Gelatin silver print
$9\frac{1}{2} \times 7\frac{9}{16}$ in. (24.2 x 19.2 cm)
Ford Motor Company Collection, Gift of Ford Motor Company and John C. Waddell, 1987
1987.1100.11

EDWARD STEICHEN (1879–1973)

54. *Self-Portrait*
1899
Platinum print
$7\frac{13}{16}$ x $3\frac{5}{8}$ in. (19.8 x 9.2 cm)
Alfred Stieglitz Collection, 1933
33.43.1

55. *Woods Interior*
1899
Platinum print
$7\frac{7}{16}$ x $6\frac{5}{16}$ in. (18.9 x 16.1 cm)
Alfred Stieglitz Collection, 1933
33.43.8

56. *The Pool—Evening*
1899
Platinum print
$8\frac{1}{8}$ x $6\frac{5}{16}$ in. (20.7 x 16 cm)
Alfred Stieglitz Collection, 1949
49.55.232

57. *Voulangis*
1900–1902
Platinum print
$5\frac{13}{16}$ x $5\frac{13}{16}$ in. (14.7 x 14.7 cm)
Gift of Grace M. Mayer, 1990
1990.1042

58. *Moonlight—Winter*
1902
Platinum print with applied color
$13\frac{9}{16}$ x $16\frac{11}{16}$ in. (34.5 x 42.4 cm)
Alfred Stieglitz Collection, 1933
33.43.30

59. *The Big Cloud, Lake George*
1903, printed 1904
Direct carbon print
$15\frac{1}{2}$ x 19 in. (39.3 x 48.3 cm)
Alfred Stieglitz Collection, 1933
33.43.47

60. *The Pond—Moonrise*
1904
Platinum print with applied color
$15\frac{5}{8}$ x 19 in. (39.7 x 48.2 cm)
Alfred Stieglitz Collection, 1933
33.43.40

61. *The Flatiron*
1904
Gum bichromate over platinum print
$18\frac{13}{16}$ x $15\frac{1}{8}$ in. (47.8 x 38.4 cm)
Alfred Stieglitz Collection, 1933
33.43.43

62. *The Flatiron*
1904, printed 1909
Gum bichromate over platinum print
$18\frac{13}{16}$ x $15\frac{1}{8}$ in. (47.8 x 38.4 cm)
Alfred Stieglitz Collection, 1933
33.43.39

63. *The Flatiron*
1904, printed 1905
Gum bichromate over platinum print
$19\frac{5}{8}$ x $15\frac{5}{16}$ in. (49.9 x 38.9 cm)
Alfred Stieglitz Collection, 1933
33.43.44

64. *Figure with Iris*
1902
Direct carbon print
$13\frac{3}{8}$ x $7\frac{3}{8}$ in. (34 x 18.8 cm)
Alfred Stieglitz Collection, 1933
33.43.17

65. *La Cigale*
1901, printed 1904–5
Gum bichromate over platinum print
$10\frac{7}{16}$ x $11\frac{7}{16}$ in. (26.5 x 29 cm)
Alfred Stieglitz Collection, 1933
33.43.22

66. *The Little Round Mirror*
1901, printed 1905
Gum bichromate over platinum print
19 x $13\frac{1}{16}$ in. (48.3 x 33.2 cm)
Alfred Stieglitz Collection, 1933
33.43.32

67. *In Memoriam*
1901, printed 1904
Gum bichromate over platinum print
$19\frac{5}{8}$ x $15\frac{7}{8}$ in. (49.8 x 40.3 cm)
Alfred Stieglitz Collection, 1933
33.43.48

68. *The Black Vase*
1901, printed 1902
Direct carbon print
8 x $6\frac{1}{16}$ in. (20.4 x 15.4 cm)
Alfred Stieglitz Collection, 1933
33.43.20

69. *Melpomene—Landon Rives*
1904–5
Gum bichromate over platinum print
$18\frac{3}{4}$ x $12\frac{13}{16}$ in. (47.6 x 32.5 cm)
Alfred Stieglitz Collection, 1933
33.43.31

70. *The Brass Bowl*
1904
Direct carbon print
12 x $10\frac{1}{16}$ in. (30.4 x 25.6 cm)
Alfred Stieglitz Collection, 1933
33.43.6

71. *Self-Portrait with Little Sister*
1900
Platinum print
$3\frac{13}{16}$ x $5\frac{3}{8}$ in. (9.7 x 13.7 cm)
Gilman Collection, Purchase, Mrs. Walter Annenberg and The Annenberg Foundation Gift, 2005
2005.100.477

72. *Alfred Stieglitz and His Daughter Katherine*
1904, printed 1905
Gum bichromate over platinum print
$17\frac{15}{16}$ x $15\frac{3}{4}$ in. (45.5 x 40 cm)
Alfred Stieglitz Collection, 1933
33.43.23

73. *Portraits—Evening*
1903, printed 1908
Gum bichromate over platinum print
$11\frac{1}{2}$ x $13\frac{1}{4}$ in. (29.2 x 33.6 cm)
Alfred Stieglitz Collection, 1933
33.43.21

74. *Lady Ian Hamilton*
1907, printed 1909
Direct carbon print
$19\frac{13}{16}$ x $15\frac{9}{16}$ in. (50.4 x 39.6 cm)
Alfred Stieglitz Collection, 1933
33.43.24

75. *Richard Strauss*
1904, printed 1906
Direct carbon print
$18\frac{3}{8}$ x $12\frac{7}{8}$ in. (46.7 x 32.7 cm)
Alfred Stieglitz Collection, 1949
49.55.168

76. *Cyclamen—Mrs. Philip Lydig*
Ca. 1905
Direct carbon print
$12\frac{3}{8}$ x $8\frac{1}{2}$ in. (31.5 x 21.6 cm)
Alfred Stieglitz Collection, 1933
33.43.9

77. *J. Pierpont Morgan, Esq.*
1903, printed 1909–10
Gum bichromate over platinum print
$20\frac{5}{16}$ x $16\frac{3}{16}$ in. (51.6 x 41.1 cm)
Alfred Stieglitz Collection, 1949
49.55.167

78. *Rodin—The Thinker*
1902
Gum bichromate print
$15\frac{9}{16}$ x 19 in. (39.6 x 48.3 cm)
Gilman Collection, Purchase, Harriette and Noel Levine Gift, 2005
2005.100.289

79. *Balzac, The Silhouette—4 A.M.*
1908
Gum bichromate print
$14\frac{15}{16}$ x $18\frac{1}{8}$ in. (37.9 x 46 cm)
Alfred Stieglitz Collection, 1933
33.43.36

80. *Balzac, The Open Sky—11:00 P.M.*
1908, printed 1909
Direct carbon print
$19\frac{3}{16}$ x $15\frac{3}{16}$ in. (48.7 x 38.5 cm)
Alfred Stieglitz Collection, 1933
33.43.46

81. *Balzac, Towards the Light, Midnight*
1908
Direct carbon print
$14\frac{3}{8}$ x 19 in. (36.5 x 48.2 cm)
Alfred Stieglitz Collection, 1933
33.43.38

82. *Rodin—The Eve*
1907
Autochrome
$6\frac{1}{4}$ x $3\frac{7}{8}$ in. (15.9 x 9.8 cm)
Alfred Stieglitz Collection, 1955
55.635.9

83. *Late Afternoon—Venice*
1907
Direct carbon print
$11\frac{1}{16}$ x $13\frac{3}{16}$ in. (28.1 x 33.5 cm)
Alfred Stieglitz Collection, 1933
33.43.50

84. *After the Grand Prix—Paris*
1907, printed 1911
Direct carbon print
$10\frac{11}{16}$ x $11\frac{5}{8}$ in. (27.1 x 29.5 cm)
Alfred Stieglitz Collection, 1933
33.43.51

85. *Steeplechase Day, Paris—The Grandstand*
1907, printed 1911
Direct carbon print
$10\frac{3}{4}$ x $13\frac{7}{8}$ in. (27.3 x 35.2 cm)
Alfred Stieglitz Collection, 1933
33.43.49

86. *Vaux #2, After Attack*
1918
Gelatin silver print
$6\frac{1}{4}$ x $8\frac{5}{8}$ in. (15.8 x 21.9 cm)
Ford Motor Company Collection, Gift of Ford Motor Company and John C. Waddell, 1987
1987.1100.109

87. *Between the Walls, New York*
Ca. 1922
Palladium print
$9\frac{5}{8}$ x $7\frac{5}{8}$ in. (24.5 x 19.4 cm)
Gift of Grace M. Mayer, 1991
1991.1310

88. *[Brancusi's Studio]*
Ca. 1920
Gelatin silver print
$9\frac{5}{8}$ x $7\frac{5}{8}$ in. (24.4 x 19.4 cm)
Gift of Grace M. Mayer, 1992
1992.5149

89. *Triumph of the Egg*
1921
Gelatin silver print
$9\frac{5}{8}$ x $7\frac{5}{8}$ in. (24.5 x 19.3 cm)
Bequest of Edward Steichen by direction of Joanna T. Steichen and the International Museum of Photography at George Eastman House, 1983
1983.1158.1

90. *Time-Space Continuum*
Ca. 1920
Gelatin silver print
$7\frac{7}{8}$ x $9\frac{9}{16}$ in. (20 x 24.3 cm)
Ford Motor Company Collection, Gift of Ford Motor Company and John C. Waddell and Gift of Grace Mayer, 1988
1987.1100.468

91. *Self-Portrait*
1916
Platinum print
$9\frac{15}{16}$ x $7\frac{11}{16}$ in. (25.2 x 19.5 cm)
Gift of Grace M. Mayer, in honor of William S. Lieberman, 1987
1987.1003

92. *Princess Yusupov*
1924
Gelatin silver print
$9\frac{13}{16}$ x $7\frac{7}{8}$ in. (24.9 x 20 cm)
Gilman Collection, Purchase, Ann Tenenbaum and Thomas H. Lee Gift, 2005
2005.100.157

PAUL STRAND (1890–1976)

93. ***Winter, Central Park, New York***
1913–14
Platinum print
$10\frac{1}{8} \times 11\frac{3}{16}$ in. (25.7 x 28.4 cm)
Gilman Collection, Purchase, Jennifer and Joseph Duke Gift, 2005
2005.100.117

94. ***Wall Street***
1916
Photogravure from *Camera Work*, no. 48 (October 1916)
$5 \times 6\frac{7}{16}$ in. (12.7 x 16.3 cm)
Alfred Stieglitz Collection, by exchange, 1953
53.701.49

95. ***From the El***
1915
Platinum print
$13\frac{1}{4} \times 10\frac{3}{16}$ in. (33.6 x 25.9 cm)
Alfred Stieglitz Collection, 1949
49.55.221

96. ***Pears and Bowls***
1916
Silver-platinum print
$10\frac{1}{8} \times 11\frac{5}{16}$ in. (25.7 x 28.8 cm)
Gilman Collection, Purchase, Ann Tenenbaum and Thomas H. Lee Gift, 2005
2005.100.137

97. ***Jug and Fruit***
1916
Silver-platinum print
$13\frac{3}{8} \times 9\frac{11}{16}$ in. (34 x 24.6 cm)
Gilman Collection, Purchase, Ann Tenenbaum and Thomas H. Lee Gift, 2005
2005.100.341

98. ***Bowls***
1916
Silver-platinum print
$13\frac{3}{8} \times 9\frac{13}{16}$ in. (33.9 x 25 cm)
Alfred Stieglitz Collection, 1949
49.55.317

99. ***Abstraction, Twin Lakes, Connecticut***
1916
Silver-platinum print
$12\frac{15}{16} \times 9\frac{5}{8}$ in. (32.8 x 24.4 cm)
Ford Motor Company Collection, Gift of Ford Motor Company and John C. Waddell, 1987
1987.1100.10

100. ***Geometric Backyards, New York***
1917
Platinum print
$10 \times 13\frac{1}{8}$ in. (25.4 x 33.3 cm)
Ford Motor Company Collection, Gift of Ford Motor Company and John C. Waddell, 1987
1987.1100.12

101. ***Harold Greengard, Twin Lakes, Connecticut***
1916
Silver-platinum print
10 x 13 in. (25.4 x 33 cm)
Ford Motor Company Collection, Purchase, Joseph Pulitzer Bequest and The Horace W. Goldsmith Foundation Gift through Joyce and Robert Menschel, and Gift of Ford Motor Company and John C. Waddell, by exchange, 1997
1997.25

102. ***Conversation***
1916
Platinum print
$10\frac{7}{16} \times 12\frac{1}{16}$ in. (26.5 x 30.7 cm)
Alfred Stieglitz Collection, 1949
49.55.316

103. ***Blind***
1916
Platinum print
$13\frac{3}{8} \times 10\frac{1}{8}$ in. (34 x 25.7 cm)
Alfred Stieglitz Collection, 1933
33.43.334

104. ***[Irish Washerwoman]***
1916
Photogravure, from *Camera Work*, no. 49/50 (June 1917)
$8\frac{1}{2} \times 6\frac{1}{2}$ in. (21.6 x 16.4 cm)
Alfred Stieglitz Collection, by exchange, 1953
53.701.50

105. ***[Office Buildings from Below, New York]***
1917
Platinum print
$13\frac{7}{16} \times 9\frac{5}{8}$ in. (34.1 x 24.4 cm)
Alfred Stieglitz Collection, 1933
33.43.335

106. ***The White Fence***
1916
Photogravure from *Camera Work*, no. 49/50 (June 1917)
$6\frac{1}{2} \times 8\frac{1}{2}$ in. (16.5 x 21.6 cm)
Alfred Stieglitz Collection, by exchange, 1953
53.701.50

107. ***Wire Wheel***
1917
Silver-platinum print
$13 \times 10\frac{1}{4}$ in. (33.1 x 26.1 cm)
Alfred Stieglitz Collection, 1949
49.55.318

108. ***Akeley Motion Picture Camera***
1922
Gelatin silver print
$9\frac{5}{8} \times 7\frac{11}{16}$ in. (24.5 x 19.5 cm)
Ford Motor Company Collection, Gift of Ford Motor Company and John C. Waddell, 1987
1987.1100.3

109. ***Henry Churchill***
1922
Palladium print
$11\frac{5}{8} \times 7\frac{5}{8}$ in. (29.5 x 19.3 cm)
Gift of Mary S. Churchill, 1979
1979.559.1

110. ***Rebecca, New York***
Ca. 1923
Palladium print
$7\frac{5}{8} \times 9\frac{11}{16}$ in. (19.4 x 24.6 cm)
Gift of Marilyn Walter Grounds, 1989
1989.1135

111. ***Garden Iris—Georgetown, Maine***
1928
Gelatin silver print
$9\frac{9}{16} \times 7\frac{5}{8}$ in. (24.3 x 19.3 cm)
Alfred Stieglitz Collection, 1955
55.635.1a

112. ***Wild Iris, Maine***
1927–28
Gelatin silver print
$9\frac{3}{4} \times 7\frac{13}{16}$ in. (24.8 x 19.8 cm)
Alfred Stieglitz Collection, 1955
55.635.1b

113. ***Ghost Town***
1930
Platinum print
$9\frac{5}{8} \times 7\frac{5}{8}$ in. (24.5 x 19.3 cm)
Gilman Collection, Purchase, The Horace W. Goldsmith Foundation Gift, through Joyce and Robert Menschel, 2005
2005.100.917

114. ***Woman and Boy, Tenancingo***
1933, printed 1940
Photogravure
$6\frac{7}{16} \times 5\frac{1}{8}$ in. (16.4 x 13 cm)
David Hunter McAlpin Fund, 1940
40.107.9

115. ***Ocoyococ***
1933
Gelatin silver print
$4\frac{5}{8} \times 5\frac{13}{16}$ in. (11.8 x 14.8 cm)
Gilman Collection, Purchase, William Talbott Hillman Foundation Gift, 2005
2005.100.481

116. ***Man with a Hoe, Los Remedios***
1933, printed 1940
Photogravure
$5\frac{5}{16} \times 4\frac{15}{16}$ in. (16 x 12.6 cm)
David Hunter McAlpin Fund, 1940
40.107.11

117. ***Coapiaxtla, Church***
1933, printed 1940
Photogravure
$6\frac{3}{8} \times 5$ in. (16.2 x 12.7 cm)
David Hunter McAlpin Fund, 1940
40.107.2

118. ***Men of Santa Anna, Michoacan***
1933, printed 1940
Photogravure
$6\frac{5}{16} \times 5$ in. (16.1 x 12.7 cm)
David Hunter McAlpin Fund, 1940
40.107.5

119. ***Cristo, Oaxaca***
1933, printed 1940
Photogravure
$10 \times 7\frac{15}{16}$ in. (25.4 x 20.2 cm)
David Hunter McAlpin Fund, 1940
40.107.8

120. ***Alfred Stieglitz***
1939
Gelatin silver print
$9\frac{1}{2} \times 7\frac{9}{16}$ in. (24.1 x 19.2 cm)
Alfred Stieglitz Collection, 1955
55.635.2

ACKNOWLEDGMENTS

Naturally, we all owe our deepest thanks to the brilliant photographers Stieglitz, Steichen, and Strand for enriching our lives with their work; to Stieglitz and Georgia O'Keeffe for the magnificent gifts that form the foundation of the Metropolitan's photography collection; and to those who have followed their lead and enriched our collection in the years since, especially The Ford Motor Company and John C. Waddell; The Georgia O'Keeffe Foundation and Jennifer and Joseph Duke; Grace Mayer; and all those who made possible the acquisition of the Gilman Collection.

This publication has benefited enormously from the attention of many people. I owe a special debt of gratitude to those who read drafts and made invaluable suggestions with respect to fact and interpretation: Maria Morris Hambourg, whose inspiring example and devoted mentorship have shaped my work far beyond the present volume; Sarah Greenough, whose decades-long scholarship on Stieglitz now provides the essential resource for any work on the artist, and whose always generous collegiality I have enjoyed on this and other projects; and the book's editor, Dale Tucker, whose delicate crafting of my text has made it more readable than it would otherwise have been. I also thank Russell Lord for his valuable research assistance and Joel Smith for sharing his knowledge of Steichen's early work. For the visual pleasure on and between the covers of this volume, I thank Abbott Miller, Kristen Spilman, and Susan Brzozowski of Pentagram; Eileen Travell for her subtle and accurate copy photography of the original photographs; Pat Goley of Professional Graphics for the color separations; Gwen Roginsky, Peter Antony, Bonnie Laessig and Chris Zichello for expertly seeing to all details of production and printing; Jane Tai for securing the permissions for reproduction; and Lucy von Brachel, who coordinated many of the details that made it all possible.

The exhibition that this book accompanies could not have been realized without the attention and patience of many members of the Metropolitan Museum staff. I thank conservators Nora Kennedy, Lisa Barro, Hanako Murata, Angeletta Leggio, Georgia Southworth, and Luisa Casella for their examination and analysis of the original photographs, for treating and preparing the prints for exhibition, and for creating the conservation component of the exhibition and its educational programming. Predrag Dimitrijevic brought his discerning eye and exquisite skills to the matting and framing of the photographs. Daniel Kershaw and Sophia Geronimus applied their extraordinary talents to the exhibition and graphic design. That the stage sets are ready when the curtain rises is thanks to Linda Sylling, Patricia Gilkison, Taylor Miller, and the incomparable crews of the Met's carpentry, plexi, and electrical shops. I also thank Joseph Loh, John Welch, Nicole Leist, and Vivian Wick for organizing a variety of public education programs to accompany the exhibition. For their direct contributions to the book and exhibition and for their forbearance while I was occupied by the project, I thank Doug Eklund, Mia Fineman, Laura Harris, Brian Novatny, Rebecca Phillips, Karan Rinaldo, and Jeff Rosenheim, all of the Department of Photographs. Also for his patience and calming influence on my life, Darryl Morrison. Finally, on behalf of the Metropolitan and its public, I extend my heartfelt thanks to Joseph M. Cohen for his generous support of the exhibition "Stieglitz, Steichen, Strand."

MD

Malcolm Daniel is Curator in Charge of the
Department of Photographs, The Metropolitan
Museum of Art, New York.